Test Bank

for

For All Practical Purposes

Introduction to Contemporary Mathematics

Kay Roebuck
John Emert
Ball State University

W. H. Freeman and Company
New York

ISBN: 0-7167-3067-7

Printed in the United States of America.

First printing 1997, VB

Contents

Chapter 1 Multiple-Choice Questions
Street Networks

1. What is the valence of vertex A in the graph below?

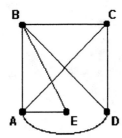

a) 2   b) 3   c) 4   d) 5

2. What is the valence of vertex A in the graph below?

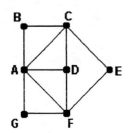

a) 3   b) 5   c) 7   d) 11

3. What is the valence of vertex A in the graph below?

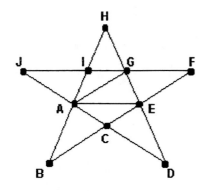

a) 3   b) 4   c) 5   d) 6

4. What is the valence of vertex A in the graph below?

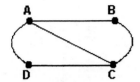

a) 3   b) 4   c) 5   d) 6

5. Which of the following defines the *valence of vertex A* of a graph?
a) The total number of vertices of the graph   c) The total number of edges of the graph
b) The number of edges meeting at vertex A   d) None of the above

6. The valence of vertex A in the graph shown below is 1.

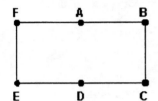

a) true   b) false

7. Which of the graphs below are connected?

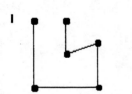   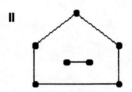

a) I only   b) II only   c) I and II both   d) Neither I or II

8. Which of the graphs below are connected?

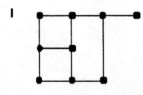   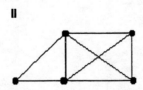

a) I only   b) II only   c) I and II both   d) Neither I or II

9. Which of the graphs below are connected?

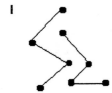
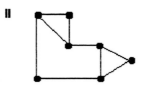

a) I only   b) II only   c) I and II both   d) Neither I or II

10. Which of the following statements about a connected graph is always true?
a) Every pair of vertices is joined by a single edge.
b) A path of edges exists between any two vertices of the graph.
c) There are an even number of vertices on the graph.
d) There are an even number of edges on the graph.

11. A graph which is not connected must have at least one vertex with valence 0.
a) True   b) False

12. If a graph of four vertices has a vertex with valence 0, then the graph is not connected.
a) True   b) False

13. If a graph of six vertices has only four edges it is not connected.
a) True   b) False

14. Which of the graphs below have Euler circuits?

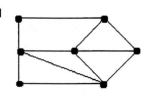

a) I only   b) II only   c) I and II both   d) Neither I or II

15. Which of the graphs below have Euler circuits?

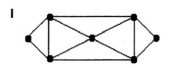

a) I only   b) II only   c) I and II both   d) Neither I or II

16. Which of the graphs below have Euler circuits?

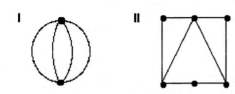

a) I only   b) II only   c) I and II both   d) Neither I or II

17. Which of the graphs below have Euler circuits?

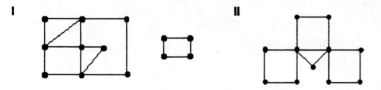

a) I only   b) II only   c) I and II both   d) Neither I or II

18. Every graph with an Euler circuit has an even number of vertices.
a) True   b) False

19. Every graph with an Euler circuit has an even number of edges.
a) True   b) False

20. Every graph that has an Euler circuit is connected.
a) True   b) False

21. Every connected graph has an Euler circuit.
a) True   b) False

22. Every graph with an Euler circuit has only vertices with even valences.
a) True   b) False

23. It is possible for a graph with all vertices of even valence to *not* have an Euler circuit.
a) True   b) False

24. Consider the paths represented by the numbered sequence of edges on the graphs below. Which path represents an Euler circuit?

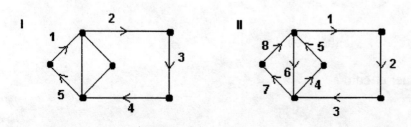

a) I only   b) II only   c) I and II both   d) Neither I or II

25. Consider the paths represented by the numbered sequence of edges on the graphs below. Which path represents an Euler circuit?

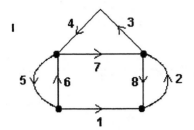 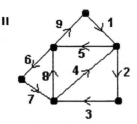

a) I only   b) II only   c) I and II both   d) Neither I or II

26. Consider the paths represented by the numbered sequence of edges on the graphs below. Which path represents an Euler circuit?

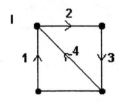 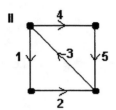

a) I only   b) II only   c) I and II both   d) Neither I or II

27. Consider the path represented by the sequence of numbered edges on the graph below. Why does the path *not* represent an Euler circuit?

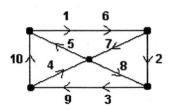

a) The path does not start and stop at the same vertex.
b) The path does not cover every edge of the graph.
c) The path uses some edges more than one time.
d) The path does not touch each vertex of the graph.

28. Consider the path represented by the sequence of numbered edges on the graph below. Why does the path *not* represent an Euler circuit?

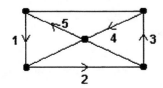

a) The path does not start and stop at the same vertex.
b) The path does not cover every edge of the graph.
c) The path uses some edges more than one time.
d) The path does not touch each vertex of the graph.

29. Consider the path represented by the numbered sequence of edges of the graph below. Which statement is true?

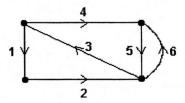

a) The path is not a circuit.
b) The path is an Euler circuit.

c) The path is a circuit, but not an Euler circuit.
d) None of the above

30. Consider the path represented by the numbered sequence of edges on the graph below. Which statement is true?

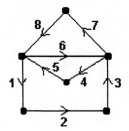

a) The path is not a circuit.
b) The path is an Euler circuit.

c) The path is a circuit, but not an Euler circuit.
d) None of the above

31. Consider the path represented by the numbered sequence of edges on the graph below. Which statement is true?

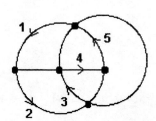

a) The path is not a circuit.
b) The path is an Euler circuit.

c) The path is a circuit, but not an Euler circuit.
d) None of the above

32. For which of the two situations below is it desirable to find an Euler circuit or an efficient eulerization of

a graph?

I. A pizza delivery person takes pizzas to ten houses in a neighborhood and then returns to pick up the next set to be delivered.

II. A postal carrier picks up mail from six collection boxes around a city.

a) I only   b) II only   c) I and II both   d) Neither I or II

33. For which of the two situations below is it desirable to find an Euler circuit or an efficient eulerization of a graph?

I. After a storm, a health department worker inspects all the houses of a small village to check for damage.

II. A veteran planning a visit to all the war memorials in Washington D.C. plots a route to follow.

a) I only   b) II only   c) I and II both   d) Neither I or II

34. For which of the two situations below is it desirable to find an Euler circuit or an efficient eulerization of a graph?

I. A street department employee must check the traffic signals at each intersection in a downtown area to be certain they are working.

II. An employee of a power company reads the electric meters outside each house along the streets in a residential area.

a) I only   b) II only   c) I and II both   d) Neither I or II

35. For which of the two situations below is it desirable to find an Euler circuit or an efficient eulerization of a graph?

I. Plowing the streets of a small village after a snow.

II. Painting the lines down the center of the roads in a town with only two way roads.

a) I only   b) II only   c) I and II both   d) Neither I or II

36. After a major natural disaster, such as a flood, hurricane or tornado, many tasks need to be completed as efficiently as possible. For which situation below would finding an Euler circuit or an efficient eulerization of a graph, be the appropriate mathematical technique to apply?

a) Relief food supplies must be delivered to 8 emergency shelters located at different sites in a large city.

b) The Department of Public Works must inspect traffic lights at intersections in the city to determine which are still working.

c) An insurance claims adjuster must visit 10 homes in various neighborhoods to write reports.

d) The Department of Public Works must inspect all streets in the city to remove dangerous debris.

37. After a major natural disaster, such as a flood, hurricane or tornado, many tasks need to be completed as efficiently as possible. For which situation below would finding an Euler circuit or an efficient eulerization of a graph, be the appropriate mathematical technique to apply?

a) The electric company must check several substations for malfunctions.

b) The gas company must check along all gas lines for possible leaks.

c) The phone company must respond to customers' needs in several parts of town.

d) The water company must spot check the integrity of 8 water towers located throughout the city.

38. In order to eulerize the graph below, give the fewest number of edges that need to be added or duplicated?

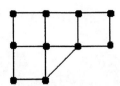

a) 1 b) 2 c) 3 d) 4

39. In order to eulerize the graph below, give the fewest number of edges that need to be added or duplicated?

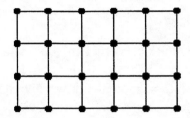

a) 4 b) 6 c) 10 d) 12

40. In order to eulerize the graph below, give the fewest number of edges that need to be added or duplicated?

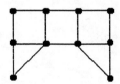

a) 1 b) 2 c) 3 d) 4

41. If a graph had 8 vertices of odd valence, what is the absolute minimum number of edges that would need to be added (duplicated) to eulerize the graph?
a) 2 b) 4 c) 6 d) 8

42. If a graph had 12 vertices of odd valence, what is the absolute minimum number of edges that would need to be added (duplicated) to eulerize the graph?
a) 2 b) 4 c) 6 d) 8

43. Which of the graphs shown below gives the best eulerization of the given graph. (In the graphs below, added edges are denoted with zig-zag lines.)

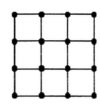

a.

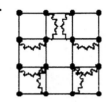

b.

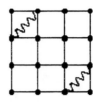

c.

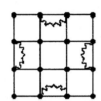

d.

44. Which of the graphs shown below gives the best eulerization of the given graph. (In the graphs below, added edges are denoted with zig-zag lines.)

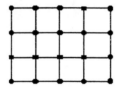

a.

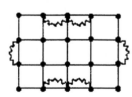

b.

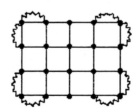

c.

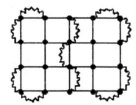

d.

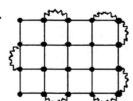

45. Which of the graphs shown below gives the best eulerization of the given graph. (In the graphs below, added edges are denoted with zig-zag lines.)

a.
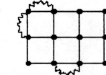

b.
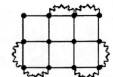

c.
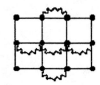

d.
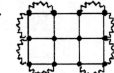

46. Which of the graphs shown below gives the best eulerization of the given graph. (In the graphs below, added edges are denoted with zig-zag lines.)

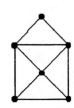

a.
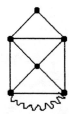

b.
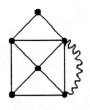

c.
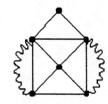

d.
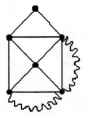

47. Suppose the edges of a graph represent streets that must be checked by a worker from the Department of Public Works. In order to eulerize the graph, we must add 3 edges. The real world interpretation of this is:

a) We must travel 3 blocks twice in our circuit.

b) The street department will build 3 new streets.

c) Three blocks will not be checked by the Department of Public Works.

d) It will take three workers to check all the streets in the city.

48. The map shown below illustrates part of a postal carrier's territory. The dots indicate mailboxes to which mail must be delivered. Which graph would be most useful for finding an efficient route for mail delivery?

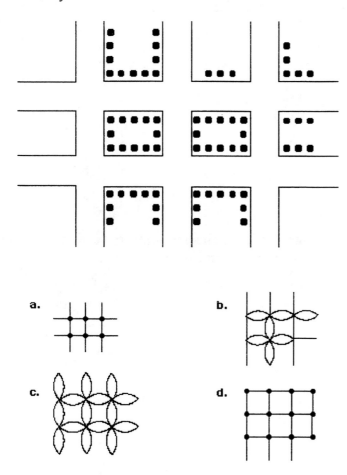

49. For the street network shown below, which graph would be most useful for routing a garbage truck? Assume all streets are two way and that passing down a street once would be sufficient to collect from both sides.

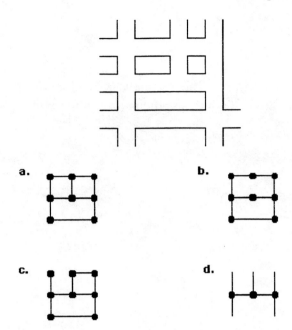

50. The map below shows the territory for a parking control officer. The dots represent parking meters that need to be checked. Which graph would be useful for finding an efficient route?

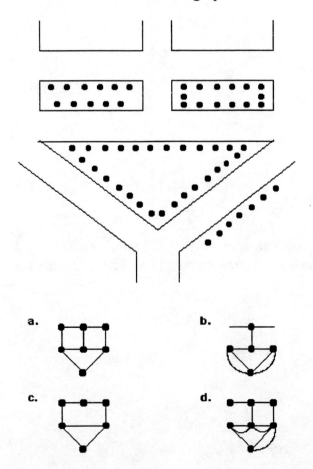

Free-Response Questions

1. On a graph that represents six cities and the roads between them, the valence of vertex A is 4. What does this mean in real world terms?

2. A graph that represents six cities and the roads between them is not connected. What does this mean in real world terms?

3. Draw a graph representing four cities A, B, C, and D with a road that connects each pair of cities given:
   AB,   AC,   BC,   BD,   CD

4. Draw a graph with vertices A, B, C, and D in which the valence of vertices A and D is 3 and the valence of vertices B and C is 2.

5. Draw a graph with vertices A, B, C, and D in which the valence of each vertex is 3.

6. Consider the path represented by the sequence of numbered edges on the graph below. Explain why the path is *not* an Euler circuit.

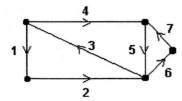

7. Consider the path represented by the sequence of numbered edges on the graph below. Explain why the path is *not* an Euler circuit.

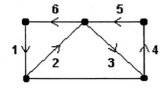

8. Draw a graph with 8 vertices, with the valence of each vertex even, that does *not* have an Euler circuit.

9. Explain why the graph shown below does not have an Euler circuit.

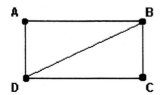

10. Explain why the graph shown below does *not* have an Euler circuit.

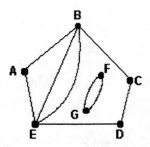

Identify an Euler circuit on the graphs below by numbering the sequence of edges in the order traveled.

11.

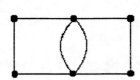

12.

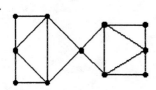

13.

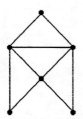

14.

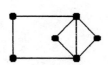

Add wiggly edges to find an efficient Eulerization of the graphs shown below.

15.

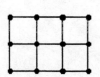

16.

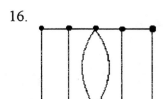

17.

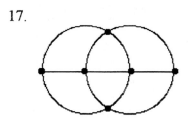

18.

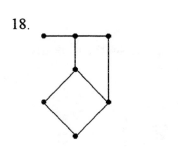

19. The map below gives the territory of a parking control officer. The dots represent meters that must be checked. Draw the graph that would be useful for finding an efficient route.

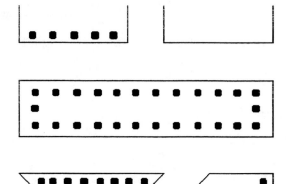

20. For the street network shown below, draw a graph that would be useful for routing a garbage truck. Assume all streets are two way and that passing once down the street is sufficient for collecting trash from both sides.

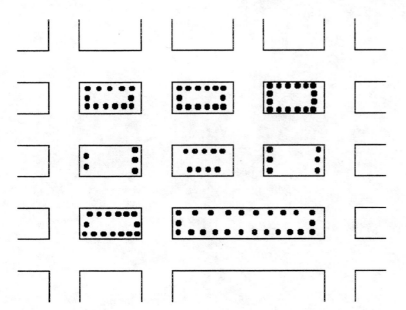

21. Find an Euler circuit on the graph on the left and use it to find a circuit on the graph on the right that reuses one edge.

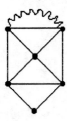   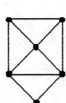

22. Find an Euler circuit on the graph on the left and use it to find a circuit on the graph on the right that reuses 4 edges.

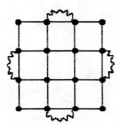   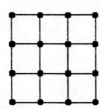

23. Find an Euler circuit on the graph on the left and use it to find a circuit on the graph on the right that reuses 3 edges.

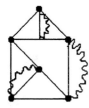 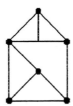

24. Why would a city street department want its snow plow operator's path to follow an Euler circuit if possible?

25. Give three real world applications in which a worker would want to find an Euler circuit on a street network.

Chapter 2 Multiple-Choice Questions
Visiting Vertices

1. Which of the following describes a Hamiltonian circuit for the graph below?

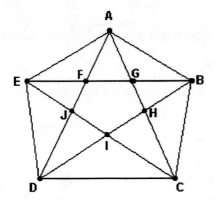

a) ABCDEFJIHG   b) ABCDEAFJDIHBGFEJICHGA   c) ABCDEAGHIJFA   d) AEDCBGHIJFA

2. Which of the following describes a Hamiltonian circuit for the graph below?

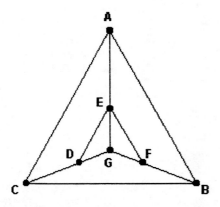

a) ABCDEFGA   b) ACBAEGFDEA   c) ACBFGDEA   d) ABCDGEF

3. Which of the following describes a Hamiltonian circuit for the graph below?

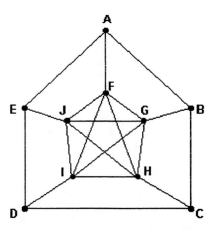

a) ABCDEJHIGF   b) AEDCBGIHJFA   c) ABCDEAFGHIJFA   d) ABCDEAFGBGIDIHCHJEJFA

4. On the graph below, which routing is produced by using the nearest-neighbor algorithm to solve the traveling salesman problem?

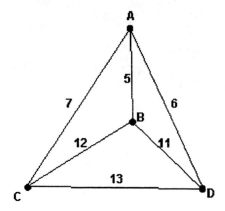

a) ABCDA   b) ABDCA   c) ACBDA   d) ABCD

5. For the graph below, what is the cost of the Hamiltonian circuit obtained by using the nearest-neighbor algorithm, starting at A?

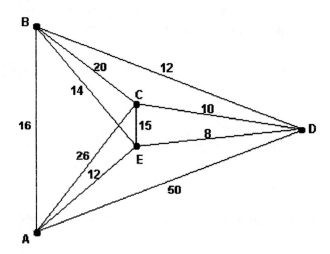

a) 60   b) 54   c) 62   d) 66

6. For the graph below, what is the cost of the Hamiltonian circuit obtained by using the nearest-neighbor algorithm, starting at A?

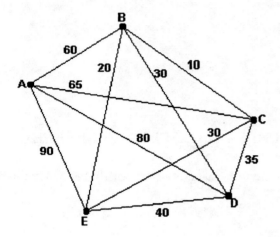

a) 215   b) 220   c) 235   d) 295

7. Which path listed forms a Hamiltonian circuit on the graph below?

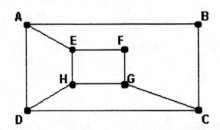

a) ADCBFGHEA   b) ABCDHGFE   c) ABCDHGFEA   d) ABCDHGFEHDA

8. On a map there are roads from town A of length 10, 26, 12, and 50 miles. Using the nearest-neighbor algorithm for finding a Hamiltonian circuit starting at town A, which road would be traveled first?
a) road of length 10   b) road of length 26   c) road of length 12   d) road of length 50

9. For the traveling salesman problem (Hamiltonian circuit) applied to six cities, how many tours are possible?
a) 60   b) 120   c) 360   d) 720

10. For the traveling salesman problem (Hamiltonian circuit) applied to five cities, how many distinct tours are possible?
a) 120   b) 60   c) 24   d) 12

11. For the traveling salesman problem (Hamiltonian circuit) applied to four cities, how many distinct tours are possible?

a) 3 b) 6 c) 12 d) 24

12. For the traveling salesman problem applied to seven cities, how many distinct tours are possible?
 a) 360 b) 720 c) 2520 d) 5040

13. On the graph below, which routing is produced by using the sorted-edges algorithm to solve the traveling salesman problem?

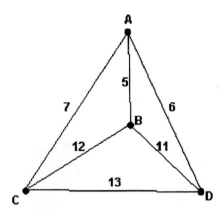

 a) ABCDA b) ABDCA c) ACBDA d) ABCD

14. For the graph below, what is the cost of the Hamiltonian circuit obtained by using the sorted-edges algorithm?

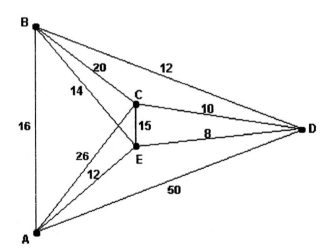

 a) 40 b) 58 c) 60 d) 66

15. For the graph below, what is the cost of the Hamiltonian circuit obtained by using the sorted-edges algorithm?

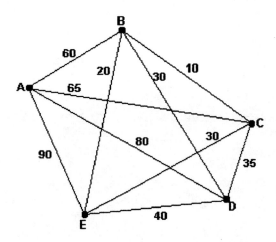

a) 220   b) 225   c) 235   d) 295

16. Use Kruskal's algorithm for minimum-cost spanning trees on the graph below. The cost of the tree found is:

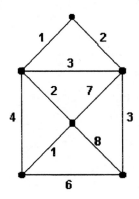

a) 5   b) 9   c) 12   d) 15

17. Use Kruskal's algorithm for minimum-cost spanning trees on the graph below. The cost of the tree found is:

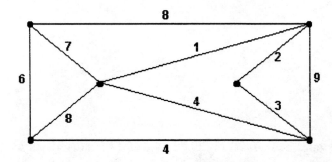

a) 23   b) 20   c) 16   d) 5

18. Use Kruskal's algorithm for minimum-cost spanning trees on the graph below. The cost of the tree found is:

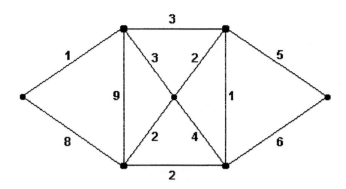

a) 20   b) 14   c) 19   d) 22

19. Use Kruskal's algorithm for minimum-cost spanning trees on the graph below. The cost of the tree found is:

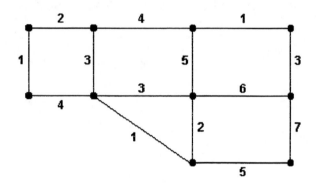

a) 47   b) 25   c) 22   d) 15

20. Use Kruskal's algorithm for minimum-cost spanning trees on the graph below. The cost of the tree found is:

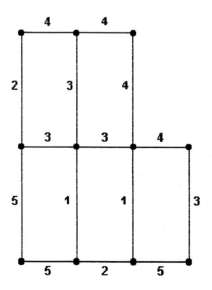

a) 22   b) 28   c) 32   d) 49

21. Given the order-requirement digraph for a collection of tasks shown below, the critical path would be:

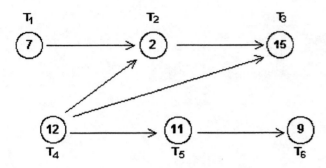

a) T_1, T_2, T_3 b) T_4, T_2, T_3 c) T_4, T_3 d) T_4, T_5, T_6

22. If the order-requirement digraph for a collection of tasks is shown below, then what is the minimum completion time for the collection of tasks?

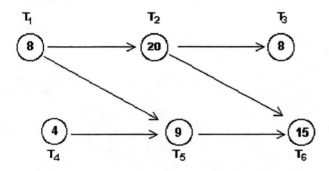

a) 64 minutes   b) 43 minutes   c) 36 minutes   d) 28 minutes

23. What is the earliest possible completion time for a job whose order-requirement is shown below?

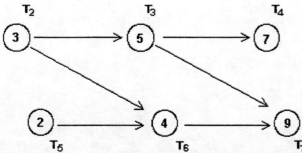

a) 10   b) 17   c) 40   d) 15

24. What is the earliest possible completion time for a job whose order-requirement digraph is shown below?

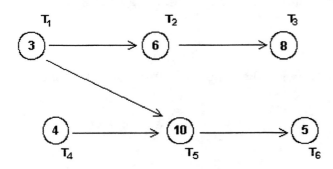

a) 15 b) 22 c) 34 d) 19

25. What is the earliest possible completion time for a job whose order-requirement is shown below?

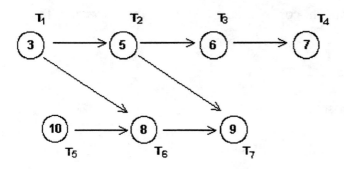

a) 27 b) 17 c) 21 d) 48

26. The nearest-neighbor algorithm for solving the traveling salesman problem always gives optimal results.
   a) True   b) False

27. The sorted-edges algorithm for solving the traveling salesman problem always gives optimal results.
   a) True   b) False

28. Kruskal's algorithm for finding minimum-cost spanning trees always gives optimal results.
   a) True   b) False

29. The nearest-neighbor algorithm for solving the traveling salesman problem always produces the same result as the sorted-edges algorithm.
   a) True   b) False

30. The path produced by the nearest-neighbor algorithm when solving the traveling salesman problem may be dependent on the starting city.
   a) True   b) False

31. The path produced by the sorted-edges algorithm when solving the traveling salesman problem may be dependent on the starting city.

a) True   b) False

32. The minimum-cost spanning tree produced by applying Kruskal's algorithm will always contain the lowest cost edge of the graph.
a) True   b) False

33. The minimum-cost spanning tree produced by applying Kruskal's algorithm may contain the most expensive edge of the graph.
a) True   b) False

34. A heuristic algorithm will always produce optimal results.
a) True   b) False

35. A heuristic algorithm may produce optimal results.
a) True   b) False

36. When Kruskal's algorithm is used to find a minimum-cost spanning tree on a graph, which of the following is false?
a) Circuits are not permitted in the tree.
b) The tree contains the edge of the graph of minimum cost.
c) The tree is not necessarily connected.
d) The tree may contain the edge of the highest cost.

37. A spanning tree of a graph must contain every edge of the graph.
a) True   b) False

38. A digraph is a graph with exactly two vertices.
a) True   b) False

39. Suppose an architect needs to design an intercom system for a large office building. The technique most likely to be useful in solving this problem is
a) finding a Euler circuit on a graph.
b) applying the nearest-neighbor algorithm for the traveling salesman problem.
c) applying Kruskal's algorithm for finding a minimum-cost spanning tree for a graph.
d) None of these techniques is likely to apply.

40. Suppose a veteran is planning a visit to all the war memorials in Washington D.C. The technique most likely to be useful in solving this problem is
a) finding a Euler circuit on a graph.
b) applying the nearest-neighbor algorithm for the traveling salesman problem.
c) applying Kruskal's algorithm for finding a minimum-cost spanning tree for a graph.
d) None of these techniques is likely to apply.

41. Suppose an employee of a power company needs to read the electricity meters outside of each house along the streets in a residential area. The technique most likely to be useful in solving this problem is
a) finding a Euler circuit on a graph.

b) applying the nearest-neighbor algorithm for the traveling salesman problem.
c) applying Kruskal's algorithm for finding a minimum-cost spanning tree for a graph.
d) None of these techniques is likely to apply.

42. Suppose a pizza delivery person needs to take pizzas to ten houses in different neighborhoods and then return to pick up the next set to be delivered. The technique most likely to be useful in solving this problem is
a) finding a Euler circuit on a graph.
b) applying the nearest-neighbor algorithm for the traveling salesman problem.
c) applying Kruskal's algorithm for finding a minimum-cost spanning tree for a graph.
d) None of these techniques is likely to apply.

43. Suppose a college campus decides to install its own phone lines connecting all of the buildings where calls may be relayed through one or more buildings before reaching their destination. The technique most likely to be useful in solving this problem is
a) finding a Euler circuit on a graph.
b) applying the nearest-neighbor algorithm for the traveling salesman problem.
c) applying Kruskal's algorithm for finding a minimum-cost spanning tree for a graph.
d) None of these techniques is likely to apply.

44. Suppose that after a storm an inspection needs to be made of the sewers along the streets in a small village to make sure local flooding is not due to clogging. The technique most likely to be useful in solving this problem is
a) finding a Euler circuit on a graph.
b) applying the nearest-neighbor algorithm for the traveling salesman problem.
c) applying Kruskal's algorithm for finding a minimum-cost spanning tree for a graph.
d) None of these techniques is likely to apply.

45. Suppose a maintenance worker needs to empty garbage dumpsters from five locations on the grounds of a park in the most efficient way possible. The technique most likely to be useful in solving this problem is
a) finding a Euler circuit on a graph.
b) applying the nearest-neighbor algorithm for the traveling salesman problem.
c) applying Kruskal's algorithm for finding a minimum-cost spanning tree for a graph.
d) None of these techniques is likely to apply.

46. Phyllis has her office in Middletown and must visit four clients, each in a different city. The graph below shows each city and the distances between each pairs of cities. How many miles would Phyllis travel is she chooses the Hamiltonian circuit for her trip by using the sorted-edges algorithm?

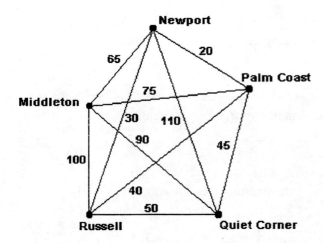

a) 265 miles   b) 300 miles   c) 285 miles   d) 345 miles

47. The graph below shows the cost of installing telephone wires (in hundreds of dollars) between the work spaces in an office complex. Use Kruskal's algorithm for minimum-cost spanning trees to find the cost for establishing this phone network.

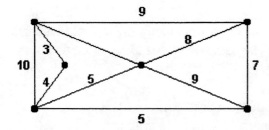

a) $2100   b) $2400   c) $2900   d) $6200

48. A local cafeteria offers a choice of 5 meats, 6 vegetables, and 3 salads. A complete dinner includes 1 meat, 1 vegetable, and 1 salad. How many different dinners can be created?
a) 14   b) 45   c) 90   d) 120

49. Kris has 3 pairs of pants of different colors, 5 shirts of different colors, and 2 pairs of shoes. How many different outfits can Kris create?
a) 2   b) 10   c) 30   d) 50

50. Given the two graphs shown below, which one represenst a tree?

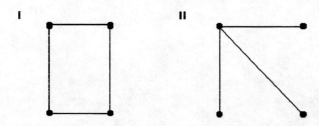

a) I only   b) II only   c) I and II both   d) Neither I or II

51. Given the two graphs shown below, which one represenst a tree?

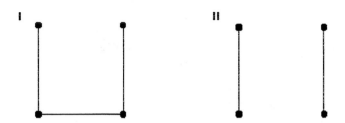

a) I only b) II only c) I and II both d) Neither I or II

52. In which of the diagrams below do the wiggled edges represent spanning trees?

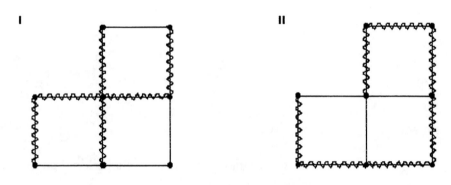

a) I only b) II only c) I and II both d) Neither I or II

53. In which of the diagrams below do the wiggled edges represent spanning trees?

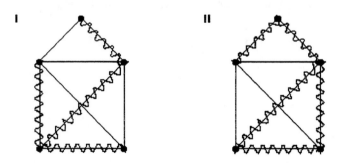

a) I only b) II only c) I and II both d) Neither I or II

Free-Response Questions

1. Construct a complete graph on 4 vertices.

2. Construct a complete graph whose vertices represent the six largest islands of Hawaii: Kauai, Oahu, Molokai, Lanai, Maui, and Hawaii.

3. Construct an example of a spanning tree on the graph given below.

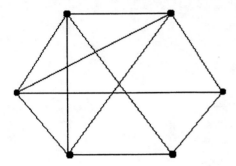

4. Construct an example of a graph with no Hamiltonian circuit.

5. Construct a digraph for the following tasks necessary when building a house: get a building permit, install wiring, pour foundation, build walls, build doghouse, pass final inspection.

6. Identify six tasks necessary when building a sandwich, and construct a digraph for these tasks.

7. Identify six tasks necessary when preparing for a picnic, and construct a digraph for these tasks.

8. Use the brute force algorithm to solve the traveling salesman problem for the graph of the four cities shown below.

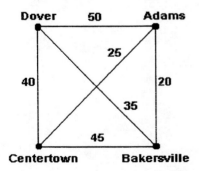

9. Use the brute force algorithm to solve the traveling salesman problem for the graph of the four cities shown below.

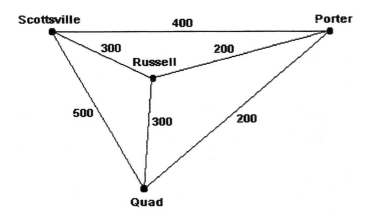

10. Use the brute force algorithm to solve the traveling salesman problem for the graph of the four cities shown below.

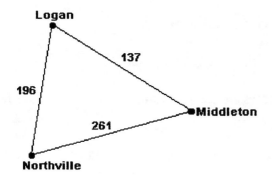

11. You own a chain of twelve apartment complexes (including your residence) and you want to plan a trip to visit each of your properties. If it takes 1/2 minute to compute the total length of a tour, how long will it take to apply the brute force algorithm to find the optimal tour?

12. You own a chain of ten one-day photo development kiosks and a lab where the photos are developed. Each morning and evening a delivery truck leaves the lab, visits each kiosk and returns to the lab. If it takes 1/3 minute to compute the total length of a tour, how long will it take to apply the brute force algorithm to find the optimal tour for the delivery truck?

13. You want to create a mileage grid showing the distance between every pair of the 50 U.S. state capitals. How many numbers will you have to compute?

14. You want to create a mileage grid showing the distance between every pair of the 10 Canadian provincial and territorial capitals. How many numbers will you have to compute?

15. The local cafe offers 3 different entrees, 10 different vegetables, and 4 different salads. A "blue plate special" includes an entree, a vegetable, and a salad. How many different ways can a special be constructed?

16. A nearby ice cream shop offers 31 different flavors and 3 different types of cones. How many different

single scoop cones can be ordered?

17. In some states, license plates use a mixture of letters and numerals. How many possible plates could be constructed using three letters followed by three numerals?

18. In some states, license plates use a mixture of letters and numerals. How many possible plates could be constructed using two letters followed by four numerals?

19. What is an advantage of a *heuristic* algorithm?

20. What is a disadvantage of a *heuristic* algorithm?

21. What is *critical* about the *critical path* of an order-requirement digraph?

22. Can a graph have an Euler circuit, but not a Hamiltonian circuit? Explain your answer.

23. Can a graph have a Hamiltonian circuit, but not an Euler circuit? Explain your answer.

24. Will the nearest-neighbor algorithm ever use the most expensive edge of a graph?

25. The route of a neighborhood garbage truck generally follows an Euler circuit. Under what circumstances should it instead follow a Hamiltonian circuit?

26. The route of a delivery truck generally follows a Hamiltonian circuit. Under what circumstances should it instead follow an Euler circuit?

Chapter 3 Multiple-Choice Questions
Planning and Scheduling

1. Given the order-requirement digraph below (with time given in minutes) and the priority list T_1, T_2, T_3, T_4, T_5, T_6, apply the list-processing algorithm to construct a schedule using two processors. How much time does the resulting schedule require?

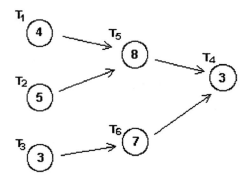

a) 15 minutes   b) 16 minutes   c) 17 minutes   d) 18 minutes

2. Given the order-requirement digraph below (with time given in minutes) and the priority list T_1, T_2, T_3, T_4, T_5, T_6, apply the list-processing algorithm to construct a schedule using two processors. How much time does the resulting schedule require?

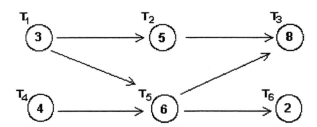

a) 14 minutes   b) 15 minutes   c) 16 minutes   d) 18 minutes

3. Given the order-requirement digraph below (with time given in minutes) and the priority list T_1, T_2, T_3, T_4, T_5, T_6, T_7, apply the list-processing algorithm to construct a schedule using two processors. How much time does the resulting schedule require?

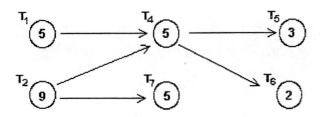

a) 16 minutes b) 17 minutes c) 18 minutes d) 21 minutes

4. Given the order-requirement digraph below (with time given in minutes) and the priority list T_1, T_2, T_3, T_4, T_5, T_6, T_7, T_8, apply the list-processing algorithm to construct a schedule using two processors. How much time does the resulting schedule require?

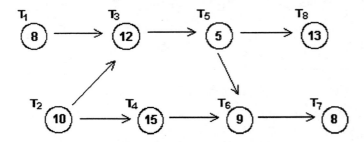

a) 40 minutes b) 44 minutes c) 45 minutes d) 49 minutes

5. Given the order-requirement digraph below (with time given in minutes) and the priority list T_1, T_2, T_3, T_4, T_5, T_6, apply the list-processing algorithm to construct a schedule using two processors. How much time does the resulting schedule require?

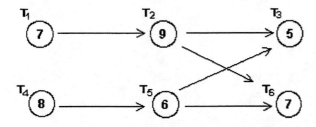

a) 21 minutes b) 22 minutes c) 23 minutes d) 24 minutes

6. Given the order-requirement digraph below (with time given in minutes) and the priority list T_1, T_2, T_3, T_4, T_5, T_6, apply the critical-path scheduling algorithm to construct a schedule using two processors. How much time does the resulting schedule require?

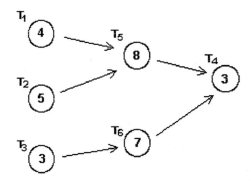

a) 15 minutes   b) 16 minutes   c) 17 minutes   d) 18 minutes

7. Given the order-requirement digraph below (with time given in minutes) and the priority list T_1, T_2, T_3, T_4, T_5, T_6, apply the critical-path scheduling algorithm to construct a schedule using two processors. How much time does the resulting schedule require?

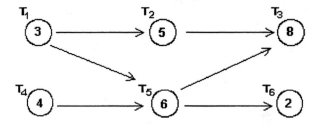

a) 14 minutes   b) 15 minutes   c) 16 minutes   d) 18 minutes

8. Given the order-requirement digraph below (with time given in minutes) and the priority list T_1, T_2, T_3, T_4, T_5, T_6, T_7, apply the critical-path scheduling algorithm to construct a schedule using two processors. How much time does the resulting schedule require?

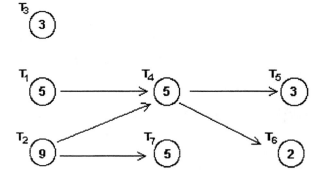

a) 16 minutes   b) 17 minutes   c) 18 minutes   d) 21 minutes

9. Given the order-requirement digraph below (with time given in minutes) and the priority list T_1, T_2, T_3, T_4, T_5, T_6, T_7, T_8, apply the critical-path scheduling algorithm to construct a schedule using two processors. How much time does the resulting schedule require?

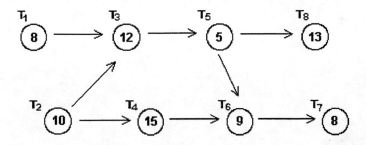

a) 40 minutes   b) 44 minutes   c) 45 minutes   d) 49 minutes

10. Given the order-requirement digraph below (with time given in minutes) and the priority list T_1, T_2, T_3, T_4, T_5, T_6, apply the critical-path scheduling algorithm to construct a schedule using two processors. How much time does the resulting schedule require?

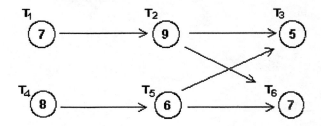

a) 21 minutes   b) 22 minutes   c) 23 minutes   d) 24 minutes

11. What is the minimum time required to complete nine independent tasks on three processors when the sum of all the times of the nine tasks is 72 minutes?
a) 3 minutes   b) 8 minutes   c) 24 minutes   d) 27 minutes

12. What is the minimum time required to complete eight independent tasks on two processors when the sum of all the times of the eight tasks is 72 minutes?
a) 4 minutes   b) 9 minutes   c) 16 minutes   d) 36 minutes

13. What is the minimum time required to complete twelve independent tasks on two processors when the sum of all the times of the twelve tasks is 84 minutes?
a) 6 minutes   b) 14 minutes   c) 24 minutes   d) 42 minutes

14. What is the minimum time required to perform six independent tasks with a total task time of 48 minutes on 3 machines?
a) 2 minutes   b) 8 minutes   c) 16 minutes   d) 18 minutes

15. What is the minimum time required to perform eight independent tasks with a total task time of 48 minutes on 4 machines?
a) 2 minutes   b) 6 minutes   c) 12 minutes   d) 24 minutes

16. Use the decreasing-time-list algorithm to schedule these tasks on two machines:
    4 minutes, 5 minutes, 8 minutes, 3 minutes, 3 minutes, 7 minutes
How much time does the resulting schedule require?

a) 15 minutes   b) 16 minutes   c) 17 minutes   d) 18 minutes

17. Use the decreasing-time-list algorithm to schedule these tasks on two machines:
         3 minutes, 5 minutes, 8 minutes, 4 minutes, 6 minutes, 2 minutes
     How much time does the resulting schedule require?
a) 14 minutes   b) 15 minutes   c) 16 minutes   d) 18 minutes

18. Use the decreasing-time-list algorithm to schedule these tasks on two machines:
         9 minutes, 6 minutes, 3 minutes, 4 minutes, 8 minutes
     How much time does the resulting schedule require?
a) 14 minutes   b) 15 minutes   c) 16 minutes   d) 17 minutes

19. Use the decreasing-time-list algorithm to schedule these tasks on two machines:
         9 minutes, 2 minutes, 8 minutes, 5 minutes, 4 minutes, 8 minutes
     How much time does the resulting schedule require?
a) 17 minutes   b) 18 minutes   c) 19 minutes   d) 22 minutes

20. Use the decreasing-time-list algorithm to schedule these tasks on two machines:
         9 minutes, 8 minutes, 7 minutes, 9 minutes, 2 minutes, 5 minutes.
     How much time does the resulting schedule require?
a) 19 minutes   b) 20 minutes   c) 21 minutes   d) 22 minutes

21. Choose the packing that results from the use of the first fit (FF) bin-packing algorithm to pack the
     following weights into bins that can hold no more than 8 lbs.
         6 lbs, 2 lbs, 4 lbs, 3 lbs, 5 lbs, 3 lbs, 2 lbs, 4 lbs

22. Choose the packing that results from the use of the next fit (NF) bin-packing algorithm to pack the
     following weights into bins that can hold no more than 8 lbs.
         6 lbs, 2 lbs, 4 lbs, 3 lbs, 5 lbs, 3 lbs, 2 lbs, 4 lbs

a. 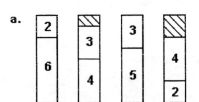 **b.**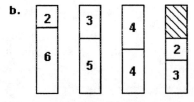

c. 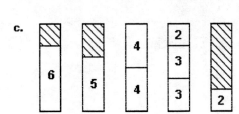 **d.**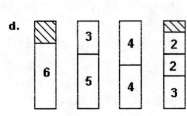

23. Choose the packing that results from the use of the worse fit (WF) bin-packing algorithm to pack the following weights into bins that can hold no more than 8 lbs.

 6 lbs, 2 lbs, 4 lbs, 3 lbs, 5 lbs, 3 lbs, 2 lbs, 4 lbs

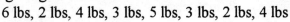

a. 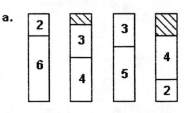 **b.**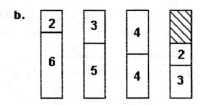

c. 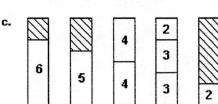 **d.**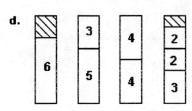

24. Choose the packing that results from the use of the first-fit decreasing (FFD) bin-packing algorithm to pack the following weights into bins that can hold no more than 8 lbs.

 6 lbs, 2 lbs, 4 lbs, 3 lbs, 5 lbs, 3 lbs, 2 lbs, 4 lbs

a. **b.**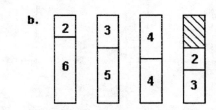

c. 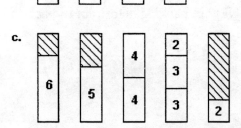 **d.**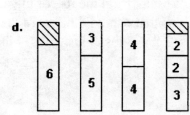

25. Choose the packing that results from the use of the next-fit decreasing (NFD) bin-packing algorithm to pack the following weights into bins that can hold no more than 8 lbs.

6 lbs, 2 lbs, 4 lbs, 3 lbs, 5 lbs, 3 lbs, 2 lbs, 4 lbs

a.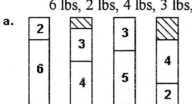

b.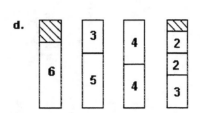

c.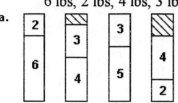

d.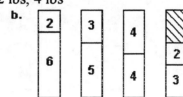

26. Choose the packing that results from the use of the worst-fit decreasing (WFD) bin- packing algorithm to pack the following weights into bins that can hold no more than 8 lbs.

6 lbs, 2 lbs, 4 lbs, 3 lbs, 5 lbs, 3 lbs, 2 lbs, 4 lbs

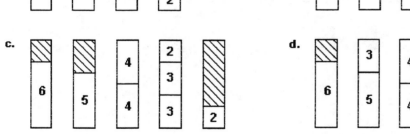

27. Choose the packing that results from the use of the first fit (FF) bin-packing algorithm to pack the following weights into bins that can hold no more than 9 lbs.

4 lbs, 5 lbs, 3 lbs, 2 lbs, 7 lbs, 6 lbs, 4 lbs, 2 lbs

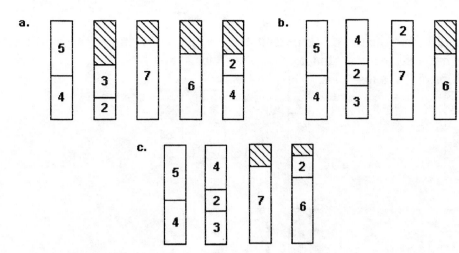

d. Another packing

28. Choose the packing that results from the use of the next fit (NF) bin-packing algorithm to pack the following weights into bins that can hold no more than 9 lbs.

4 lbs, 5 lbs, 3 lbs, 2 lbs, 7 lbs, 6 lbs, 4 lbs, 2 lbs

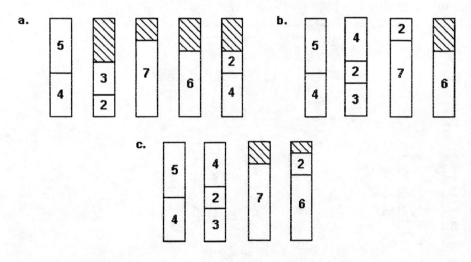

d. Another packing

29. Choose the packing that results from the use of the worst fit (WF) bin-packing algorithm to pack the following weights into bins that can hold no more than 9 lbs.

4 lbs, 5 lbs, 3 lbs, 2 lbs, 7 lbs, 6 lbs, 4 lbs, 2 lbs

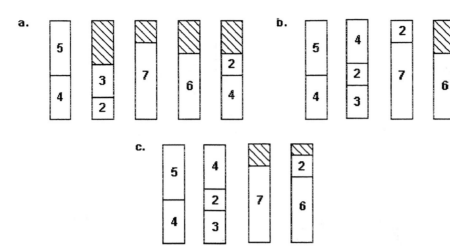

d. Another packing

30. Choose the packing that results from the use of the first-fit decreasing (FFD) bin-packing algorithm to pack the following weights into bins that can hold no more than 9 lbs.
    4 lbs, 5 lbs, 3 lbs, 2 lbs, 7 lbs, 6 lbs, 4 lbs, 2 lbs

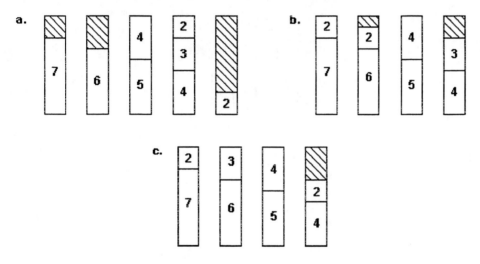

d. Another packing

31. Choose the packing that results from the use of the next-fit decreasing (NFD) bin-packing algorithm to pack the following weights into bins that can hold no more than 9 lbs.
    4 lbs, 5 lbs, 3 lbs, 2 lbs, 7 lbs, 6 lbs, 4 lbs, 2 lbs

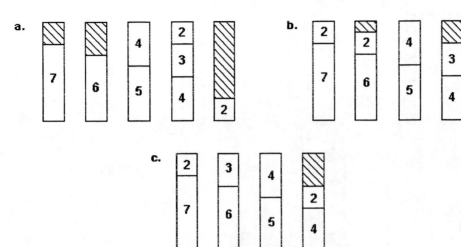

d. Another packing

32. Choose the packing that results from the use of the worst-fit decreasing (WFD) bin- packing algorithm to pack the following weights into bins that can hold no more than 9 lbs.

    4 lbs, 5 lbs, 3 lbs, 2 lbs, 7 lbs, 6 lbs, 4 lbs, 2 lbs

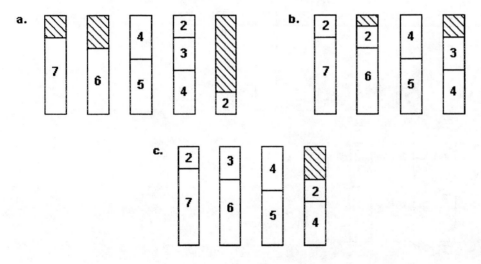

d. Another packing

33. Choose the packing that results from the use of the first fit (FF) bin-packing algorithm to pack the following weights into bins that can hold no more than 8 lbs.

    5 lbs, 7 lbs, 1 lb, 2 lbs, 4 lbs, 5 lbs, 1 lb, 1 lb, 3 lbs, 6 lbs, 2 lbs

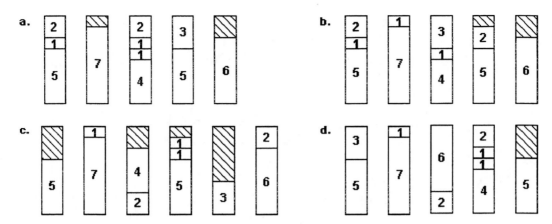

34. Choose the packing that results from the use of the next fit (NF) bin-packing algorithm to pack the following weights into bins that can hold no more than 8 lbs.

    5 lbs, 7 lbs, 1 lb, 2 lbs, 4 lbs, 5 lbs, 1 lb, 1 lb, 3 lbs, 6 lbs, 2 lbs

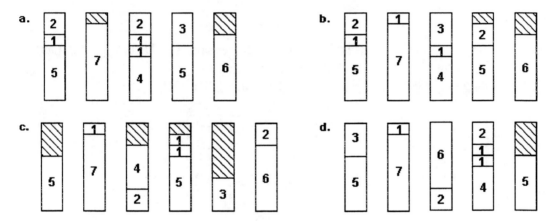

35. Choose the packing that results from the use of the worst fit (WF) bin-packing algorithm to pack the following weights into bins that can hold no more than 8 lbs.

    5 lbs, 7 lbs, 1 lb, 2 lbs, 4 lbs, 5 lbs, 1 lb, 1 lb, 3 lbs, 6 lbs, 2 lbs

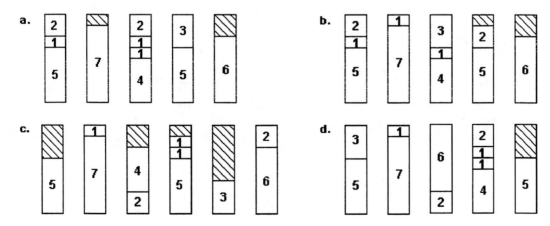

36. Choose the packing that results from the use of the first-fit decreasing (FFD) bin-packing algorithm to pack the following weights into bins that can hold no more than 8 lbs.

5 lbs, 7 lbs, 1 lb, 2 lbs, 4 lbs, 5 lbs, 1 lb, 1 lb, 3 lbs, 6 lbs, 2 lbs

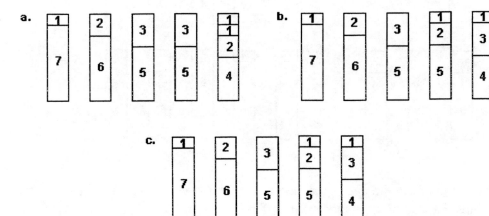

d. Another packing

37. Choose the packing that results from the use of the next-fit decreasing (NFD) bin- packing algorithm to pack the following weights into bins that can hold no more than 8 lbs.

5 lbs, 7 lbs, 1 lb, 2 lbs, 4 lbs, 5 lbs, 1 lb, 1 lb, 3 lbs, 6 lbs, 2 lbs

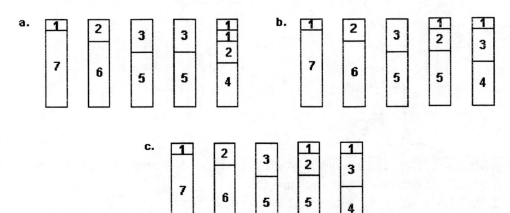

d. Another packing

38. Choose the packing that results from the use of the worst-fit decreasing (WFD) bin- packing algorithm to pack the following weights into bins that can hold no more than 8 lbs.

5 lbs, 7 lbs, 1 lb, 2 lbs, 4 lbs, 5 lbs, 1 lb, 1 lb, 3 lbs, 6 lbs, 2 lbs

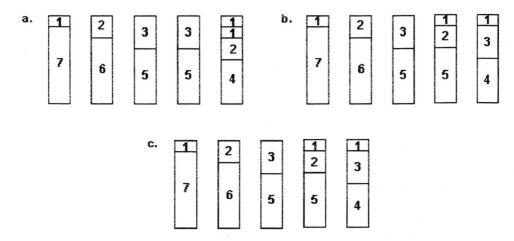

d. Another packing

39. A talent show producer needs to fit 17 acts of varying lengths into three segments. The segments should be as short as possible and are to be separated by intermissions.

    This problem could be solved by using
    a) the list processing algorithm for independent tasks.
    b) the worst-fit algorithm for bin packing.
    c) the critical-path scheduling algorithm.
    d) None of these techniques would work to find a solution.

40. A talent show producer needs to fit 17 acts of varying lengths into several segments. The segments will be no more than 45 minutes long, and are to be separated by intermissions.

    This problem could be solved by using
    a) the list processing algorithm for independent tasks.
    b) the worst-fit algorithm for bin packing.
    c) the critical-path scheduling algorithm.
    d) None of these techniques would work to find a solution.

41. Suppose that a crew can currently complete in a minimum amount of time the job whose order-requirement digraph is shown below. If Task T_1 is shortened from 7 minutes to 4 minutes, then what is the maximum amount by which the completion time of the entire job can be shortened?

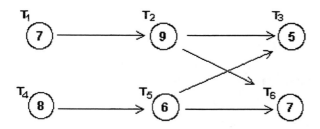

a) It cannot be reduced. b) 1 minute c) 2 minutes d) 3 minutes

42. Suppose that a crew can currently complete in a minimum amount of time the job whose order-requirement digraph is shown below. If Task T_2 is shortened from 9 minutes to 6 minutes, then what is the maximum amount by which the completion time of the entire job can be shortened?

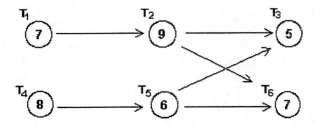

a) It cannot be reduced.   b) 1 minute   c) 2 minutes   d) 3 minutes

43. Suppose that a crew can currently complete in a minimum amount of time the job whose order-requirement digraph is shown below. If Task T_4 is shortened from 8 minutes to 5 minutes, then what is the maximum amount by which the completion time of the entire job can be shortened?

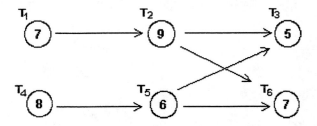

a) It cannot be reduced.   b) 1 minute   c) 2 minutes   d) 3 minutes

44. Suppose that a crew can currently complete in a minimum amount of time the job whose order-requirement digraph is shown below. If Task T_5 is shortened from 6 minutes to 3 minutes, then what is the maximum amount by which the completion time of the entire job can be shortened?

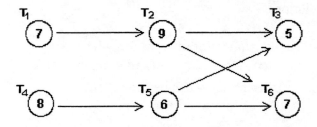

a) It cannot be reduced.   b) 1 minute   c) 2 minutes   d) 3 minutes

45. Suppose that a crew can currently complete in a minimum amount of time the job whose order-requirement digraph is shown below. If Task T_6 is shortened from 7 minutes to 4 minutes, then what is the maximum amount by which the completion time of the entire job can be shortened?

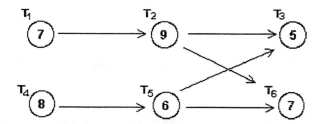

a) It cannot be reduced.   b) 1 minute   c) 2 minutes   d) 3 minutes

46. The first fit (FF) algorithm never uses more boxes than the next fit (NF) algorithm.
a) True   b) False

47. The worst fit (WF) algorithm never uses more boxes than the first fit (FF) algorithm.
a) True   b) False

48. When scheduling tasks using the list-processing algorithm, increasing the number of machines always reduces the completion time.
a) True   b) False

49. When scheduling tasks using the list-processing algorithm, decreasing the time of each task always decreases the completion time.
a) True   b) False

50. The list-processing algorithm for scheduling tasks is guaranteed to always produce an optimal solution.
a) True   b) False

51. The worst-fit decreasing (WFD) algorithm for bin packing is guaranteed to always produce an optimal solution.
a) True   b) False

Free-Response Questions

1. Which of the algorithms: first fit (FF), next fit (NF), or worst fit (WF) would be most preferable when filling boxes on an assembly line? Why?

2. Which of the algorithms: first fit (FF), next fit (NF), or worst fit (WF) would be most preferable when packing cloth dolls? Why?

3. Which of the algorithms: first fit (FF), next fit (NF), or worst fit (WF) would be most preferable when packing china dishes? Why?

4. Which of the algorithms: first fit (FF), next fit (NF), or worst fit (WF) would be most preferable when cutting wooden shelves from planks? Why?

5. Which of the algorithms: first fit (FF), next fit (NF), or worst fit (WF) would be most preferable when cutting quilt pieces? Why?

6. Use the first fit (FF) bin-packing algorithm to pack the following weights into bins that can hold no more than 9 lbs.
    5 lbs, 7 lbs, 1 lb, 2 lbs, 4 lbs, 5 lbs, 1 lb, 1 lb, 3 lbs, 6 lbs, 2 lbs

7. Use the next fit (NF) bin-packing algorithm to pack the following weights into bins that can hold no more than 9 lbs.
    5 lbs, 7 lbs, 1 lb, 2 lbs, 4 lbs, 5 lbs, 1 lb, 1 lb, 3 lbs, 6 lbs, 2 lbs

8. Use the worst fit (WF) bin-packing algorithm to pack the following weights into bins that can hold no more than 9 lbs.
    5 lbs, 7 lbs, 1 lb, 2 lbs, 4 lbs, 5 lbs, 1 lb, 1 lb, 3 lbs, 6 lbs, 2 lbs

9. Use the first-fit decreasing (FFD) bin-packing algorithm to pack the following weights into bins that can hold no more than 9 lbs.
    5 lbs, 7 lbs, 1 lb, 2 lbs, 4 lbs, 5 lbs, 1 lb, 1 lb, 3 lbs, 6 lbs, 2 lbs

10. Use the next-fit decreasing (NFD) bin-packing algorithm to pack the following weights into bins that can hold no more than 9 lbs.
    5 lbs, 7 lbs, 1 lb, 2 lbs, 4 lbs, 5 lbs, 1 lb, 1 lb, 3 lbs, 6 lbs, 2 lbs

11. Use the worst-fit decreasing (WFD) bin-packing algorithm to pack the following weights into bins that can hold no more than 9 lbs.
    5 lbs, 7 lbs, 1 lb, 2 lbs, 4 lbs, 5 lbs, 1 lb, 1 lb, 3 lbs, 6 lbs, 2 lbs

12. Given the order-requirement digraph below (with time given in minutes) and the priority list T_1, T_2, T_3, T_4, T_5, T_6, apply the list-processing algorithm to construct a schedule using two processors.

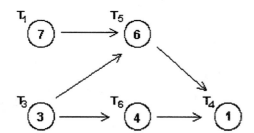

13. Given the order-requirement digraph below (with time given in minutes) and the priority list T_1, T_2, T_3, T_4, T_5, T_6, apply the list-processing algorithm to construct a schedule using three processors.

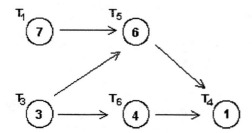

14. Given the order-requirement digraph below (with time given in minutes) and the priority list T_1, T_2, T_3, T_4, T_5, T_6, apply the critical-path scheduling algorithm to construct a schedule using two processors.

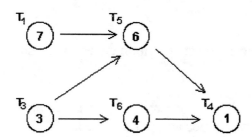

15. Given the order-requirement digraph below (with time given in minutes) and the priority list T_1, T_2, T_3, T_4, T_5, T_6, apply the critical-path scheduling algorithm to construct a schedule using three processors.

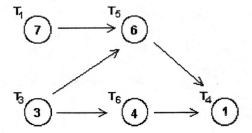

16. What is the minimum time required to complete 12 independent tasks on 3 processors when the sum of all the times of the 12 tasks is 60 minutes?

17. What is the minimum time required to complete 8 independent tasks on 2 processors when the sum of the times of the 8 tasks is 64 minutes?

18. Give an example of an order-requirement digraph with six tasks T_1, T_2, T_3, T_4, T_5, T_6 for which the critical-path is T_1, T_3, T_4.

19. Give an example of an order-requirement digraph with six tasks T_1, T_2, T_3, T_4, T_5, T_6 that requires 10 minutes when scheduled on 2 processors.

20. Give an example in which six independent tasks require 12 minutes when scheduled on 3 processors.

21. Give an example in which the first fit (FF) and next fit (NF) bin-packing algorithms produce the same packing.

22. Give an example in which the first-fit Decreasing (FFD) and worst-fit decreasing (WFD) bin-packing algorithms produce the same packing.

23. Why are there several different algorithms for the bin-packing problem?

24. When scheduling independent tasks, why does the decreasing-time-list algorithm generally produce good schedules? Does it always produce an optimal schedule?

25. When scheduling tasks using an order-requirement digraph, why does the critical-path scheduling algorithm generally produce good schedules? Does it always produce an optimal schedule?

Chapter 4 Multiple-Choice Questions
Linear Programming

1. Find the graph of the equation $3x + 5y = 30$.

a.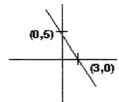

(0,5)

(3,0)

b.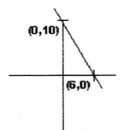

(0,10)

(6,0)

c.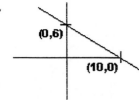

(0,6)

(10,0)

d.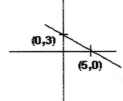

(0,3)

(5,0)

2. Find the graph of the equation $4x + 2y = 12$.

a.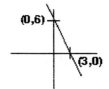

(0,6)

(3,0)

b.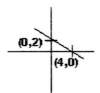

(0,2)

(4,0)

c.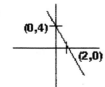

(0,4)

(2,0)

d.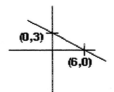

(0,3)

(6,0)

3. Find the graph of the equation $4x + 6y = 18$.

a.
(0,6)
(4,0)

b.
(0,3)
(4.5,0)

c.
(0,4.5)
(3,0)

d.
(0,4)
(6,0)

4. Find the graph of the equation $5x + 2y = 15$.

a.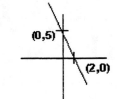
(0,5)
(2,0)

b.
(0,7.5)
(3,0)

c.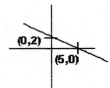
(0,2)
(5,0)

d.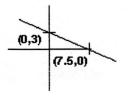
(0,3)
(7.5,0)

5. Find the graph of the inequality $3x + 4y \leq 12$.

a.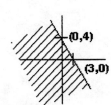
(0,4)
(3,0)

b.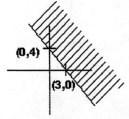
(0,4)
(3,0)

c.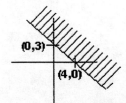
(0,3)
(4,0)

d.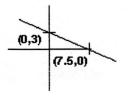
(0,3)
(4,0)

6. Find the graph of the inequality $4x + 5y \le 40$.

a.
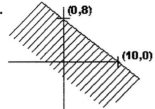
(0,8)
(10,0)

b.
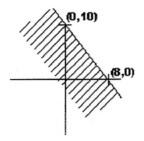
(0,10)
(8,0)

c.
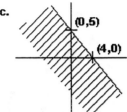
(0,5)
(4,0)

d.
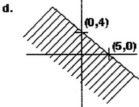
(0,4)
(5,0)

7. Find the graph of the inequality $6x + 4y \le 48$.

a.
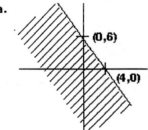
(0,6)
(4,0)

b.
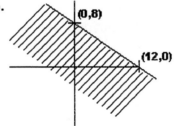
(0,8)
(12,0)

c.
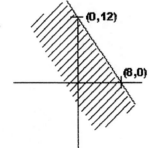
(0,12)
(8,0)

d.
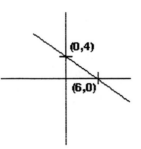
(0,4)
(6,0)

8. Find the graph of the inequality $3x + 7y \le 21$.

a.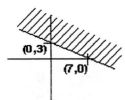

b.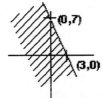

c.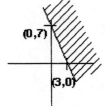

d.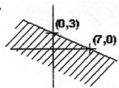

9. Find the point of intersection of the lines whose equations are $2x + 3y = 12$ and $1x + 5y = 13$.
    a) $(2, 3)$ b) $(3, 2)$ c) $(6, 0)$ d) $(-2, 3)$

10. Find the point of intersection of the lines whose equations are $4x + 2y = 12$ and $3x + 9y = 39$.
    a) $(5, -4)$ b) $(10, 1)$ c) $(1, 4)$ d) $(2, 2)$

11. Find the point of intersection of the lines whose equations are $3x + 2y = 21$ and $2x + 1y = 13$.
    a) $(5, 3)$ b) $(29, 45)$ c) $(8, -3)$ d) $(3, 5)$

12. Find the point of intersection of the lines whose equations are $2x + 5y = 6$ and $3x + 2y = 9$.
    a) $(3, 0)$ b) $(2, 1)$ c) $(-3, 0)$ d) $(1, 2)$

13. Graph the constraint inequalities for a linear programming problem shown below. Which feasible region shown is correct?

    $$2x + 3y \le 12$$
    $$x \ge 0, y \ge 0$$

a.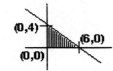

b.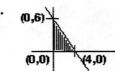

c.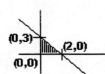

d.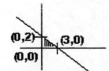

14. Graph the constraint inequalities for a linear programming problem shown below. Which feasible region shown is correct?

    $$4x + 3y \le 24$$

a.

b.

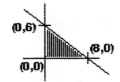

c.

d.

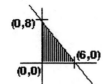

15. Graph the constraint inequalities for a linear programming problem shown below. Which feasible region shown is correct?

$$6x + 4y \leq 12$$
$$x \geq 0, y \geq 0$$

a.

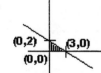

b.

c.

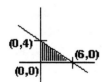

d.

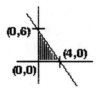

16. Graph the constraint inequalities for a linear programming problem shown below. Which feasible region shown is correct?

$$1x + 4y \leq 8$$
$$x \geq 0, y \geq 0$$

a.
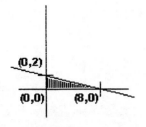

b.
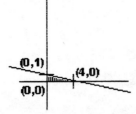

c.
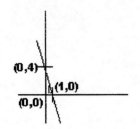

d.
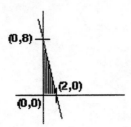

17. Write a resource constraint for this situation: A lawn service company has 40 hours of worker time available. Mowing a lawn (x) takes 3 hours and trimming (y) takes 2 hours. The profit from mowing is $15 and the profit from trimming is $10.
 a) $3x + 2y \le 40$ b) $(40/3)x + 10y \le 40$ c) $15x + 10y \le 40$ d) $5x + 5y \le 40$

18. Write a resource constraint for this situation: Producing a plastic ruler (x) requires 10 grams of plastic while producing a pencil box (y) requires 30 grams of plastic. There are 2000 grams of plastic available.
 a) $200x + (2000/30)y \le 2000$ b) $30x + 10y \le 2000$ c) $10x + 30y \le 2000$ d) $x + y \le 2000$

19. Write the constraint inequalities for this situation: Kim and Lynn produce pottery vases and bowls. A vase requires 35 oz. of clay and 5 oz. of glaze. A bowl requires 20 oz. of clay and 10 oz. of glaze. There are 500 oz. of clay available and 200 oz. of glaze available. The profit on one vase is $5 and the profit on one bowl is $4.
 a) $35x + 5y \le 5, 20x + 10y \le 4, x \ge 0, y \ge 0$
 b) $35x + 5y \le 500, 20x + 10y \le 200, x \ge 0, y \ge 0$
 c) $35x + 20y \le 500, 5x + 10y \le 200, x \ge 0, y \ge 0$
 d) $35x + 20y \le \$5, 5x + 10y \le \$4, x \ge 0, y \ge 0$

20. Write the constraint inequalities for this situation: A cheeseburger requires 5 oz. of meat and 0.7 oz. of cheese while a superburger requires 7 oz. of meat and 0.6 oz. of cheese. The burger stand has 350 oz. of meat and 42 oz. of cheese available. The profit on a cheeseburger is 10 cents and the profit on a superburger is 40 cents.
 a) $5x + 7y \le 350, 0.7x + 0.6y \le 42, x \ge 0, y \ge 0$
 b) $5x + 0.7y \le 10, 7x + 0.6y \le 40, x \ge 0, y \ge 0$
 c) $5x + 7y \le 10, 0.7x + 0.6y \le 40, x \ge 0, y \ge 0$
 d) $70x + 50y \le 350, 60x + 70y \le 42, x \ge 0, y \ge 0$

21. Write the resource constraints for this situation: A small stereo manufacturer makes a receiver and a CD player. Each receiver takes eight hours to assemble and one hour to test and ship. Each CD player takes fifteen hours to assemble and two hours to test and ship. The profit on each receiver is $30 and the profit on each CD player is $50. There are 160 hours available in the assembly department and 22 hours available in the testing and shipping department.
 a) $8x + 1y \le 30, 15x + 2y \le 50, x \ge 0, y \ge 0$
 b) $8x + 1y \le 160, 15x + 2y \le 22, x \ge 0, y \ge 0$
 c) $8x + 15y \le 30, 1x + 2y \le 50, x \ge 0, y \ge 0$
 d) $8x + 15y \le 160, 1x + 2y \le 22, x \ge 0, y \ge 0$

22. Write the resource constraints for this situation: Kim and Lynn produce tables and chairs. Each piece is assembled, sanded, and stained. A table requires 2 hours to assemble, 3 hours to sand, and 3 hours to stain. A chair requires 4 hours to assemble, 2 hours to sand, and 3 hours to stain. The profit earned on each table is $20 and on each chair is $12. Together Kim and Lynn spend at most 16 hours assembling, 10 hours sanding, and 13 hours staining.

a) $2x + 4y \leq 16,\ 3x + 2y \leq 10,\ 3x + 3y \leq 13,\ x \geq 0, y \geq 0$

b) $2x + 3y + 3z \leq 20,\ 4x + 2y + 3z \leq 12,\ x \geq 0, y \geq 0, z \geq 0$

c) $16x + 10y + 13z \leq 0,\ 2x + 3y + 3z \leq 20,\ 4x + 2y + 3z \leq 12,\ x \geq 0, y \geq 0, z \geq 0$

d) $8x + 4y \leq 16,\ (10/3)x + 5y \leq 10,\ (13/3)x + (13/3)y \leq 13,\ x \geq 0, y \geq 0$

23. Write the resource constraints for this situation: A company manufacturers patio chairs and rockers. Each piece is made of wood, plastic, and aluminum. A chair requires 1 unit of wood, 1 unit of plastic, and 2 units of aluminum. A rocker requires 1 unit of wood, 2 units of plastic, and 5 units of aluminum. The company's profit on a chair is $7 and on a rocker is $12. The company has available 400 units of wood, 500 units of plastic, and 1450 units of aluminum.

a) $1x + 1y + 2z \leq 7,\ 1x + 2y + 5z \leq 12,\ x \geq 0, y \geq 0, z \geq 0$

b) $1x + 1y \leq 400,\ 1x + 2y \leq 500,\ 2x + 5y \leq 1450,\ x \geq 0, y \geq 0$

c) $400x + 500y + 1450z \leq 0,\ 1x + 1y + 2z \leq 7,\ 1x + 2y + 5z \leq 12,\ x \geq 0, y \geq 0, z \geq 0$

d) $7x + 12y \leq 400,\ 2x + 5y \leq 1450,\ x \geq 0, y \geq 0$

24. Graph the feasible region identified by the inequalities:

$$2x + 3y \leq 12$$
$$1x + 5y \leq 10$$
$$x \geq 0, y \geq 0$$

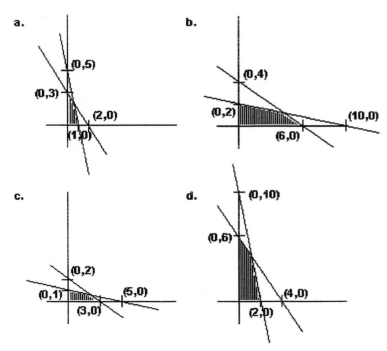

25. Graph the feasible region identified by the inequalities:

$$4x + 1y \le 12$$
$$2x + 7y \le 28$$
$$x \ge 0, y \ge 0$$

a.
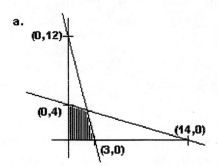

b.
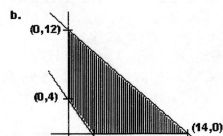

c.
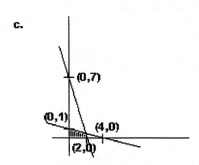

d.
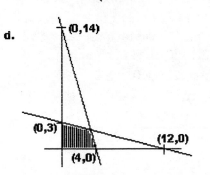

26. Graph the feasible region identified by the inequalities:

$$5x + 1y \le 10$$
$$3x + 3y \le 18$$
$$x \ge 0, y \ge 0$$

a.
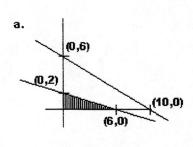

b.
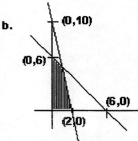

c.
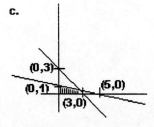

d.
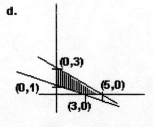

27. Graph the feasible region identified by the inequalities:

$$4x + 3y \le 12$$
$$3x + 3y \le 18$$
$$x \ge 0, y \ge 0$$

a.
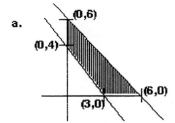

b.
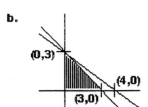

c.
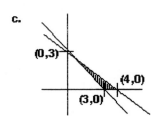

d.
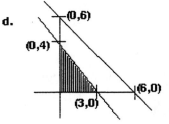

28. Given below is the sketch of the feasible region in a linear programming problem. Which point is *not* in the feasible region?

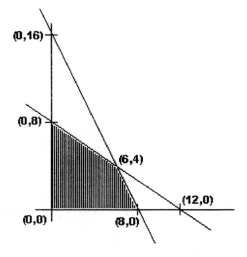

a) (0, 8)   b) (12, 0)   c) (6, 4)   d) (2, 2)

29. Given below is the sketch of the feasible region in a linear programming problem. Which point is *not* in the feasible region?

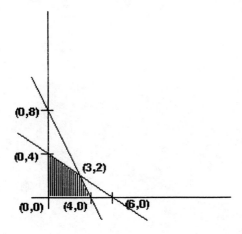

a) (0, 4)   b) (4, 0)   c) (6, 0)   d) (1, 2)

30. Given below is the sketch of the feasible region in a linear programming problem. Which point is *not* in the feasible region?

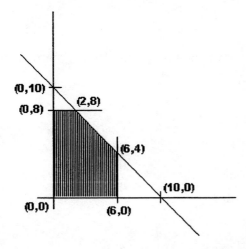

a) (6, 4)   b) (0, 10)   c) (2, 6)   d) (0, 8)

31. Given below is the sketch of the feasible region in a linear programming problem. Which point is *not* in the feasible region?

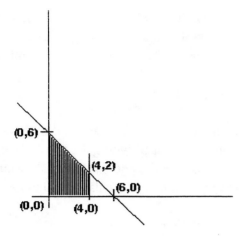

a) $(0, 6)$ b) $(4, 0)$ c) $(4, 2)$ d) $(6, 0)$

32. Given below is the sketch of the feasible region in a linear programming problem. Which point is *not* in the feasible region?

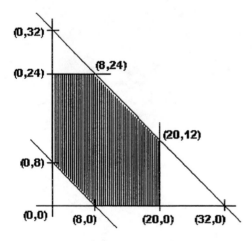

a) $(0, 32)$ b) $(0, 24)$ c) $(8, 16)$ d) $(20, 12)$

33. Write a profit formula for this mixture problem: Kim and Lynn produce pottery vases and bowls. A vase requires 35 oz. of clay and 5 oz. of glaze. A bowl requires 20 oz. of clay and 10 oz. of glaze. There are 500 oz. of clay available and 200 oz. of glaze available. The profit on one vase is $5 and the profit on one bowl is $4.
a) $P = 500x + 200y$ b) $P = 35x + 20y$ c) $P = 5x + 4y$ d) $P = 5x + 10y$

34. Write a profit formula for this mixture problem: A small stereo manufacturer makes a receiver and a CD player. Each receiver takes eight hours to assemble, one hour to test and ship, and earns a profit of $30. Each CD player takes fifteen hours to assemble, two hours to test and ship, and earns a profit of $50. There are 160 hours available in the assembly department and 22 hours available in the testing and shipping department.
a) $P = 8x + 1y$ b) $P = 160x + 22y$ c) $P = 15x + 2y$ d) $P = 30x + 50y$

35. Write a profit formula for this mixture problem: Kim and Lynn produce tables and chairs. Each piece is

assembled, sanded, and stained. A table requires 2 hours to assemble, 3 hours to sand, and 3 hours to stain. A chair requires 4 hours to assemble, 2 hours to sand, and 3 hours to stain. The profit earned on each table is $20 and on each chair is $12. Together Kim and Lynn spend at most 16 hours assembling, 10 hours sanding, and 13 hours staining.

a) $P = 20x + 12y$ b) $P = 2x + 3y + 3z$ c) $P = 16x + 10y + 13z$ d) $P = 8x + 9y$

36. Write a profit formula for this mixture problem: A company manufacturers patio chairs and rockers. Each piece is made of wood, plastic, and aluminum. A chair requires 1 unit of wood, 1 unit of plastic, and 2 units of aluminum. A rocker requires 1 unit of wood, 2 units of plastic, and 5 units of aluminum. The company's profit on a chair is $7 and on a rocker is $12. The company has available 400 units of wood, 500 units of plastic, and 1450 units of aluminum.

a) $P = 400x + 500y + 1450z$ b) $P = 4x + 8y$ c) $P = 7x + 12y$ d) $P = 1x + 2y + 5z$

37. The graph of the feasible region for a mixture problem is shown below. Find the point that maximizes the profit function $P = 2x + y$.

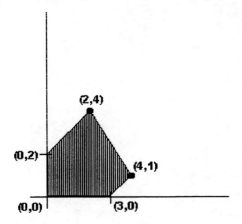

a) (0, 2)   b) (2, 4)   c) (4, 1)   d) (3, 0)

38. The graph of the feasible region for a mixture problem is shown below. Find the point that maximizes the profit function $P = x + 4y$.

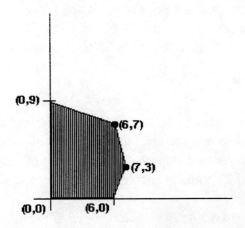

a) (0, 9)   b) (6, 7)   c) (7, 3)   d) (6, 0)

39. The graph of the feasible region for a mixture problem is shown below. Find the point that maximizes the profit function P = 2x + 5y.

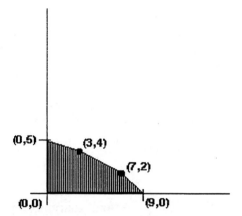

a) (0, 5)   b) (3, 4)   c) (7, 2)   d) (9, 0)

40. The graph of the feasible region for a mixture problem is shown below. Find the point that maximizes the profit function P = 3x + 6y.

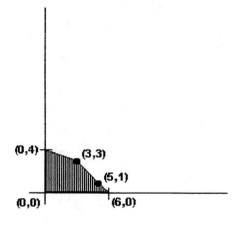

a) (0, 4)   b) (3, 3)   c) (5, 1)   d) (6, 0)

41. The graph of the feasible region for a mixture problem is shown below. Find the point which maximizes the profit function P = 3x + 6y.

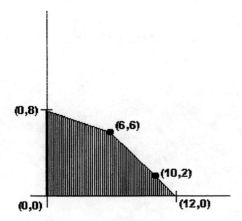

a) (0, 8)   b) (6, 6)   c) (10, 2)   d) (12, 0)

42. The graph of the feasible region for a mixture problem is shown below. Find the point that maximizes the profit function $P = 3x + y$.

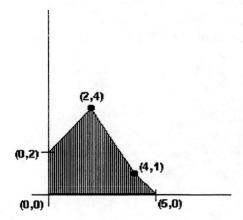

a) (0, 2)   b) (2, 4)   c) (4, 1)   d) (5, 0)

43. The simplex algorithm always gives optimal solutions to linear programming problems.
a) True   b) False

44. An optimal solution for a linear programming problem will always occur at a corner point of the feasible region.
a) True   b) False

45. Any linear programming problem has at most two products.
a) True   b) False

46. An optimal production policy for a linear programming mixture problem may eliminate one product.
a) True   b) False

47. The graph of the inequality $2x + 7y \leq 10$ is a straight line.
a) True   b) False

48. The ordered pair (200, 400) satisfies the inequality $x + 2y \leq 1500$.
   a) True   b) False

49. The feasible region for a linear programming mixture problem may have holes in it.
   a) True   b) False

50. The feasible region for a linear programming mixture problem with two products is in the first quadrant of the Cartesian plane.
   a) True   b) False

Free-Response Questions

1. Sketch the graph of the equation $3x + 5y = 30$.

2. Sketch the graph of the equation $4x + 3y = 24$.

3. Sketch the graph of the equation $x + 3y = 9$.

4. Sketch the graph of the inequality $2x + 4y \leq 12$.

5. Sketch the graph of the inequality $5x + y \leq 15$.

6. Sketch the graph of the inequality $4x + 6y \leq 12$.

7. Find the point of intersection for the lines represented by the equations $2x + 4y = 12$ and $3x + y = 13$.

8. Find the point of intersection for the lines represented by the equations $x + 5y = 28$ and $4x + 3y = 27$.

9. Find the point of intersection for the lines represented by the equations $3x + 2y = 14$ and $4x + 5y = 28$.

10. Find the point of intersection for the lines represented by the equations $2x + 7y = 61$ and $3x + 4y = 46$.

11. With the given the constraints for the following linear programming mixture problem, graph the feasible region.
    $$2x + 3y \leq 1800$$
    $$x \geq 0$$
    $$y \geq 0$$

12. With the given the constraints for the following linear programming mixture problem, graph the feasible region.
    $$x + 6y \leq 110$$
    $$x \geq 0$$
    $$y \geq 0$$

13. With the given the constraints for the following linear programming mixture problem, graph the feasible region.
    $$2x + 3y \leq 180$$
    $$5x + 2y \leq 230$$
    $$x \geq 0$$
    $$y \geq 0$$

14. With the given the constraints for the following linear programming mixture problem, graph the feasible region.
    $$x + 6y \leq 1100$$

$$4x + y \leq 2100$$
$$x \geq 0$$
$$y \geq 0$$

15. With the given the constraints for the following linear programming mixture problem, graph the feasible region.

$$x + 3y \leq 23$$
$$3x + 7y \leq 50$$
$$x \geq 2$$
$$y \geq 4$$

16. Find the constraint inequalities and the profit formula for this linear programming mixture problem: Toni has a small business producing dried floral wreaths and table arrangements. Each wreath takes 7 hours to produce, uses 12 stems of flowers, and earns a profit of $23. Each table arrangement takes 5 hours to produce, uses 20 stems of flowers, and earns a profit of $26. Toni can work no more than 30 hours per week and has a steady supply of 100 stems of dried flowers per week. What should Toni's production schedule be to optimize profit?

17. Find the constraint inequalities and the profit formula for this linear programming mixture problem: The Acme construction company builds two types of houses. Plan A requires 200 man-hours for rough construction and 70 man-hours for finish work. Plan B requires 300 man-hours for rough construction and 50 man-hours for finish work. Acme has carpenters available to provide up to 900 hours of rough construction per month and 260 hours of finish work per month. If Acme clears $7000 profit on a plan A house and $8000 profit on a plan B house, how should they schedule production to maximize profit?

18. Write the constraint inequalities and the profit formula for this linear programming mixture problem: The "Dig-The -Pig" ham shop sells regular and special ham and cheese sandwiches. The regular is made of 5 oz. of meat, 0.7 oz. of cheese, and requires 3 minutes of preparation time. The special is made of 7 oz. of meat, 0.6 oz. of cheese, and requires 11 minutes of preparation time. The profit on a regular sandwich is 10 cents while the profit on a special sandwich is 40 cents. If "Dig-The-Pig" has 350 oz. of meat, 42 oz. of cheese and 330 minutes of preparation time available each lunch period, how many of each type sandwich should they try to sell to maximize profit?

19. Write the constraint inequalities and the profit formula for this linear programming mixture problem: Amazin' Raisin Baking Co. makes both raisin cake and raisin pie. A batch of raisin cakes requires 5 lbs. of flour, 2 lbs. of sugar, and 1 lb. of raisins. A batch of raisin pies requires 2 lbs. of flour, 3 lbs. of sugar, and 4 lbs. of raisins. There are 165 lbs. of flour, 110 lbs. of sugar, and 120 lbs. of raisins available each week. Standing orders require at least 5 batches of raisin cakes and 8 batches of raisin pies per week. If profit on a batch of raisin cakes is $35 and profit on a batch of raisin pies is $40, how many batches of each should be made per week to maximize profit?

20. Solve this linear programming mixture problem: Kim and Lynn produce pottery vases and bowls. A vase requires 25 oz. of clay and 5 oz. of glaze. A bowl requires 20 oz. of clay and 10 oz. of glaze. There are 500 oz of clay available and 160 oz. of glaze available. The profit on one vase is $5 and the profit on one bowl is $3.

21. Solve this linear programming mixture problem: A small stereo manufacturer makes a receiver and a CD player. Each receiver takes eight hours to assemble, one hour to test and ship, and earns a profit of $30. Each CD player takes fifteen hours to assemble, two hours to test and ship, and earns a profit of $50. There are 160 hours available in the assembly department and 26 hours available in the testing and shipping department. What should the production schedule be to maximize profit?

22. Explain what the real world implications are if the optimal production policy for a linear programming mixture problem is represented by a point on the x axis of the Cartesian plane.

23. Describe the shape of the feasible region for linear programming mixture problems with two products.

24. Name two alternatives to the graphical approach for solving linear programming problems.

25. Explain why a linear programming mixture problem might have minimum constraints other than zero.

26. Explain why the feasible region for a linear programming mixture problem must be in the first quadrant of the Cartesian plane.

Chapter 5 Multiple-Choice Questions
Producing Data

1. A polling company conducted a survey of voters to obtain data for a political campaign. They selected 3500 voters randomly from the 168,000 names on the voter registration lists of the county and found that 1372 intended to vote for candidate Doe. The 3500 voters represent
   a) the population.   b) the sample.

2. A polling company conducted a survey of voters to obtain data for a political campaign. They selected 3500 voters randomly from the 168,000 names on the voter registration lists of the county and found that 1372 intended to vote for candidate Doe. The 168,000 names represent
   a) the population.   b) the sample.

3. A marketing company conducted a survey of college students to obtain data for an advertising campaign. They selected 1421 students randomly from campus directories of 132 colleges and universities. The 1421 students represent
   a) the population.   b) the sample.

4. A marketing company conducted a survey of college students to obtain data for an advertising campaign. They selected 1421 students randomly from campus directories of 132 colleges and universities. The students in the directories at the 132 colleges and universities represent
   a) the population.   b) the sample.

5. To determine the proportion of voters who favor a certain candidate for governor, the campaign staff phones 2500 residents of the state chosen from the state property tax rolls. The 2500 residents represent
   a) the population.   b) the sample.

6. To determine the proportion of voters who favor a certain candidate for governor, the campaign staff phones 2500 residents of the state chosen from the state property tax rolls. All property owners in the state represent
   a) the population.   b) the sample.

7. In order to determine the mean weight of bags of chips filled by its packing machines, a company inspects 50 bags per day and weighs them. In this example, the population is
   a) the 50 bags inspected each day.   c) all bags of chips produced by the company.
   b) all potato chips produced by the company.   d) the weight of the 50 bags inspected.

8. To estimate the proportion of voters in a town likely to favor a tax increase for road repair, a random sample of people chosen from the voter registration list is surveyed and the proportion who favor the increase is found to be 43%. The actual proportion in the town is 40%. This difference is most likely an example of sampling
   a) bias.   b) variability.

9. To determine the proportion of students at a university who favor the construction of a parking garage, a sample of people driving through the student center parking lot is surveyed and it is found that 45% favor

the garage. The actual proportion of the student body who favor the garage is 40%. This difference is most likely an example of sampling

a) bias.   b) variability.

10. To determine the proportion of students at a university who favor the construction of a parking garage, a sample of people on the current enrollment list is surveyed and it is found that 45% favor the garage. The actual proportion of the student body who favor the garage is 40%. This difference is most likely an example of sampling

a) bias.   b) variability.

11. To estimate the mean income of all residents in a town, a sample of people chosen from the telephone directory is surveyed and the mean is found to be $43,000. The actual mean income in the town is $40,000. This difference is most likely an example of sampling

a) bias.   b) variability.

12. A polling company surveys 200 people outside a county courthouse concerning tighter restrictions on smoking in public buildings. Their results indicate that 34% of those surveyed favor tighter restrictions. The actual proportion of county residents who favor tighter restrictions in 65%. The difference is most likely due to

a) variability in sampling.
b) bias due to the use of a convenience sample.
c) confounding variables in the survey.
d) the wording of the survey.

13. You wish to survey the students at your college to determine their feelings about the quality of services in the Student Center. Which of the following sampling designs is best for avoiding bias?
a) Place an ad in the student newspaper asking all readers to mail in their opinions.
b) Obtain a list of student names from the registrar and select 250 names to contact.
c) Air an announcement on the campus radio station asking all listeners to phone in their opinions.
d) Survey every tenth student who enters the Student Center.

14. To determine the proportion of students at a university who favor the construction of a parking garage, a student senate member surveys students as they leave the student union. This type of sample is a
a) convenience sample.
b) simple random sample.
c) multi-stage random sample.
d) voluntary response sample.

15. In order to determine the proportion of voters in a small town who favor a candidate for mayor, the campaign staff takes out an ad in the paper asking voters to call in their preference for mayor. This type of sample is a
a) convenience sample.
b) simple random sample.
c) multi-stage random sample.
d) voluntary response sample.

16. A marketing company conducts a survey of college students to obtain data for a marketing campaign. They randomly select 5 in-state colleges and then randomly choose 100 students from the registration lists of these colleges. This type of sample is a
a) convenience sample.
b) simple random sample.
c) multi-stage random sample.
d) voluntary response sample.

17. To estimate the number of motorists likely to favor a tax increase for road repair, a polling company chooses 1000 names at random from a list of registered car owners provided by the county license office. This type of sample is a
a) convenience sample.
b) simple random sample.
c) multi-stage random sample.
d) voluntary response sample.

18. Which of the following sampling techniques is most likely to produce biased results?
a) multi-stage random sampling
b) sampling using a random digits table
c) voluntary response sampling
d) simple random sampling

19. A polling company conducted a survey of voters to obtain data for a political campaign. They selected 3500 voters randomly from the 16,800 names on the voter registration lists of the county and found that 1365 intended to vote for candidate Doe. The sample percent is
a) 8.1%. b) 20.8%. c) 39%. d) 13.65%.

20. A poll of 80 students selected at random at Midtown University found that 20 were in favor of a fee increase to support extra maintenance of gardens on campus. In the example, the sample proportion is
a) 20%. b) 8%. c) 80%. d) 25%.

21. A sample of 50 people at a local fast-food restaurant found 15 in favor of new fat-free menu items. In this example, the sample proportion is
a) 15%. b) 25%. c) 30%. d) 50%.

22. A poll of 60 students selected at random at State University found that 12 were in favor of higher parking fees to support extra police patrols of parking lots on campus. In this example, the sample proportion is
a) 20%. b) 12%. c) 5%. d) 60%.

23. A random sample of 600 voters in Centralville indicated that 48 of them believed their congressional representative was honest and trustworthy. The sample proportion is
a) 8%. b) 12.5%. c) 48%. d) 80%.

24. A soft drink bottler selects 80 cans at random from a production line and finds that 32 are under filled. The sample proportion of under-filled cans is
a) 2.5%. b) 4%. c) 32%. d) 40%.

Use the following random digits to answer the following question(s):

```
101    01033 08705 42934 79257 89138 21506 26797
102    49105 00755 39242 50772 44036 54518 56865
103    61589 35486 59500 20060 89769 54870 75586
104    08900 87788 73717 19287 69954 45917 80026
105    75029 51052 25648 02523 84300 83093 39852
106    91276 88988 12439 73741 30492 19280 41255
107    74008 72750 70742 67769 72837 27098 07049
108    98406 27011 76385 15212 03806 85928 76385
```

25. A large group of people are eating dinner at a Chinese restaurant. They are very hungry. The menus are printed in Chinese but no one in the group can read Chinese. Use the portion of the random digits table above, starting at line 105 to choose 5 dishes from the menu numbered 01 to 50.
   a) 2, 5, 7, 9, 10   b) 02, 10, 23, 25, 25   c) 02, 10, 23, 25, 30   d) 02, 05, 09, 25, 30

26. Beginning with line 102 of the random digits table above, select three individuals from the list below to serve on a student affairs committee.

01 Crosby	06 Jones	11 Turner	16 Bush
02 Hunter	07 Smith	12 Baker	17 Thompson
03 Cooper	08 Davis	13 Wilson	18 Goodman
04 Grant	09 Ewing	14 Adams	19 Stevens
05 Riley1	0 Doe	15 Hill	20 Williams

   a) Cooper, Doe, Smith   b) Doe, Ewing, Grant   c) Doe, Smith, Smith   d) Crosby, Ewing, Grant

27. Beginning with line 104 of the random digits table above, select three individuals to receive a prize in contest.

01 Anderson	06 Hall	11 Opus	16 Thompson
02 Butts	07 Hunsaker	12 Parson	17 Ubet
03 Calvin	08 Jones	13 Quayle	18 Watson
04 Ernest	09 Miller	14 Riley	19 Wilson
05 Gaynor	10 Norton	15 Stone	20 Ziggy

   a) Jones, Jones, Ubet   b) Hunsaker, Jones, Miller   c) Jones, Ubet, Wilson   d) Butts, Jones, Ubet

28. Use the random digits table above, starting at line 102, to choose five people from a list numbered 001 to 500 to receive a survey.
   a) 491, 050, 075, 242, 403   b) 491, 007, 392, 440, 354   c) 49, 10, 50, 07, 55   d) 49, 61, 08, 75, 91

29. Use the random digits table above, starting at line 103, to choose five people from a list numbered 01 to 99 to receive a survey.
   a) 01, 03, 30, 87, 05   b) 10, 36, 15, 89, 35   c) 61, 58, 93, 54, 86   d) 61, 58, 35, 48, 59

30. Use the random digits table above, starting at line 104, to choose four people from a list numbered 001 to 500 to call for a poll.
   a) 089, 008, 778, 873   b) 089, 008, 192, 445   c) 089, 008, 77, 88   d) 089, 192, 459, 256

31. Use the random digits table above, starting at line 105 to select four people from a list numbered 00 to 99
   a) 75, 02, 95, 10   b) 75, 51, 25, 02   c) 10, 57, 50, 29   d) 01, 00, 05, 07

32. Random selection of subjects in a survey is used to eliminate variability in results.
   a) True   b) False

33. Random selection of subjects for surveys is used to avoid
   a) placebo effects.   b) variability.   c) double blindness.   d) bias.

34. A ten-year study of low-birth-weight babies is performed to determine if birth weight affects IQ and

performance in elementary school. Children are identified in hospitals at birth and their performance is tracked until they are ten years old. This type of study is a(n)

a) comparative experiment. c) observational study.
b) experiment with compounding variables. d) biased survey.

35. A group of 200 students are identified, half took Latin in high school and half did not. The students are compared to see if the students who took Latin received higher SAT verbal scores. This type of study is a(n)

a) comparative experiment. c) prospective study.
b) experiment with compounding variables. d) simple random sample.

36. A group of 100 students are randomly chosen and divided into two groups, one group is taught typing using a set of new materials and the other using traditional methods. After instruction, typing speeds are compared to determine if the new materials improve learning. This type of study is a(n)

a) comparative experiment. b) observational study. c) prospective study. d) biased survey.

37. Consider the following situation: A group of 300 students are randomly selected at a local high school and required to fill out yearly questionnaires on family income. Students' performance on standardized tests is then followed throughout their high school years to determine if socio-economic status affects SAT scores. This describes an experiment.

a) True b) False

38. Consider the following situation: Doctors identify 500 women, half of whom had mothers with breast cancer and half of whom did not. The medical records of the women are followed for 20 years to determine if heredity plays a role in breast cancer. This describes a prospective study.

a) True b) False

39. Consider the following situation: Doctors question 5000 women who have had breast cancer to determine if there is a genetic factor which increases the likelihood of cancer. Each woman is asked about her family background and incidences of breast or other types of cancer among her relatives. This describes a prospective study.

a) True b) False

40. A prospective study may be used to show cause and effect.

a) True b) False

41. An observational study may be used to show cause and effect.

a) True b) False

42. An experiment may be used to show cause and effect.

a) True b) False

43. A dummy medication (such as a salt tablet) will often help a patient who trusts the doctor who administers the medicine. This is called

a) confidentiality. b) double blindness. c) confounding variables. d) the placebo effect.

44. A study gathered data on 1000 randomly selected students and showed that students who took Latin in high school had much higher scores on a test of verbal English skills than those who did not take Latin. The study *cannot* conclude that taking Latin improves verbal English skills because
a) the study was not an experiment.
b) the study was not double blind.
c) of the placebo effect.
d) the verbal English test was faulty.

45. A survey is sent to 100 employees at a community hospital asking if they support a law requiring motorcycle riders to wear helmets. The results indicate 88% support the law. If the actual proportion of the community's residents who support the law is 72%, the difference is most likely a result of
a) sampling bias.
b) sampling variability.
c) an insufficient sample size.
d) a poorly worded questionnaire.

46. A physical education researcher wishes to determine if walking every day affects the health of middle-aged men. The researcher randomly identifies 400 participants in two groups. Members of one group belong to a health club and walk on its track and members of the other do not. After 2 months, the researcher decides the group who walks daily is healthier and concludes that walking positively affects men's health. This conclusion is of questionable validity because
a) of the placebo effect.
b) of confounding variables in the study.
c) the study is not double blind.
d) the researcher is not a doctor.

47. In a medical study that is double blind, participants do not know whether or not they are taking the experimental drug. This is to avoid
a) selection bias.   b) the placebo effect.   c) having too small a sample.   d) statistical significance.

48. In an experiment, an observed effect is called *statistically significant* if
a) the experiment will help a large number of people.
b) the study was double blind.
c) the experiment was well designed.
d) the effect is too large to attribute to chance.

49. The type of statistical study that can show cause and effect is
a) an experimental study.   b) an observational study.   c) a prospective study.   d) a survey study.

50. Nonresponse occurs when
a) all participants surveyed answer "no" to a question.
b) a sample for a study is not chosen at random.
c) an individual selected for a sample cannot be contacted.
d) a study does not produce statistically significant results.

Free-Response Questions

1. A polling company working for a candidate for governor surveys a sample of 2500 registered voters in the state to determine if they are in agreement with the candidate's stand on gun control. Describe the population for this study.

2. A biologist draws a sample of 200 fish from a lake to test for mercury levels. She finds that 8% have levels above limits set as healthy. Describe the population for this study.

3. In order to determine if students on a college campus are in favor of a tuition hike to pay for expanded parking services, a member of the student senate surveys 25 people in a commuter parking lot. Why is this a poor sampling technique?

4. Convenience samples are said to be highly likely to produce bias in survey results. Explain why this is true.

5. Explain the difference between bias and variability in sampling results.

6. We wish to know what proportion of students at a major university believe too much emphasis is placed on athletics at the school. Explain how we could choose a sample of 500 students to reduce the possibility of bias in the results.

7. In order to determine what proportion of a town's residents approve of a new plan for trash collection, the town council placed an ad in the newspaper asking residents to phone in their opinions. Explain why the results of this poll may differ from the actual beliefs of all residents in the town.

8. Define a *simple random sample.*

9. Can we eliminate variability in results of sampling? Why or why not?

10. Use the random digits table, beginning at line 103, to choose a sample of four people from the following list:

01 Adams	06 Ford	11 Kramer	16 Post
02 Brown	07 Goodman	12 Loomis	17 Quayle
03 Cook	08 Harris	13 Martin	18 Rogers
04 Davis	09 Inez	14 Norton	19 Stevens
05 Elliot	10 Jones	15 O'Hare	20 Thompson

11. We must use a random digits table to choose a sample of 8 names from the roster of a club with 100 members. Why can we use two-digit numbers from the table to select our sample?

12. The marketing department of a large national corporation wishes to determine what proportion of the residents of a state may be interested in buying its new product. Describe how the corporation might use a multi-stage random sampling process to choose a sample of the state's residents to survey.

13. A high school principal wishes to determine what proportion of the school's students like the new school mascot. The principal decides to survey every 25th name from the school enrollment records, (an alphabetical list of all students at the school). Is this a valid simple random sampling technique? Why or Why not?

14. In a poll of 2500 residents of a state it is found that 480 are in favor of naming the grasshopper the state insect. What is the sample proportion for this poll?

15. A marketing department surveys 1500 shoppers and finds that 950 would visit a new store more often if were open Sunday evenings. What is the sample proportion in this survey?

16. Why do opinion polls usually report a "margin of error" with the results of a survey? What does the margin of error mean?

17. What is the difference between an observational study and an experiment?

18. One July, the city council of a small town decides to impose an experimental curfew on all residents under 18 to cut down on loitering in the town square. After four months, the number of teens found in the square after dark has decreased 80%, and the council declares the curfew a success. Explain why this conclusion may not be valid.

19. A farmer believes that exposing chickens to classical music will cause them to produce more eggs. Describe how the farmer may design a randomized comparative experiment to test this theory.

20. A school superintendent believes a new approach to teaching children to read will produce better standardized test scores in the district. Describe how the superintendent may design a randomized comparative experiment to test this theory.

21. A school principal is concerned with the increasing level of absenteeism in the school. A meeting of parents, teachers, and students is called at which the principal expresses her concern and describes an experimental program that will be instituted to try to curb absenteeism. After two months, absenteeism is down by 15%. Explain how confounding variables may have affected the results of the experiment.

22. Medical experiments are frequently double blind. Explain what this means and why medical experiments are designed this way.

23. Describe what is meant by *the placebo effect* in an experiment.

24. How does a randomized comparative experiment control the effects of confounding variables?

25. What does it mean to say that the results of an experiment are *statistically significant*?

Chapter 6 Multiple-Choice Questions
Describing Data

1. Below are listed the ages of children in a home day care. Choose the correct dotplot of the data.

   1.5, 2, 2, 3, 3, 3.5, 4, 4, 4, 5

   a.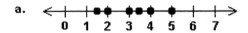

   b.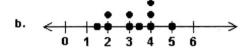

   c.

   d.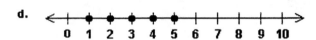

2. Below are listed the numbers of children in the classrooms of a small elementary school. Choose the correct boxplot of the data.

   12, 14, 20, 21, 21, 25, 27, 30, 30, 30

   a.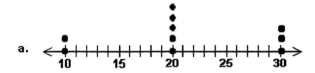

   b.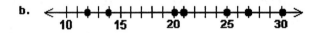

   c.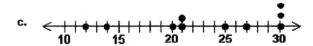

   d.

3. Given the dotplot below, which description is true?

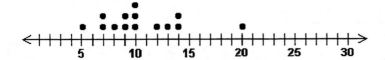

a) There are no outliers on the dotplot.
b) The numbers 5 and 20 are outliers on the dotplot.
c) The number 20 is the only outlier on the dotplot.
d) The number 5 is the only outlier on the dotplot.

4. Given the dotplot below, which description is true?

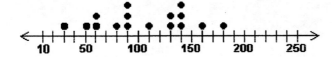

a) There are no outliers on the dotplot.
b) The number 30 is the only outlier on the dotplot.
c) The numbers 30 and 180 are both outliers on the dotplot.
d) The number 180 is the only outlier on the dotplot.

5. Given the dotplot below, which description is true?

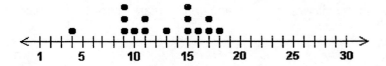

a) There are no outliers on the dotplot.
b) The number 4 is the only outlier on the dotplot.
c) The numbers 4 and 13 are both outliers on the dotplot.
d) The number 13 is the only outlier on the dotplot.

6. Below is a histogram of waiting times for patients at a health clinic. How many patients waited between 20 and 29 minutes?

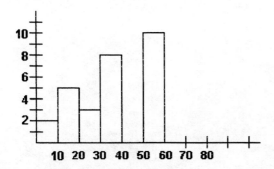

a) 2   b) 3   c) 6   d) 8

7. Given the histogram below of waiting times for patients at a health clinic, which statement must be true?

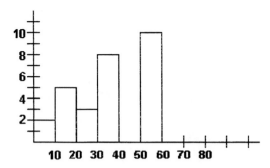

a) There are no gaps in the histogram.
b) Eight patients waited exactly 35 minutes.
c) Two patients were seen immediately on arrival at the clinic.
d) More patients waited longer than one-half hour than waited less than one-half hour.

8. Given the histogram of waiting times for patients at a health clinic, which statement is true?

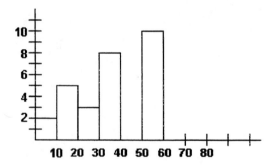

a) The histogram is roughly symmetric.
b) The class from 50 to 59 minutes represents 10 outliers.
c) There is a gap in the histogram.
d) The histogram is skewed to the right.

9. Below is a histogram of the ages of people attending a concert. Which statement is true?

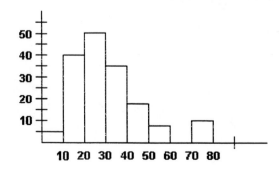

a) The histogram is roughly symmetric.
b) There is a gap in the histogram.

c) The histogram is skewed to the left.
d) The center of the distribution is at about age 50.

10. Given the histogram below, which statement is true?

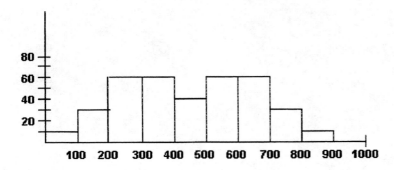

a) The histogram has an outlier between 400 and 500.
b) The histogram is skewed to the right.
c) The histogram is symmetric.
d) The histogram has a gap between 400 and 500.

11. Given the histogram below, which statement is true?

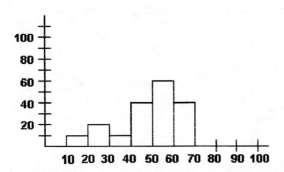

a) The histogram has a gap.
b) There is an outlier at 100.

c) The histogram is skewed to the left.
d) The histogram is roughly symmetric.

12. Below are the ages of 15 students in a college class. Find the median age.

27, 50, 33, 25, 86, 25, 85, 31, 37, 44, 20, 36, 59, 34, 28

a) 34   b) 31   c) 41.3   d) 20.6

13. Below are the ages of 15 students in a college class. Find the mean age.

27, 50, 33, 25, 86, 25, 85, 31, 37, 44, 20, 36, 59, 34, 28

a) 34   b) 31   c) 41.3   d) 20.6

14. Below are the ages of 15 students in a college class. Find the standard deviation of the ages.

27, 50, 33, 25, 86, 25, 85, 31, 37, 44, 20, 36, 59, 34, 28

a) 34   b) 31   c) 41.3   d) 20.6

15. Below are the ages of 15 students in a college class. Find the first quartile of the ages.

    27, 50, 33, 25, 86, 25, 85, 31, 37, 44, 20, 36, 59, 34, 28
a) 20   b) 25   c) 27   d) 50

16. Below are the heights (in inches) of students in a third-grade class. Find the mean height.

    39, 37, 48, 49, 40, 42, 48, 53, 47, 42, 49, 51, 52, 45, 47, 48
a) 47.5   b) 50   c) 46.0625   d) 47

17. Below are the heights (in inches) of students in a third-grade class. Find the median height.

    39, 37, 48, 49, 40, 42, 48, 53, 47, 42, 49, 51, 52, 45, 47, 48
a) 47.5   b) 50   c) 46.0625   d) 47

18. Below are the number of errors made by a typist on various pages of typing. Find the mean number of errors.

    14, 6, 12, 19, 2, 35, 5, 4, 3, 7, 5, 8
a) 6.5   b) 7   c) 9.583   d) 10

19. Below are the number of errors made by a typist on various pages of typing. Find the median number of errors.

    14, 6, 12, 19, 2, 35, 5, 4, 3, 7, 5, 8
a) 6.5   b) 7   c) 9.583   d) 10

20. Below are the number of errors made by a typist on various pages of typing. Find the third quartile for the number of errors.

    14, 6, 12, 19, 2, 35, 5, 4, 3, 7, 5, 8
a) 5   b) 13   c) 15.5   d) 4.5

21. Below are the number of errors made by a typist on various pages of typing. Find the first quartile for the number of errors.

    14, 6, 12, 19, 2, 35, 5, 4, 3, 7, 5, 8
a) 5   b) 13   c) 15.5   d) 4.5

22. Given the set of data below, find the mean.

    2, 4, 4, 5, 6, 9
a) 4.5   b) 5   c) 7   d) 30

23. Given the set of data below, find the median.

2, 4, 4, 5, 6, 9

a) 4.5   b) 5   c) 7   d) 30

24. Given the set of data below, find the variance.

2, 4, 4, 5, 6, 9

a) 2.366   b) 4.5   c) 5.598   d) 7

25. Given the set of data below, find the standard deviation.

2, 4, 4, 5, 6, 9

a) 2.366   b) 4.5   c) 5.598   d) 7

26. Given the set of data below, find the mean.

25, 16, 50, 19, 42, 37

a) 34.5   b) 31   c) 31.5   d) 50

27. Given the set of data below, find the median.

25, 16, 50, 19, 42, 37

a) 34.5   b) 31   c) 31.5   d) 50

28. Given the set of data below, find the variance.

25, 16, 50, 19, 42, 37

a) 184.3   b) 184.6   c) 921.5   d) 923

29. Given the set of data below, find the standard deviation.

25, 16, 50, 19, 42, 37

a) 6.07   b) 13.58   c) 184.3   d) 921.5

30. Below are the numbers of pages in seven chapters of a textbook. Find the mean number of pages.

14, 14, 20, 38, 47, 48, 57

a) 34   b) 38   c) 37.33   d) 42.5

31. Below are the numbers of pages in seven chapters of a textbook. Find the median number of pages.

14, 14, 20, 38, 47, 48, 57

a) 34   b) 38   c) 37.33   d) 42.5

32. Below are the numbers of pages in seven chapters of a textbook. Find the variance.

14, 14, 20, 38, 47, 48, 57

a) 312.4   b) 317.67   c) 324   d) 343

33. Below are the numbers of pages of seven chapters of a textbook. Find the standard deviation.

    14, 14, 20, 38, 47, 48, 57
    a) 18.52   b) 18   c) 17.82   d) 17.67

34. Below are the lengths (in minutes) of phone calls made on an 800 line to a business on one day. Find the five-number summary for this data.

    14, 6, 12, 19, 2, 35, 5, 4, 3, 7, 5, 8
    a) 5, 8, 14, 15.5, 20   b) 2, 4, 7, 14, 35   c) 2, 4, 6, 12, 19   d) 2, 4.5, 6.5, 13, 35

35. Below are the numbers of accidents occurring at a certain corner on 15 consecutive days. Find the five-number summary of the data.

    0, 1, 3, 4, 5, 2, 2, 6, 7, 2, 0, 1, 3, 6, 3
    a) 0, 1.5, 3.5, 5.5, 7   b) 0, 1, 3, 5, 7   c) 0, 4, 6, 1, 3   d) 0, 1.5, 3, 5.5, 7

36. Below are the scores of 21 students on a history exam. Find the five-number summary of the scores.

    50, 60, 60, 60, 65, 65, 70, 75, 75, 75, 75, 80, 80, 80, 85, 85, 90, 95, 95, 95, 100
    a) 50, 65, 75, 85, 100   b) 50, 65, 75, 87.5, 100   c) 50, 65, 76.9, 87.5, 100   d) 50, 65, 77.5, 90, 100

37. A typing service keeps data on the number of pages in a manuscript and the length of time (in hours) it takes to complete the typing. The least squares regression line for the data is given by $y = 20 + 0.273x$. Use this to predict the length of time needed to type a 40-page manuscript.
    a) 810.92   b) 60.273   c) 30.92   d) 16.38

38. An airline has determined that the relationship between the number of passengers on a flight and the total weight (in pounds) of luggage stored in the baggage compartment can be estimated by the least squares regression equation $y = 250 + 27x$. Predict the weight of luggage for a flight with 125 passengers.
    a) 402   b) 3625   c) 10,125   d) 34,625

39. The least squares regression equation $y = 50 + 0.1x$ gives the yield in bushels per acre of corn when x pounds of fertilizer are applied. Predict the yield for a farmer who plans to use 320 pounds of fertilizer.
    a) 82   b) 16,032   c) 37   d) 50.32

40. Which of the following statements about measures of the center of a distribution of data is true?
    a) Neither the mean nor the median is strongly affected by an outlier in the data.
    b) The mean is strongly affected by an outlier in the data but the median is not.
    c) The median is strongly affected by an outlier in the data but the mean is not.
    d) Both the mean and the median are strongly affected by an outlier in the data.

41. Which of the following statements about measures of the spread of data is true?
    a) Neither the quartiles nor the standard deviation is strongly affected by an outlier in the data.
    b) The quartiles are strongly affected by an outlier in the data but the standard deviation is not.
    c) The standard deviation is strongly affected by an outlier in the data but the quartiles are not.
    d) Both the quartiles and the standard deviation are strongly affected by an outlier in the data.

42. Given the histogram below for a set of data, which of the following statements is true?

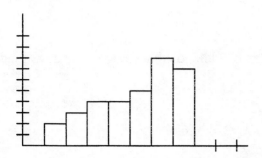

a) The five-number summary would describe the data better than the mean and standard deviation.
b) The mean and standard deviation would describe the data better than the five- number summary.
c) Either the mean and standard deviation or the five-number summary would be equally good to describe the data.
d) Neither the mean and standard deviation nor the five-number summary could be used to describe the data.

43. Given the histogram below for a set of data, which statement is true?

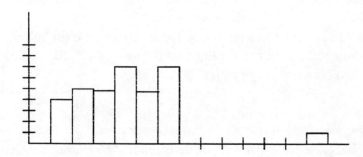

a) Either the mean or the median would describe the center of the data well.
b) The mean would be a better measure of the center of the data than the median.
c) The median would be a better measure of the center of the data than the mean.
d) Neither the mean nor the median would be a good measure of the center of the data.

44. Given the histogram below for a set of data, which statement is true?

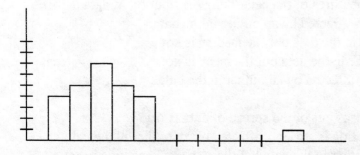

a) For the set of data shown, the mean and the median are about equal.
b) For the set of data shown, the mean is greater than the median.

c) For the set of data shown, the median is greater than the mean.
d) For the set of data shown, the relationship between the mean and the median cannot be determined.

45. Given the histogram below for a set of data, which statement is true?

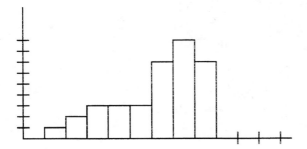

a) For the set of data shown, the mean and the median are about equal.
b) For the set of data shown, the mean is greater than the median.
c) For the set of data shown, the median is greater than the mean.
d) For the set of data shown, the relationship between the mean and the median cannot be determined.

46. Given the histogram below for a set of data, which statement is true?

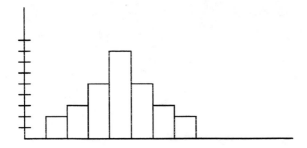

a) For the set of data shown, the mean and the median are about equal.
b) For the set of data shown, the mean is greater than the median.
c) For the set of data shown, the median is greater than the mean.
d) For the set of data shown, the relationship between the mean and the median cannot be determined.

47. A bank collects data on the savings and incomes of families to predict an expected increase in certificate of deposit accounts due to a 10% increase in salaries of employees at a local company. Which variable, savings or income, would be the explanatory variable?
a) Family savings   b) Family income

48. A university admissions counselor wishes to predict the performance of freshmen by considering their SAT scores. Which variable, freshman GPA or SAT score, would be the explanatory variable in a least squares regression equation?
a) Freshman GPA   b) SAT score

49. To choose advertising media, a marketing analyst studies the relationship between a consumer's income and the amount spent on restaurant dining. Which variable, consumer's income or dining expenditures, would be the response variable for a least squares regression equation?

a) Consumers income   b) Dining expenditures

50. To determine the effectiveness of group study sessions a college instructor gathers data on hours of attendance and exam scores for students in the class. Which variable, hours of attendance or exam scores, would be the response variable for a least squares regression equation?

a) Hours of attendance   b) Exam scores

Free-Response Questions

1. Below are family income figures (in thousands of dollars) for fifteen residents of a neighborhood. Make a dotplot of the income data.

17	31	25	30	21
25	28	19	32	25
32	27	21	26	21

2. The data below represent the numbers of auto accidents at a certain intersection each month for a year. Make a dotplot of the data.

    0, 1, 3, 4, 5, 2, 2, 6, 7, 2, 0, 1

3. The fifty measurements given below represent the weights, in ounces, of zucchini grown in a garden one summer. Make a histogram of the weights using classes of width of 5 oz. Does the distribution appear to be symmetric?

12	8	23	14	25	22	16	28	35	26
27	26	30	18	37	26	31	37	20	28
42	21	27	7	25	18	23	11	23	32
30	29	36	22	38	32	26	6	17	33
28	11	20	32	24	28	12	32	19	38

4. Below are exam scores for 26 students in an English course. Make a histogram of the scores.

84	77	67	94	90	77	79
81	56	89	77	88	72	93
74	76	28	80	58	94	
66	77	89	81	78	93	

5. Below are exam scores for 26 students in an English course. Find the median exam score.

84	77	67	94	90	77	79
81	56	89	77	88	72	93
74	76	28	80	58	94	
66	77	89	81	78	93	

6. Below are family income figures (in thousands of dollars) for fifteen residents of a neighborhood. Find the median family income.

17	31	25	30	21
25	28	19	32	25
32	27	21	26	21

7. Find the mean of the following set of data

23, 45, 26, 18, 11, 42, 35, 16, 32

8. Below are the ages of students attending an art exhibit. Find the mean age of the students.

    11, 11, 12, 12, 13, 1 3, 13, 13, 13, 14, 14, 15, 15, 15, 16, 16, 17, 17, 18

9. Below are the ages of students attending an art exhibit. Find the first and third quartiles of the data.

    11, 11, 12, 12, 13, 1 3, 13, 13, 13, 14, 14, 15, 15, 15, 16, 16, 17, 17, 18

10. A linguist is studying the lengths of paragraphs in a given text. The number of words in 20 paragraphs are given below. Find the five-number summary for the data.

42	88	37	75	98	93	73	62	96	80
52	76	66	54	73	69	83	62	53	79

11. Find the five-number summary for the following set of data.

2	11	6	4	18
1	9	2	2	15
8	16	12	11	17

12. Below are the exam scores of thirty students. Make a boxplot of this data.

24	31	38	49	51	55	56	59	62	63
65	66	69	72	72	74	76	81	84	84
86	86	86	88	88	88	91	91	92	99

13. Below are the ages of thirty people who died in a city hospital in one month. Make a boxplot of this data.

7	22	25	31	37	38	41	48	49	50
55	58	62	62	64	65	66	66	72	75
76	76	76	85	86	88	88	88	92	94

14. Find the variance of the following set of data.

    5, 7, 17, 31, 45, 47, 68, 85, 96, 99

15. Below are the ages of 6 patients seen by a pediatrician on one day. Find the variance of the ages.

    3, 6, 7, 9, 15, 20

16. Two towns both have a mean income for their residents of \$30,000. The standard deviation of incomes of residents in town A is \$2600 and the standard deviation of incomes of residents in town B is \$25,000. Explain what this says about the difference in the distribution of incomes in the two towns.

17. Below are the ages of 6 patients seen by a pediatrician on one day. Find the standard deviation of the

ages.

3, 6, 7, 9, 15, 20

18. Find the standard deviation of the following set of measurements.

4, 7, 9, 11, 13, 22

19. Below are data on the age of ten cars and the amount spent on auto repairs in one year. Make a scatterplot of the data.

Age (years)	Auto repairs ($)
2	120
3	175
3	160
5	250
6	325
7	380
10	500
12	615
12	630
15	770

20. Below are data on two related variables. Make a scatterplot of the data.

X	Y
118	66
99	50
120	73
121	69
123	72
108	65
111	62

21. Below is a histogram of car prices on a used car lot. An advertisement for the lot says the average price of a car for sale is $12,000. Could the advertisement be true? Why or why not?

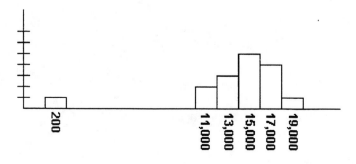

22. Below is a histogram for a set of data. Would you use the five-number summary or the mean and standard deviation to describe these data? Why?

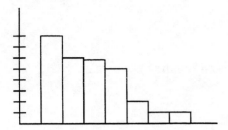

23. Below is the scatterplot for data collected on two variables. Would a least squares regression equation be useful in describing the relationship between the variables? Why or why not?

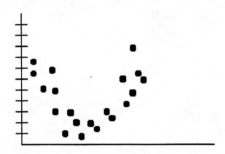

24. In the list of five measurements shown below, one is blurred. What *must* this value be, if the mean of the five measurements is 6?

     8   5   10   3   #

25. In the list of five measurements shown below, one is blurred. Supply a fifth value that would make the median 8.

     8   5   10   3   #

Chapter 7 Multiple-Choice Questions
Probability: The Mathematics of Chance

1. A die is rolled and a coin is flipped simultaneously. The number rolled on the die and whether the coin lands heads or tails is recorded. How many outcomes are in the sample space?
a) 8   b) 6   c) 10   d) 12

2. Two coins are flipped at the same time and it is recorded whether each coin lands heads or tails. The sample space for this is
a) {H, T}.   b) {HH, HT, TT}.   c) {HH, HT, TH, TT}.   d) {H, H, T, T}.

3. A spinner numbered 1 through 10 is spun and one die is tossed simultaneously. The number spun and the number rolled are recorded. How many outcomes are in the sample space?
a) 60   b) 16   c) 10   d) 6

4. A spinner numbered 1 through 10 is spun and one die is rolled simultaneously. The sum of the number spun and the number rolled is recorded. How many outcomes are in the sample space?
a) 60   b) 16   c) 15   d) 10

5. Three dice are tossed. The number rolled on each die is recorded. How many outcomes are in the sample space?
a) 18   b) 72   c) 216   d) 42

6. Three dice are tossed. The sum of the numbers rolled is recorded. How many outcomes are in the sample space?
a) 18   b) 12   c) 16   d) 72

7. Three dice are rolled and the number rolled on each die is recorded. The outcomes in the sample space are all equally likely.
a) True   b) False

8. Three dice are rolled and the sum of the numbers rolled is recorded. The outcomes in the sample space are all equally likely.
a) True   b) False

9. Two coins are flipped and the number that landed on heads is recorded. The outcomes in the sample space are all equally likely.
a) True   b) False

10. Two coins are flipped and whether each one landed heads or tails is recorded. The outcomes in the sample space are all equally likely.
a) True   b) False

11. There are seven blue and six black socks in a drawer. One is pulled out at random. Find the probability that it is black.
a) 6/13   b) 6/7   c) 1/2   d) 1/6

12. Two fair dice are rolled and the sum rolled is recorded. Find the probability that the sum is 4.
 a) 1/3   b) 1/12   c) 4/11   d) 1/9

13. A fair coin is tossed three times. Find the probability of getting exactly 2 heads.
 a) 1/2   b) 1/3   c) 2/3   d) 3/8

14. If a fair die is rolled once, what is the probability of getting a number less than five?
 a) 1/6   b) 1/2   c) 2/3   d) 5/6

15. A computer is programmed to randomly print two letters in a row without repeating a letter. What is the probability that the first combination printed is the word "DO?"
 a) 1/325   b) 1/650   c) 2/325   d) 1/26

16. We need to create three-digit code numbers that must begin with a 7. How many such codes can be made?
 a) 700   b) 107   c) 100   d) 27

17. We need to create serial numbers that start with one of the letters a, b, c, d, or f followed by three non-repeating digits. How many serial numbers can be created?
 a) 32   b) 2520   c) 725   d) 3600

18. We need to create code words that use three letters of the alphabet. Repeating of letters is allowed. How many code words can be created?
 a) 17,576   b) 15,600   c) 78   d) 75

19. A computer system requires users to have an access code that consists of a three-digit number that is not allowed to start with zero and cannot repeat digits. How many such codes are possible?
 a) 990   b) 648   c) 729   d) 720

20. The Olympic flag consists of five intertwined circles, one in each of the colors black, blue, green, red, and yellow. What is the probability that a random coloring of the five circles using these colors will produce the exact match of the Olympic symbol?
 a) 1/5   b) 1/3125   c) 5/120   d) 1/120

21. Either Terry, Chris, or Kim will attend a party. The probability Terry attends is 0.31 and the probability Chris attends is 0.5. What is the probability that Kim attends?
 a) 0.33   b) 0.5   c) 0.81   d) 0.19

22. If there is a 0.8 probability of rain today, what is the probability it will not rain?
 a) 0.8   b) 0.5   c) 0.2   d) 0.1

23. A sample space has three outcomes, A, B, and C. The probability of outcome A is 0.39 and the probability of outcome B is 0.25. What is the probability of outcome C?
 a) 0.36   b) 0.33   c) 0.5   d) 0.64

24. A sample space contains three outcomes, A, B, and C. Which of the following could be a legitimate assignment of probabilities to the outcomes?
a) P(A) = 0.2   P(B) = 0.4   P(C) = 0.6
b) P(A) = 0.2   P(B) = 0.2   P(C) = 0.6
c) P(A) = 2   P(B) = 3   P(C) = 1
d) P(A) = 0.3   P(B) = 0.3   P(C) = 0.3

25. A sample space consists of three outcomes, X, Y, and Z. Which of the following could be a legitimate assignment of probabilities to the outcomes?
a) P(X) = 0.3   P(Y) = 0.6   P(Z) = 0.9
b) P(X) = 0.3   P(Y) = 0.2   P(Z) = 0.5
c) P(X) = 0.3   P(Y) = 0.3   P(Z) = 0.3
d) P(X) = 0.7   P(Y) = -0.3   P(Z) = 0.6

26. A raffle ticket costs $5. First and second prize winners will be drawn at random. The probability of winning the $100 first prize is 1/40 and the probability of winning the $25 second prize is 1/20. What is the mean winnings for one play, taking into account the $5 cost of the ticket?
a) 3.75   b) 3.375   c) -0.875   d) -1.25

27. Suppose a game has three outcomes, A, B, and C with probabilities P(A) = 0.2, P(B) = 0.3 and P(C) = 0.5. A player will receive $3 when outcome A occurs, $4 when outcome B occurs, and will have to pay $2 when outcome C occurs. What is the mean value of one trial of the game?
a) 0.80   b) 1.66   c) 1.00   d) 5.00

28. At a certain discount store, the number of people in checkout lines varies. The probability model for the number of people in a randomly chosen line is

Number in line	0	1	2	3	4	5
Probability	0.08	0.15	0.20	0.22	0.15	0.20

What is the mean number of people in a line?
a) 2.5   b) 15.92   c) 2.81   d) 2.89

29. A fair die is rolled. If a number 1 or 2 appears, you will receive $5. If any other number appears, you will pay $2. What is the mean value of one trial of this game?
a) $1/3   b) $3   c) $3/2   d) -$3

30. The marketing department of an electronics manufacturer has done research on the number of television sets owned by families in a large town. The probability model for the number of sets owned by a randomly chosen family is given below. What is the mean number of sets per family?

Number of sets	0	1	2	3
Probability	0.04	0.34	0.47	0.15

a) 0.96   b) 1.5   c) 1.77   d) 1.73

31. The shelf life of a battery produced by one major company is known to be normally distributed, with a mean life of 3.5 years and a standard deviation of 0.75 years. What is the upper quartile of battery shelf life?
a) 4.0025 years   b) 4.25 years   c) 4.17 years   d) 5.25 years

32. The length of students' college careers at Anytown University is known to be normally distributed, with a mean length of 5.5 years and a standard deviation of 1.75 years. What is the lower quartile for the length of students' careers at Anytown University?
a) 4.83 years   b) 3.75 years   c) 4.3275 years   d) 2.75 years

33. The scores of students on standardized test form a normal distribution with a mean of 300 and a standard deviation of 40. What are the lower and upper quartile scores for this test?
a) 299.33 and 300.67   b) 273.2 and 326.8   c) 260 and 340   d) 150 and 450

34. The mean length of time, per week, that students at a certain school spend on their homework is 24.3 hours, with a standard deviation of 1.4 hours. Assuming the distribution of study times is normal, what percent of students spend more than 25.238 hours per week on homework?
a) 16.5%   b) 5%   c) 12.5%   d) 25%

35. The scores of students on a standardized test are normally distributed with a mean of 300 and a standard deviation of 40. What is the probability that a randomly chosen student scores below 273.2 on the test?
a) 0.025   b) 0.25   c) 0.165   d) 0.125

36. The annual income of residents in a county is $42,000 with a standard deviation of $10,000. Between what two values do 95% of the incomes of county residents lie?
a) $40,000 and $44,000   b) $22,000 and $62,000   c) $32,000 and $52,000   d) $30,000 and $50,000

37. The shelf life of a battery produced by one major company is known to be normally distributed, with a mean life of 3.5 years and a standard deviation of 0.75 years. What range of years contains 68% of all battery shelf lives?
a) 2 to 5 years   b) 2.5 to 4.5 years   c) 2.83 to 4.17 years   d) 2.75 to 4.25

38. The scores of students on a standardized test are normally distributed with a mean of 300 and a standard deviation of 40. Between what two values do 99.7% of the test scores lie?
a) 260 to 340   b) 220 to 380   c) 297 to 303   d) 180 to 420

39. The mean length of time, per week, that students at a certain school spend on their homework is 24.3 hours, with a standard deviation of 1.4 hours. Assuming the distribution of study times is normal, what percent of students study between 22.9 and 25.7 hours?
a) 99.7%   b) 95%   c) 68%   d) 50%

40. The length of students' college careers at Anytown University is known to be normally distributed, with a mean length of 5.5 years and a standard deviation of 1.75 years. What percent of students have college careers lasting between 2 and 9 years?
a) 50%   b) 99.75   c) 68%   d) 95%

41. The shelf life of a battery produced by one major company is known to be normally distributed, with a mean life of 3.5 years and a standard deviation of 0.75 years. What percent of batteries last between 1.25 and 5.75 years?
    a) 99.7% b) 95% c) 68% d) 50%

42. The annual income of residents in a certain county is normally distributed, with a mean of $42,000 and a standard deviation of $10,000. What is the probability that a randomly chosen resident has income over $52,000?
    a) 16% b) 32% c) 50% d) 68%

43. The weight of potato chip bags filled by a machine at a packaging plant is normally distributed, with a mean of 15.0 ounces and a standard deviation of 0.2 ounces. What is the probability that a randomly chosen bag will weigh less than 14.6 ounces?
    a) 50% b) 5% c) 2.5% d) 2%

44. The weight of potato chip bags filled by a machine at a packaging plant is normally distributed, with a mean of 15.0 ounces and a standard deviation of 0.2 ounces. What is the probability that a randomly chosen bag will weigh more than 15.6 ounces?
    a) 5% b) 2.5% c) 0.3% d) 0.15%

45. Using the Central Limit Theorem for a normally distributed variable, how would the standard deviation of the sample mean for a sample of size 200 be related to that of size 3200?
    a) It would be one-sixteenth as large.
    b) It would be one-fourth as large.
    c) It would be four times as large.
    d) It would be sixteen times as large.

46. The weight of bags of potato chips produced by one machine at a packaging plant has a standard deviation of 0.2 ounces. Suppose a sample of 25 bags is drawn from a production run and weighed. What is the standard deviation σ_x of the mean result?
    a) 0.008 b) 0.04 c) 0.2 d) 1.0

47. A poll of 60 students found that 20% were in favor of raising parking fees to pave two new parking lots. The standard deviation of this poll is about 5.2%. What would be the standard deviation if the sample size was increased from 60 students to 120 students?
    a) 10.4% b) 7.3% c) 2.6% d) 3.67%

48. The batteries used by a calculator have useful lives that follow a normal distribution, with an average life of 2000 hours and a standard deviation of 200 hours. In the production process, the manufacturer draws random samples of 100 batteries and determines the mean useful life of the sample. What is the standard deviation σ_x of this mean?
    a) 25 hours b) 100 hours c) 2 hours d) 20 hours

49. A poll of 60 students found that 20% were in favor of raising parking fees to pave two new parking lots. The standard deviation of this poll is about 5.2%. How large a sample would be needed to reduce this standard deviation to 2.6%?
    a) 30 b) 1200 c) 120 d) 240

50. The weight of bags of potato chips produced by one machine at a packaging plant has a standard deviation of 0.3 ounces. A sample of chip bags is to be drawn and the mean weight calculated. How large must the sample be if the standard deviation of the sampling distribution is to be 0.1 ounce?

a) 9 bags   b) 3 bags   c) 6 bags   d) 10 bags

Free-Response Questions

1. A spinner with regions numbered 1 to 4 is spun and a coin is tossed. Both the number spun and whether the coin lands heads or tails is recorded. Write the sample space.

2. Three coins are flipped simultaneously and it is recorded whether each coin lands heads or tails. List the sample space.

3. A pair of dice is rolled. Sam says there are 36 outcomes in the sample space for this procedure and Sally says there are 11 outcomes in the sample space. Explain how they could both be correct.

4. Exactly one of three contestants will win a game show. The probability that Terry wins is 0.25 and the probability that Chris wins is 0.65. What is the probability that Toni wins?

5. If the probability that Kerry gets an "A" in English class is 0.82, what is the probability that Kerry does not get an "A?"

6. Suppose three fair coins are tossed and the number of heads that appear is recorded. What is the probability of getting exactly two heads?

7. A pair of fair dice is rolled and the sum of the faces showing is recorded. What is the probability of getting a sum greater than 9?

8. We wish to make a spinner that will be numbered 1 to 4, but will have the probability of spinning a "1" be 0.5. Draw the face for such a spinner.

9. Find the probability of drawing a three or a heart from a regular (bridge) deck of cards. (Such a deck consists of four suits of thirteen cards each. The suits are hearts, spades, diamonds, and clubs. The cards are 1 through 10, Jack, Queen, and King.)

10. We must create a license plate code that consists of two letters followed by three digits. The letters cannot repeat, but the digits may. How many such license plate codes can be formed?

11. A pizza can be made with any of the following toppings: Cheese, pepperoni, sausage, mushrooms, anchovies, green peppers, or olives. How many different three-topping pizzas can be made? Doubling of any topping is not allowed.

12. A license plate code consists of two letters followed by three digits. The letters cannot repeat, but the digits can. What is the probability that a randomly chosen plate has all three digits the same?

13. A pizza can be made with any of the following toppings: Cheese, pepperoni, sausage, mushrooms, anchovies, green peppers, or olives. Doubling of any topping is not allowed. What is the probability that a randomly created three-topping pizza will contain mushrooms?

14. A student is taking a five-question "True"/"False" Test. If the students chooses answers at random, what is the probability of getting all questions correct?

15. Below is a probability model for the number of automobiles owned by a randomly chosen family in a large town. What is the mean number of automobiles owned?

Number of automobiles	0	1	2	3
Probability	0.15	0.20	0.55	0.10

16. Suppose a game has four outcomes, A, B, C, and D. The probability of outcome A is 0.4, the probabilities of each of the other outcomes is 0.2. A player receives $2 if outcome A occurs, $3 if outcome B occurs, $1 if outcome C occurs and must pay $5 if outcome D occurs. What is the mean value of one trial of this game?

17. The mean value of one trial of a carnival game is -$.05. Explain what this means.

18. The scores of students on a standardized test form a normal distribution with a mean score of 500 and a standard deviation of 100. Between what two values do the middle 50% of scores lie?

19. The average length of time, per week, that students at a certain university spend on homework is normally distributed with a mean of 24.3 hours and a standard deviation of 1.4 hours. Jane tells her parents she spends more time studying than 75% of the students on campus. How many hours per week must Jane spend on homework for this to be true?

20. The scores of students on a standardized test form a normal distribution with a mean of 300 and a standard deviation of 40. Two thousand students took the test. Find the number of students who score above 380.

21. The mean weight of a collection of potatoes in a shipment to a fruit market is 1.3 lbs, with a standard deviation of 0.35 lbs. The distribution of weights is approximately normal. What is the probability that one potato chosen at random will weigh more than 1.65 lbs?

22. The mean weight of a collection of potatoes in a shipment to a fruit market is 1.3 lbs, with a standard deviation of 0.35 lbs. The distribution of weights is approximately normal. What fraction of the potatoes in the shipment will weigh between 0.25 and 2.35 lbs?

23. In the manufacturing process for ball bearings, the mean diameter is 5 mm with a standard deviation of 0.002 mm. Between what two measurements will 95% of all diameters of ball bearings be found?

24. In the manufacturing process for ball bearings, the mean diameter is 5 mm with a standard deviation of 0.002 mm. Each hour a sample of 20 bearings is drawn, measured and the mean diameter of the sample found. What is the standard deviation σ_x of the sample mean?

25. A publisher wishes to know what percent of book pages will need graphics editing. A random sample of 25 pages in a textbook finds that 58% of the pages had drawings or figures on them. The standard deviation for this percent is 9.9%. If the publisher wishes to reduce the standard deviation to 3.3%, how many pages should the publisher sample?

Chapter 8 Multiple-Choice Questions
Statistical Interference

1. A poll of 1500 voters finds that 36% are in favor of a certain candidate. In this example, 36% is a
a) parameter.   b) population.   c) statistic.   d) sample.

2. A random sample of bags of potato chips produced by a company has a mean weight of 15.3 ozs., which is greater than the 14.9 oz. mean weight of all bags of chips produced by the company. In this example, 14.9 is called a
a) parameter.   b) population.   c) statistic.   d) sample.

3. A random sample of bags of potato chips produced by a company has a mean weight of 15.3 ozs., which is greater than the 14.9 oz. mean weight of all bags of chips produced by the company. In this example, 15.3 is called a
a) population.   b) parameter.   c) sample.   d) statistic.

4. To determine the proportion of students at a university who favor the construction of a parking garage, a random sample of people chosen from current enrollment lists is surveyed and it is found that 43% favor the garage. The actual proportion of the student body who favor the garage is 40%. In this example, 43% is a
a) population.   b) parameter.   c) sample.   d) statistic.

5. To determine the proportion of students at a university who favor the construction of a parking garage, a random sample of people chosen from current enrollment lists is surveyed and it is found that 43% favor the garage. The actual proportion of the student body who favor the garage is 40%. In this example, 40% is a
a) sample.   b) population.   c) parameter.   d) statistic.

6. In the manufacturing process for ball bearings, the mean diameter is 5 mm with a standard deviation of 0.002 mm. A random sample of 20 bearings is drawn and the mean diameter is found to be 4.996 mm. In this example, 5 mm is a
a) statistic.   b) parameter.   c) sample.   d) population.

7. In the manufacturing process for ball bearings, the mean diameter is 5 mm with a standard deviation of 0.002 mm. A random sample of 20 bearings is drawn and the mean diameter is found to be 4.996 mm. In this example, 4.996 mm is a
a) sample.   b) statistic.   c) population.   d) parameter.

8. To determine the proportion of students at a university who favor the construction of a parking garage, 500 students are randomly chosen from current enrollment lists and surveyed. It is found that 215 are in favor of the garage. What is the sample proportion?
a) 43%   b) 21.5%   c) 2.3%   d) 4.3%

9. A poll of 1500 people finds that 1140 are in favor of candidate Jones for governor. What is the sample proportion?

a) 1.3%   b) 76%   c) 13%   d) 7.6%

10. A poll of 80 students selected at random at Midtown University found that 20 were in favor of a fee increase to support extra maintenance of the gardens on campus. In this example, what is the sample proportion?
a) 20% b) 25% c) 4% d) 40%

11. A sample of 75 people at a local fast-food restaurant found 30 in favor of new fat-free menu items. In this example, what is the sample proportion?
a) 30%   b) 40%   c) 2.5%   d) 75%

12. A random sample of 300 car owners in Brownsville indicated that 36 had full insurance coverage on glass breakage for their car, with no detuctible amount. In this example, what is the sample proportion?
a) 36% b) 8.3% c) 83% d) 12%

13. In a Midwestern state, 36% of all voters favor candidate Jones for governor. A random sample of 1500 voters is to be polled. The percent who favor Jones is the statistic of interest. What is the standard deviation of the sampling distribution of this statistic?
a) 6.8%   b) 3.4%   c) 1.78%   d) 1.33%

14. Forty percent of students at a given university favor the construction of a parking garage. Five hundred students will be chosen at random and surveyed about the garage. The percent in favor is the statistic of interest. What is the standard deviation of the sampling distribution of this statistic?
a) 0.098%   b) 0.76%   c) 9.8%   d) 2.2%

15. Twenty five percent of the students at Midtown University favor a fee increase to pay for the maintenance of the campus gardens. Ninety students will be chosen at random and surveyed about the fee increase. The percent who approve is the statistic of interest. What is the standard deviation of the sampling distribution of this statistic?
a) 0.48%   b) 4.16%   c) 4.56%   d) 4.8%

16. Sixty five percent of the patrons of a fast-food restaurant approve of new fat-free menu items. Eighty people will be randomly selected and asked about the menu. The percent in favor of the fat-free items is the statistic of interest. What is the standard deviation of the sampling distribution of this statistic?
a) 3.53%   b) 0.017%   c) 5.33%   d) 1.7%

17. Twenty eight percent of the voters in a certain city favor an income tax increase to support the building of a new sports arena. Two hundred fifty people will be randomly chosen and asked about the tax increase. The percent who are in favor is the statistic of interest. What is the standard deviation of the sampling distribution of this statistic?
a) 17.9%   b) 1.52%   c) 2.84%   d) 0.18%

18. The life of a washing machine produced by one major company has a mean of 8.55 years and a standard deviation of 1.45 years. Ten washing machines are to be chosen at random and the mean life found. What is the standard deviation of the sampling distribution for the mean life?
a) 0.46 years   b) 0.38 years   c) 0.145 years   d) 0.92 years

19. In the manufacturing process for ball bearings, it is found that the mean diameter is 5 mm with a standard deviation of 0.002 mm. Each hour a random sample of 20 bearings is drawn and the mean diameter found. What is the standard deviation of the sampling distribution for the mean diameter?
    a) 0.0001 mm   b) 0.01 mm   c) 0.0022 mm   d) 0.00045 mm

20. The mean shelf life of a battery produced by one major company is known to be 3.5 years with a standard deviation of 0.75 years. A random sample of 25 batteries is selected and the mean life determined. What is the standard deviation of the sampling distribution for the mean life?
    a) 0.15 years   b) 0.03 years   c) 0.173 years   d) 0.035 years

21. A potato chip bagging machine operator knows the machine fills bags to a mean weight of 13 ozs. with a standard deviation of 0.19 ozs. The operator selects a random sample of 25 bags and finds the mean weight. What is the standard deviation of the sampling distribution for the mean weight?
    a) 0.0076 ozs.   b) 0.0174 ozs.   c) 0.038 ozs.   d) 0.087 ozs.

22. The annual income of residents in a certain county has a mean of $42,000 and a standard deviation of $10,000. For a survey, 150 residents will be polled and the mean income determined. What is the standard deviation of the sampling distribution for the mean income?
    a) $8.16   b) $0.667   c) $816.00   d) $67.00

23. A poll of 1200 randomly selected residents in a state found that 63% favored higher taxes to support education. Find a 95% confidence interval for the proportion of the state's residents who support taxes for education.
    a) 62.76 to 63.24%   b) 62.51 to 63.49%   c) 61.6 to 64.4%   d) 60.2 to 65.8%

24. A random sample of 20 pages of a textbook was made and 60% of the pages had drawings or figures on them. Find a 95% confidence interval for the actual proportion of pages on which a drawing or figure would be found.
    a) 49.1 to 70.9%   b) 44.5 to 75.7%   c) 38.1 to 81.9%   d) 29 to 91%

25. A random sample of 1540 adults were asked if they jog. Fifteen percent answered "yes." Find a 95% confidence interval for the percent of all adults who would answer "yes" when asked if they jog.
    a) 14.09 to 15.91%   b) 13.2 to 16.8%   c) 14.79 to 15.21%   d) 14.58 to 15.42%

26. A random sample of 200 college students living off-campus found that 57% had a dishwasher in their residence. Find a 95% confidence interval for the percent of all college students living off-campus with dishwashers.
    a) 53.5 to 60.5%   b) 55.4 to 58.6%   c) 51.8 to 58.2%   d) 50 to 64%

27. A random sample of 250 of the residents of a city found that 235 believe the intersection of Main and First streets is dangerous. Find a 95% confidence interval for the true percent of the city's residents who believe the intersection is dangerous.
    a) 92.5 to 95.5%   b) 91.0 to 97.0%   c) 71 to 100%   d) 93.54 to 94.46%

28. A random sample of 900 workers in Brownsville found 72 workers who had full health insurance

coverage. Find a 95% confidence interval for the true proportion of Brownsville workers who have full health insurance coverage.
a) 7.1 to 8.9%   b) 6.2 to 9.8%   c) 70.2 to 73.8%   d) 69 to 75%

29. A random sample of 300 car owners in Centralville found that 36 had collision insurance for their cars. Find a 95% confidence interval for the true percent of Centralville car owners with collision coverage.
a) 30.46 to 41.54%   b) 6.5 to 17.5%   c) 8.25 to 15.75%   d) 10.1 to 13.9%

30. A random poll of 600 voters in a state found that 48 believed their senator was honest and trustworthy. Find a 95% confidence interval for the true percent of the voters in the state who believe their senator is honest and trustworthy.
a) 43.9 to 52.1%   b) 45.8 to 50.2%   c) 6.9 to 9.1%   d) 5.8 to 10.2%

31. A machine that produces plastic jar lids is set to produce lids with a diameter of 9 cm. The standard deviation of the diameters, due to the production process, is 0.02 cm. A quality-control worker checks a sample of 25 lids from each production run and finds the mean diameter. One day, the mean diameter for the sample is 8.99 cm. Find a 95% confidence interval for the true mean diameter of lids produced that day.
a) 8.95 to 9.03 cm   b) 8.993 to 9.047 cm   c) 8.982 to 8.998 cm   d) 8.97 to 9.01 cm

32. The standard deviation of the weight of individual potatoes in a shipment to a packing plant is 0.35 lbs. A sample of 20 potatoes is drawn at random and the mean weight is found to be 1.4 lbs. Find a 95% confidence interval for the true mean weight of all potatoes in the shipment.
a) 0.7 to 2.1 lbs.   b) 1.135 to 1.665 lbs.   c) 1.243 to 1.557 lbs.   d) 1.322 to 1.4078 lbs.

33. In the manufacturing process for ball bearings, the mean diameter is supposed to be 5 mm with a standard deviation of 0.002 mm. One hour, a sample of 10 bearings is drawn and the mean diameter is found to be 4.998 mm. Find a 95% confidence interval for the true mean diameter of bearings produced that hour.
a) 4.994 to 5.002 mm   b) 4.9967 to 4.9993 mm   c) 4.97 to 5.026 mm   d) 4.9974 to 4.9986 mm

34. The standard deviation of the thickness of boards in a shipment is 0.02 in. A sample of 16 boards is chosen and found to have a mean thickness of 1.99 in. Find a 95% confidence interval for the true mean thickness of boards in the shipment.
a) 1.95 to 2.03 in   b) 1.98 to 2.00 in   c) 1.985 to 1.995 in   d) 1.92 to 2.06 in

35. A machine that produces plastic jar lids is set to produce a diameter of 9 cm. The standard deviation of the diameters, due to the production process, is 0.02 cm. A quality control worker checks a sample of five lids from each production run and finds the diameters to be 8.97 cm, 8.99 cm, 9.01 cm, 9.00 cm, and 9.01 cm. Find a 95% confidence interval for the true mean diameter of lids produced that day.
a) 8.956 to 9.036 cm   b) 8.987 to 9.005 cm   c) 8.978 to 9.014 cm   d) 8.870 to 9.122 cm

36. The standard deviation of the weight of individual potatoes in a shipment to a packing plant is 0.35 lbs. A sample of four potatoes is drawn at random and their weights are found to be 1.40 lbs, 1.39 lbs, 1.42 lbs, and 1.39 lbs. Find a 95% confidence interval for the true mean weight of all potatoes in the shipment.
a) 1.05 to 1.75 lbs   b) 0.7 to 2.1 lbs   c) 0.81 to 1.99 lbs   d) 1.11 to 1.69 lbs

37. Your bathroom scale is known to have a standard deviation of 0.5 lbs. This morning you weighed yourself four times and got the following results: 146.5 lbs, 149 lbs, 148.5 lbs, and 150 lbs. Find a 95% confidence interval for your true weight.
    a) 147.5 to 149.5 lbs   b) 147.8 to 149.2 lbs   c) 148.25 to 148.75 lbs   d) 148 to 149 lbs

38. The standard deviation of the thickness of boards in a shipment is 0.02 in. A sample of five boards is taken and their thicknesses found to be 3.99 in., 3.98 in., 3.99in., 4.00 in., and 4.01 in. Find a 95% confidence interval for the true mean thickness of boards in the shipment.
    a) 3.954 to 4.034 in.   b) 3.9851 to 4.0029 in.   c) 3.868 to 4.120 in.   d) 3.9762 to 4.0118 in.

39. A light bulb manufacturer wants to know the mean burning time of the light bulbs it produces. A random sample of 2000 bulbs is taken, each bulb is used until it burns out and the sample mean burning time is found. The company concluded that a 95% confidence interval for the true mean burning time of all its light bulbs is 2035 ± 24.6 hours.
    If the company wishes to decrease the width of the confidence interval, it may do so by
    a) decreasing the sample size to less than 2000 bulbs.
    b) decreasing the confidence level to less than 95%.
    c) increasing the mean burning time of its light bulbs.
    d) increasing the confidence level to more than 95%.

40. A control chart is a plot whose purpose is to
    a) illustrate the 68-95-99.7 rule.
    b) show the values of all items produced by a company.
    c) display a five-number summary of a set of quality control data.
    d) show whether or not a production process is operating within acceptable bounds of its target setting.

41. A soft drink can filling machine operator knows the machine is supposed to fill cans to 12 ozs. and the standard deviation for the volume of all cans filled by the machine is 0.19 ozs. In order to determine if the cans are being under or overfilled, samples of 25 cans are drawn from each production run and the mean volume of the sample found. Find the 95% control limits that would be used on a control chart for the can filling process.
    a) 11.924 to 12.076 ozs.   b) 11.62 to 12.38 ozs.   c) 11.962 to 12.038 ozs.   d) 11.83 to 12.17 ozs.

42. A soft drink can filling machine operator knows the machine is supposed to fill cans to 12 ozs. and the standard deviation for the volume of all cans filled by the machine is 0.19 ozs. In order to determine if the cans are being under or overfilled, samples of 25 cans are drawn from each production run and the mean volume of the sample found. If the company uses 95% control limits on its process control charts, would a sample mean volume of 12.08 be out of the control limits?
    a) Yes   b) No

43. A tool and die company makes dies which are to have a 2-in. diameter. the standard deviation of the produced parts is 0.003-in. Samples of 10 dies are chosen each day and the mean diameter of the sample found. What would be the 95% control limits for a process control chart used by the company?
    a) 1.9981 to 2.0019 in.   b) 1.9991 to 2.0009 in.   c) 1.994 to 2.006 in.   d) 1.9654 to 2.0346 in.

44. A tool and die company makes dies which are to have a 2 in. diameter. The standard deviation of the produced parts is 0.003 in. Samples of 10 dies are chosen each day and the mean diameter of the sample found. If the company uses 95% control limits for a process control chart, would a sample mean diameter of 1.995 in. be considered an out of control point?
a) Yes b) No

45. A small machine company expects about 2% defective parts during normal production runs. During each run, a sample of 500 parts is taken and the rate of defective parts determined. Find the 95% control limits for a process control chart for this production process.
a) 0.75 to 3.25% b) 1.375 to 2.625% c) 1.821 to 2.179% d) 0 to 4%

46. A plastics plant produces soft drink cups which are to be 6 in. tall. The standard deviation of the heights of cups produced at the plant is 0.12 in. A sample of 25 cups is drawn at random from each production run and the mean height found. Find the control limits if the company uses 95% control limits for a process control chart for this process.
a) 5.76 to 6.24 in. b) 5.976 to 5.024 in. c) 5.862 to 6.138 in. d) 5.952 to 6.048 in.

47. A plastics plant produces soft drink cups which are to be 6 in. tall. The standard deviation of the heights of cups produced at the plant is 0.12 in. A sample of 25 cups is drawn at random from each production run and the mean height found. The company uses 95% control limits for a process control chart for this process. Would a sample mean height of 5.96 in. be out of control?
a) Yes b) No

48. The two-way table for admission into a private club is shown below. Find the percentage of males accepted.

	Male	Female
Admit	15	25
Deny	35	20

a) 30% b) 37.5% c) 17% d) 15%

49. The two-way table for admission into a private club is shown below. Find the percentage of females denied.

	Male	Female
Admit	15	25
Deny	35	20

a) 36.4% b) 20% c) 21.1% d) 44.4%

50. At a certain university two courses are available on a "PASS/FAIL" basis. Men have argued that they are being discriminated against in the courses, that women in these courses are being given preferential treatment. Which of the two-way tables shown below, the combined or the separate, did the men use to make their claim?

a)   Combined courses:

	Male	Female
Pass	25	65
Fail	35	35

b)

	Course I			Course II	
	Male	Female		Male	Female
Pass	10	5		15	60
Fail	30	15		5	20

Free-Response Questions

1. A survey of voters found that 55% of them supported a particular candidate. Is 55% a parameter or a statistic? Explain your choice.

2. In a certain production process, the mean weight of a part produced is 50 g. A sample of 25 parts is taken at random, and the mean weight in the sample is found to be 49.8 g. Which value, 49.8 or 50 is the parameter and which is the statistic?

3. The campaign staff for a candidate for national office wants to determine public support for greater national control of education. They take a poll and claim that 13% of the public supports such national control. Is the 13% they announce more likely a parameter or a statistic? Why?

4. A poll of 2500 residents in a town finds that 1980 favor adopting a curbside recycling program. What is the sample proportion?

5. In a survey of students, 200 indicate they wish the library were open later on Fridays. 1300 students say they do not wish to have later Friday library hours. What is the sample proportion of students who wish the library were open later?

6. A survey of 1500 voters finds that 1100 support candidate Jones. What is the standard deviation of the sampling distribution for this survey? (Assume the survey results are very close to accurate.)

7. Approximately 27% of all the vacationers in a seaside resort will get sunburned during their vacation. A poll of 500 vacationers will be taken and each asked if they were sunburned. What is the standard deviation of the sampling distribution of the percent who will say yes?

8. A local marketing research company wishes to find out the percentage of shoppers in a town who would buy a larger size of laundry detergent if it were available. They believe the percentage of shoppers who would buy the larger size to be about 65%. The company wishes the standard deviation of the sampling distribution for the percent in their survey who say yes to be about 2.5%. How many shoppers should they survey?

9. The campaign staff for a candidate for governor wants to know how many voters agree with the candidate's stand on the death penalty. They believe the support is about 60%. If they plan to survey 2000 voters, would it be likely that they find a sample proportion of only 40%? Why or why not?

10. A plastics company produces sandbox buckets which are to have a mean diameter of 11 in. The standard deviation of the diameters of buckets produced is known to be 0.03 in. For each run, the quality control engineer takes a sample of 25 buckets and finds the mean diameter. What is the standard deviation of the sampling distribution for this mean?

11. The mean length of bolts produced by a company is 2.5 in. The standard deviation of the bolt lengths is 0.004 in. The worker in charge of quality control indicates that each hour a sample is drawn and the mean length found. He claims that the standard deviation of the sampling distribution will be 0.0008 in. What size sample is being used?

12. The marketing department for a snack food company decides to poll 250 shoppers to determine the percentage of shoppers who have tried a new snack cracker. A summer intern suggests they poll 500 people so that they "can be twice as confident in the results." How would the statisticians explain the errors in the intern's suggestion?

13. A poll finds 785 of 1000 people surveyed are in favor of a candidate's stand on gun control. Find a 95% confidence interval for the true proportion of people who favor the candidate's stand.

14. Doctors who have tested a new drug report that they are 95% confident that the drug will be effective in $70 \pm 2\%$ of the patients for whom it is prescribed. If they wish to report their results with 99.7% confidence instead of 95%, what would be the new confidence interval?

15. Eighty five percent of 2000 people polled support a council's plan for cutting the city budget. Find a 95% confidence interval for the proportion of residents who are in favor of the plan.

16. In the manufacturing process for paper clips, wire is cut to a length of 4.24 inc and then bent into a clip. The standard deviation of the lengths of wire cut is 0.05 in. To maintain quality, a sample of 25 wires is drawn each hour and measured. What is the standard deviation of the sampling distribution for the mean wire length?

17. In the manufacturing process for paper clips, wire is cut to a length of 4.24 in. and then bent into a clip. The standard deviation of the lengths of wire cut is 0.05 in. To maintain quality, a sample of 25 wires is drawn each hour and measured. A statistician has recommended to the company that they increase the sample size to 100. What effect would this have on the sampling distribution for the mean length of the cut wires?

18. In the manufacturing process for paper clips, wire is cut to a length of 4.24 in. and then bent into a clip. The standard deviation of the lengths of wire cut is 0.05 in. To maintain quality, a sample of 25 wires is drawn each hour and measured. One hour, the mean length of wires in the sample is 4.23 in. Find a 95% confidence interval for the true mean length of wires cut this hour.

19. A polling company surveys some shoppers at a store and reports that it is 95% confident that $78 \pm 9\%$ like the store's new logo. The store asks the polling company to give it results with only a 3% margin of error, but without a loss of confidence. Can the polling company comply with the request? If so, how and if not, why not?

20. A saw mill has an automatic plane set to thin boards to 1.5 in. The standard deviation of the thickness of boards planed by the machine is 0.004 in. Every three hours a sample of 25 boards is taken and the mean thickness found. Find the center line and 95% control limits for a process control chart for this planing process.

21. A saw mill has an automatic plane set to thin boards to 1.5 in. The standard deviation of the thickness of boards planed by the machine is 0.004 in. Every three hours a sample of 25 boards is taken and the mean thickness found. The mill uses 95% control limits for a process control chart for this planing process. Would a sample with mean thickness 1.4998 be within the control limits?

22. Why would a manufacturing company sample 25 parts each hour and use a process- control chart to maintain the mean diameter of parts produced rather than measure each part produced?

23. A summer sports league enrolls children aged 10 and 11 to play baseball and soccer. Two-way tables for the number of children making first and second teams for each sport are shown below. Find the percent of 10-year-olds who make the first team for soccer.

	Baseball		Soccer	
	10-year-olds	11-year-olds	10-year-olds	11-year-olds
1st team	30	8	25	100
2nd team	120	32	5	20

24. A summer sports league enrolls children aged 10 and 11 to play baseball and soccer. Two-way tables for the number of children making first and second teams for each sport are shown below. Find the percent of children enrolled for baseball who make the first team.

	Baseball		Soccer	
	10-year-olds	11-year-olds	10-year-olds	11-year-olds
1st team	30	8	25	100
2nd team	120	32	5	20

25. A summer sports league enrolls children aged 10 and 11 to play baseball and soccer. Two-way tables for the number of children making first and second teams for each sport are shown below. Combine the information into a single table for both sports and tell why such a table might be misleading to the parents of 10-year-olds.

	Baseball		Soccer	
	10-year-olds	11-year-olds	10-year-olds	11-year-olds
1st team	30	8	25	100
2nd team	120	32	5	20

Chapter 9 Multiple-Choice Questions
Identification Numbers

1. Determine the check digit which should be appended to the US Postal Service money order identification number 2384943094.
a) 1   b) 4   c) 6   d) 8

2. Determine the check digit which should be appended to the US Postal Service money order identification number 5849202911.
a) 1   b) 4   c) 5   d) 8

3. Determine the check digit which should be appended to the US Postal Service money order identification number 5428792351.
a) 1   b) 4   c) 6   d) 8

4. Suppose a US Postal Service money order is numbered x3843291010 where the first digit is obliterated. What is the missing digit?
a) 4   b) 5   c) 9   d) The missing digit can't be determined.

5. Suppose a US Postal Service money order is numbered x4839203210 where the first digit is obliterated. What is the missing digit?
a) 4   b) 5   c) 8   d) The missing digit can't be determined.

6. Determine the check digit which should be appended to the American Express Travelers Cheque identification number 483920381.
a) 2   b) 6   c) 7   d) 8

7. Determine the check digit which should be appended to the American Express Travelers Cheque identification number 483920381.
a) 2   b) 6   c) 7   d) 8

8. Determine the check digit which should be appended to the American Express Travelers Cheque identification number 293021243.
a) 1   b) 4   c) 6   d) 8

9. Suppose an American Express Travelers Cheque is numbered x483920594 where the first digit is obliterated. What is the missing digit?
a) 1   b) 6   c) 8   d) The missing digit can't be determined.

10. Suppose an American Express Travelers Cheque is numbered x392063210 where the first digit is obliterated. What is the missing digit?
a) 1   b) 4   c) 8   d) The missing digit can't be determined.

11. the check digit which should be appended to the Avis rental car identification number 483901.
a) 2   b) 5   c) 7   d) 8

12. Determine the check digit which should be appended to the Avis rental car identification number 821922.
  a) 3 b) 4 c) 7 d) 8

13. Is the number 4839212 a legitimate Avis rental car number?
  a) Yes b) No

14. Is the number 3910291 a legitimate Avis rental car number?
  a) Yes b) No

15. Determine the check digit which should be appended to the UPS identification number 102839414.
  a) 1 b) 3 c) 4 d) 6

16. Determine the check digit which should be appended to the UPS identification number 112843215.
  a) 1 b) 2 c) 5 d) 6

17. Is the number 1028343293 a legitimate UPS package number?
  a) Yes b) No

18. Is the number 1023894326 a legitimate UPS package number?
  a) Yes b) No

19. Determine the check digit which should be appended to the airline ticket identification number 28143298311.
  a) 2 b) 3 c) 4 d) 5

20. Determine the check digit which should be appended to the airline ticket identification number 85493049212.
  a) 2 b) 3 c) 4 d) 5

21. Is the number 102432854931 a legitimate airline ticket number?
  a) Yes b) No

22. Is the number 103932091202 a legitimate airline ticket number?
  a) Yes b) No

23. Determine the check digit which should be appended to the UPC identification number 0 12500 29301.
  a) 0 b) 1 c) 3 d) 9

24. Determine the check digit which should be appended to the UPC identification number 0 13500 47501.
  a) 0 b) 2 c) 3 d) 8

25. Determine the check digit which should be appended to the UPC identification number 0 15700 37501.
  a) 0 b) 1 c) 3 d) 7

26. Is the number 0 11300 84392 4 a legitimate UPC number?

a) Yes   b) No

27. Is the number 0 11300 29432 5 a legitimate UPC number?
    a) Yes   b) No

28. If the UPC number 0 11500 22810 9 is incorrectly entered as 0 11500 28810 9, will the error be detected by the check digit?
    a) Yes   b) No

29. If the UPC number 0 89901 24334 9 is incorrectly entered as 0 84401 24334 9, will the error be detected by the check digit?
    a) Yes   b) No

30. Suppose the sixth digit of the UPC number 0 5443x 30250 0 is obliterated. What is the missing digit?
    a) 0   b) 3   c) 5   d) The missing digit can't be determined.

31. Determine the check digit which should be appended to the bank identification number 01200021.
    a) 2   b) 4   c) 7   d) 8

32. Determine the check digit which should be appended to the bank identification number 05200035.
    a) 1   b) 3   c) 8   d) 9

33. Determine the check digit which should be appended to the bank identification number 04200052.
    a) 1   b) 3   c) 7   d) 9

34. Is the number 075000325 a legitimate bank identification number?
    a) Yes   b) No

35. Is the number 096000361 a legitimate bank identification number?
    a) Yes   b) No

36. Determine the check digit which should be appended to the Codabar number 312580013325001.
    a) 3   b) 4   c) 6   d) 7

37. Determine the check digit which should be appended to the Codabar number 312545006987005.
    a) 3   b) 4   c) 6   d) 7

38. Determine the check digit which should be appended to the Codabar number 312540016220550.
    a) 0   b) 1   c) 2   d) 8

39. Is the number 3125700143750015 a legitimate Codabar number?
    a) Yes

40. Is the number 3125850025490085 a legitimate Codabar number?
    a) Yes   b) No

41. Determine the check digit which should be appended to the ISBN 0-7167-6531.
 a) 4   b) 5   c) 6   d) 7

42. Determine the check digit which should be appended to the ISBN 0-7167-9811.
 a) 2   b) 5   c) 6   d) 8

43. Suppose the fourth digit of the ISBN 0-71x7-1011-0 is obliterated. What is the missing digit?
 a) 2   b) 3   c) 6   d) The missing digit can't be determined.

44. Is the number 0-7167-2431-X a legitimate ISBN?
 a) Yes   b) No

45. Is the number 0-7167-1532-0 a legitimate ISBN?
 a) Yes   b) No

46. Determine the check character which should be appended to the Code 39 number 101A00HI243320.
 a) 6   b) A   c) O   d) Z

47. Determine the check character which should be appended to the Code 39 number 2100CAP4507912.
 a) 2   b) 8   c) Y   d) Z

48. Determine the check digit which should be appended to the Postnet code for ZIP+4 code 10010-4525.
 a) 2   b) 4   c) 7   d) 8

49. Determine the check digit which should be appended to the Postnet code for ZIP+4 code 47301-5600.
 a) 3   b) 4   c) 6   d) 7

50. Suppose the third digit of the Postnet code 282x4-2486-3 is obliterated. What is the missing digit?
 a) 1   b) 3   c) 7   d) The missing digit can't be determined.

Free-Response Questions

1. If the third digit of the US Postal Service money order number 64389235311 is mistyped, can the check digit detect the error? Explain.

2. If the third digit of the American Express Travelers Cheque number 390124323 is mistyped, can the check digit detect the error? Explain.

3. If the third and fourth digits of the Avis rental car number 3960040 are exchanged, can the check digit detect the error? Explain.

4. If the last digit of the Avis rental car number 3960040 is mistyped, can the check digit detect the error? Explain.

5. A UPC code is reported to read 0-48000-03254-5, but the second digit is read in error. Can the correct second digit be determined?

6. If the last two digits of the UPC code 5-12500-65590-6 are exchanged, can the check digit detect the error? Explain.

7. A bank identification number is reported to be 017000250, but your source reports that the final digit is difficult to read and may be wrong. Is this a viable bank identification number? If not, can the correct final digit be determined?

8. If the third and fourth digits of the bank identification number 250150205 are exchanged, can the check digit detect the error? Explain.

9. If the third and fourth digits of the Codabar number 4128001234567896 are exchanged, can the check digit detect the error? Explain.

10. The last digit of the Codabar number 4128001243890110 may be wrong. Is this a viable Codabar number? If not, can the correct final digit be determined?

11. Is 0-1370-2990-X a viable ISBN number? If not, can the second digit be changed to produce a viable ISBN number?

12. If the first and second digits of the ISBN number 0-7167-2378-6 are exchanged, can the check digit detect the error? Explain.

13. If the third and fourth digits of the Code 39 number 210SA0162322ZAY are exchanged, can the check digit detect the error? Explain.

14. If the first two digits of the Postnet code 1001025001 are exchanged, can the check digit detect the error? Explain.

15. If the first digit of the Postnet code 1001025001 is mistyped, can the check digit detect the error?

Explain.

16. The ISBN code system detects all single-digit errors and single transpositions. Even so, it has a major drawback. What is it?

17. Why are there different methods of creating check digits?

18. How are bar codes used by the Postal Service to encode ZIP codes?

19. What are guard bars?

20. Give examples of some uses of the Codabar method.

21. If the first and third digits of a UPC code are exchanged, can the check digit detect the error? Explain.

22. If the first and third digits of a bank identification number are exchanged, can the check digit detect the error? Explain.

23. If the first and third digits of a Codabar number are exchanged, can the check digit detect the error? Explain.

24. Is the number 0-499290-3 a viable UPC Version E number? If not, change the final digit to produce a viable UPC Version E number.

25. Is the number 0-413882-5 a viable UPC Version E number? If not, change the final digit to produce a viable UPC Version E number.

Chapter 10 Multiple-Choice Questions
Transmitting Information

1. Use the Venn diagram method to determine the code word of the message 1010.
   a) 1010110   b) 1010111   c) 1010001   d) 1010011

2. Use the Venn diagram method to determine the code word of the message 1001.
   a) 1001111   b) 1001101   c) 1001001   d) 1001010

3. Use the nearest-neighbor Venn diagram method to decode the received word 1101101.
   a) 1001   b) 0100   c) 1101   d) 1011

4. Use the nearest-neighbor Venn diagram method to decode the received word 1011001.
   a) 1011   b) 1010   c) 1001   d) 0010

5. Suppose the Venn diagram message 1110 is received as 1110001. Will the original message be recovered?
   a) Yes   b) No

6. Suppose the Venn diagram coded message 1110 is received as 1110110. Will the original message be recovered?
   a) Yes   b) No

7. What is the distance between received words 1100101 and 1101010?
   a) 1   b) 2   c) 3   d) 4

8. What is the distance between received words 1001010 and 1010010?
   a) 1   b) 2   c) 3   d) 4

9. Add the binary sequences 1001010 and 1010010. How many 1s digits are in the sum?
   a) 2   b) 3   c) 4   d) Another answer

10. Add the binary sequences 0100110 and 1101010. How many 1s digits are in the sum?
    a) 1   b) 3   c) 5   d) Another answer

11. If two binary sequences that each have an even number of 1s are added, the sum
    a) will always have an even number of 1s.   c) will always have an odd number of 1s.
    b) will sometimes have an even number of 1s.

12. Let C be the code {1100, 1010, 1001, 0110, 0101, 0011}. Which of the following is a true statement?
    a) The code can detect and correct any single-digit error.
    b) The code can detect any single-digit error and correct some but not all single-digit errors.
    c) The code can detect any single-digit error, but cannot correct any single-digit error.
    d) The code can detect some but not all single-digit errors.

13. Let C be the code $\{110, 101, 011, 000\}$. Which of the following is a true statement?
   a) The code can detect and correct any single-digit error.
   b) The code can detect any single-digit error and can correct some but not all single-digit errors.
   c) The code can detect any single-digit error, but cannot correct any single-digit error.
   d) The code can detect some but not all single-digit errors.

14. You propose a code in which each digit of the message word is repeated to form the code word. For example, 101 is coded as 110011. Which of the following is a true statement?
   a) The code can detect and correct any single-digit error and any double error.
   b) The code can detect and correct any single-digit error and detect any double error, but cannot correct every double error.
   c) The code can detect and correct any single-digit error, but cannot detect every double error.
   d) The code can detect any single-digit error, but cannot correct every single-digit error.

15. You propose a code in which each three-digit binary message word $a_1 a_2 a_3$ has appended a parity check digit $c_1 = a_1 + a_2 + a_3$. Which of the following is a true statement?
   a) The code can detect and correct any single-digit error.
   b) The code can detect any single-digit error and correct some but not all single-digit errors.
   c) The code can detect any single-digit error, but cannot correct any single-digit error.
   d) The code can detect some but not all single-digit errors.

16. You propose a code in which each two-digit binary message word $a_1 a_2$ has appended a parity check digit $c_1 = a_1 + a_2$. Which of the following is a true statement?
   a) The code can detect and correct any single-digit error.
   b) The code can detect any single-digit error and correct some but not all single-digit errors.
   c) The code can detect any single-digit error, but cannot correct any single-digit error.
   d) The code can detect some but not all single-digit errors.

17. You propose a code in which each three-digit binary message word $a_1 a_2 a_3$ has appended two parity check digits $c_1 = a_1 + a_2$ and $c_2 = a_2 + a_3$. Which of the following is a true statement?
   a) The code can detect and correct any single-digit error.
   b) The code can detect any single-digit error and correct some but not all single-digit errors.
   c) The code can detect any single-digit error, but cannot correct any single-digit error.
   d) The code can detect some but not all single-digit errors.

18. For the code $C = \{00000, 11111\}$ how many errors would have to occur during transmission for a received word to be encoded incorrectly?
   a) 2 b) 3 c) 4 d) 5

19. For the code $C = \{000000, 111111\}$ how many errors would have to occur during transmission for a received word to be encoded incorrectly?
   a) 2 b) 3 c) 4 d) 5

20. For the code $C = \{000000, 000111, 111000, 111111\}$ how many errors would have to occur during transmission for a received word to be encoded incorrectly?

a) 1 b) 2 c) 3 d) 6

21. Let C be the code {1010, 0101, 1111, 0000}. What is the weight of this code?
a) 0 b) 1 c) 2 d) 4

22. Let C be the code {101010, 010101, 111111, 000000}. What is the weight of this code?
a) 0 b) 1 c) 3 d) 6

23. Use the encoding scheme A → 0, B → 10, C → 11 to encode the sequence ABACAB.
a) 010011010 b) 01011010 c) 01001101 d) Another sequence

24. Use the encoding scheme A → 0, B → 10, C → 11 to decode the sequence 0101101011.
a) ABCABC b) ABACABAC c) ABCBCB d) Another sequence

25. Use the Caesar cipher to encrypt the message ROME BURNS.
a) URPH EXUQV b) OLJB YROKP c) HORU VQUXE d) Another sequence

26. Use the Caesar cipher to decrypt the message ZHVW.
a) WEST b) EAST c) REST d) Another message

27. Using modular arithmetic, $(13 \cdot 21) \bmod 10$ is equal to
a) 2. b) 3. c) 7. d) Another number.

28. Using modular arithmetic, $(13 \cdot 21) \bmod 12$ is equal to
a) 3. b) 9. c) 10. d) Another number.

29. Using modular arithmetic, $4^3 \bmod 10$ is equal to
a) 2. b) 4. c) 6. d) Another number.

30. Using modular arithmetic, $5^3 \bmod 11$ is equal to
a) 0. b) 4. c) 7. d) Another number.

31. Using modular arithmetic, $15^3 \bmod 41$ is equal to
a) 0. b) 13. c) 31. d) Another number.

32. Using modular arithmetic, $13^3 \bmod 34$ is equal to
a) 13. b) 21. c) 30. d) Another number.

33. For the RSA scheme with p = 5, q = 11, and r = 7, compute the value of m.
a) 10 b) 20 c) 40 d) 55

34. For the RSA scheme with p = 5, q = 19, and r = 7, compute the value of m.
a) 18 b) 36 c) 72 d) 95

35. For the RSA scheme with p = 17 and q = 23, which of the following could be chosen as a value for r?
a) 6 b) 4 c) 9 d) 16

36. For the RSA scheme with m = 8 and r = 5, what is the value of s?
a) 1   b) 2   c) 3   d) 5

37. For the RSA scheme with m = 9 and r = 5, what is the value of s?
a) 1   b) 2   c) 4   d) 5

38. Use the RSA scheme with n = 85 and r = 7 to determine the message sent for the string "14."
a) 11   b) 13   c) 59   d) 74

39. Use the RSA scheme with n = 85 and r = 7 to determine the message sent for the string "22."
a) 13   b) 30   c) 69   d) 78

40. Use the RSA scheme with n = 133 and r = 11 to determine the message sent for the string "8."
a) 8   b) 31   c) 50   d) 88

41. Use the RSA scheme with n = 133 and r = 11 to determine the message sent for the string "10."
a) 11   b) 33   c) 110   d) 121

42. Use the RSA scheme with n = 85 and s = 3 to decode the message "7."
a) 3   b) 21   c) 62   d) 63

43. Use the RSA scheme with n = 85 and s = 3 to decode the message "13."
a) 39   b) 46   c) 63   d) 72

44. Use the RSA scheme with n = 133 and s = 5 to decode the message "32."
a) 21   b) 27   c) 53   d) 128

45. Use the RSA scheme with n = 133 and s = 5 to decode the message "29."
a) 12   b) 15   c) 17   d) 22

46. When using the Venn diagram for determining length seven binary code words for length four messages, which of the following are true statements?

     I: Every code word has an even number of 1s.
     II: Every possible string of seven binary digits is a code word.
     III: Every possible string of seven binary digits can be read as a code word or a code word with a single-digit error.
a) I only   b) I and III only   c) II only   d) III only

47. When using the Venn diagram for determining length seven binary code words for length four messages, what is the minimum distance between two code words?
a) 1   b) 2   c) 3   d) 7

48. When using the Venn diagram for determining length seven binary code words for length four messages, what is the weight of the code?
a) 1   b) 2   c) 3   d) 7

49. If a code is to detect and correct single-digit errors, which of the following are true statements?

    I: Its weight should be at least 2.
    II: The distance between any two code words should be at least 2.
    a) I only   b) II only   c) Both I and II   d) Neither I nor II

50. Which of the following are true statements?

    I: Morse code is a variable-length code.
    II: Morse code is an example of a data compression code.
    a) I only   b) II only   c) Both I and II   d) Neither I nor II

Free-Response Questions

1. Suppose you create a binary code by appending to each message word $a_1\ a_2\ a_3\ a_4$ three parity check digits $c_1 = a_1 + a_2 + a_4$, $c_2 = a_2 + a_3 + a_4$, and $c_3 = a_2 + a_3 + a_4$. Will the resulting code detect and/or correct all single-digit errors?

2. Suppose you create a binary code by appending to each message word $a_1\ a_2\ a_3$ two parity check digits $c_1 = a_1 + a_2$ and $c_2 = a_2 + a_3$. Will the resulting code detect and/or correct all single-digit errors?

3. Suppose you create a binary code by appending to each message word $a_1\ a_2\ a_3$ three parity check digits $c_1 = a_1 + a_2$, $c_2 = a_2 + a_3$, and $c_3 = a_1 + a_3$. Will the resulting code detect and/or correct all single-digit errors?

4. Append a fourth check digit to each seven-digit code created by the Venn Diagram method, $c_4 = a_1 + a_2 + a_3 + a_4$. With this additional check digit, can double errors be detected and/or corrected?

5. For the message word $a_1\ a_2\ a_3\ a_4$, append four check digits: $c_1 = a_1$, $c_2 = a_2$, $c_3 = a_3$, and $c_4 = a_4$. Will the resulting code detect and/or correct all single-digit errors? Can double errors be detected and/or corrected?

6. Construct a code for five-digit binary message words that has four parity check digits. Can it detect and/or correct single-digit errors?

7. Construct a code for five-digit binary message words that has three parity check digits. Can it detect and/or correct single-digit errors?

8. Create a binary linear code with eight possible code words that can detect and correct any single-digit error.

9. Create a binary linear code with four possible code words that can detect and correct any single-digit or double-digit error.

10. Give an example of a circumstance where the code C = {00000, 11111} could be of use.

11. Use the Caesar cipher to encrypt the message ABANDON HOPE.

12. Use the Caesar cipher to decrypt the message DOO LV ZHOO.

13. How does the weight of a code compare to the number of errors that can be detected?

14. How does the weight of a code compare to the number of errors that can be corrected?

15. Using modular arithmetic, determine $(42 \cdot 17)$ mod 23.

16. Using modular arithmetic, determine $(16 \cdot 31)$ mod 41.

17. Using modular arithmetic, determine 12^7 mod 53.

18. Using modular arithmetic, determine 17^7 mod 41.

19. Determine the value of s so that $9s = 1$ mod 17.

20. Determine the value of s so that $11s = 1$ mod 13.

21. For the RSA scheme with $p = 5$, $q = 11$, choose a value for r. Then encode the message sent for the string "23."

22. For the RSA scheme selected above, decode the message "7," if possible.

23. For the RSA scheme with $p = 17$, $q = 23$, choose a value for r. Then encode the message sent for the string "13."

24. For the RSA scheme selected above, decode the message "7," if possible.

25. Why is RSA considered a superior encryption scheme?

Chapter 11 Multiple-Choice Questions
Social Choice: The Impossible Dream

1. Majority rule is a good way to choose between two alternatives.
   a) True   b) False

2. Majority rule is a good way to choose between three alternatives.
   a) True   b) False

3. Every set of voters' preference lists produces a Condorcet winner.
   a) True   b) False

4. For a given set of voters' preference lists, different voting procedures may produce different winners.
   a) True   b) False

5. For a given set of voters' preference lists, different agendas for sequential pairwise voting may produce different winners.
   a) True   b) False

6. The Borda count method of voting satisfies the independence of irrelevant alternatives criterion.
   a) True   b) False

7. Sequential pairwise voting satisfies the Condorcet criterion.
   a) True   b) False

8. How many votes are needed for a majority winner if there are 20 voters?
   a) 10   b) 11   c) 15   d) 20

9. How many votes are needed for a majority winner if there are 25 voters?
   a) 12   b) 12.5   c) 13   d) 25

10. In how many ways can a voter rank five candidates, without allowing ties?
    a) 5   b) 32   c) 60   d) 120

11. In how many ways can a voter rank three candidates, without allowing ties?
    a) 3   b) 6   c) 8   d) 12

12. A group of twelve students have to decide among three types of pizza: Sausage (S), Mushroom (M), and Beef (B). Their preference rankings are shown below. Which choice will the group make if they use majority rule?

	Number of Students				
	3	3	2	2	2
First choice	B	M	S	B	S
Second choice	M	B	M	S	B
Third choice	S	S	B	M	M

a) S   b) M   c) B   d) No winner can be chosen.

13. A group of twelve students have to decide among three types of pizza: Sausage (S), Mushroom (M), and Beef (B). Their preference rankings are shown below. Which choice will the group make if they use plurality voting?

	Number of Students				
	3	3	2	2	2
First choice	B	M	S	B	S
Second choice	M	B	M	S	B
Third choice	S	S	B	M	M

a) S   b) M   c) B   d) No winner can be chosen.

14. A group of twelve students have to decide among three types of pizza: Sausage (S), Mushroom (M), and Beef (B). Their preference rankings are shown below. Which choice will the group make if they use the Borda count?

	Number of Students				
	3	3	2	2	2
First choice	B	M	S	B	S
Second choice	M	B	M	S	B
Third choice	S	S	B	M	M

a) S   b) M   c) B   d) No winner can be chosen.

15. A group of twelve students have to decide among three types of pizza: Sausage (S), Mushroom (M), and Beef (B). Their preference rankings are shown below. Which choice will the group make if they use the Hare system?

	Number of Students				
	3	3	2	2	2
First choice	B	M	S	B	S
Second choice	M	B	M	S	B
Third choice	S	S	B	M	M

a) S   b) M   c) B   d) No winner can be chosen.

16. A group of twelve students have to decide among three types of pizza: Sausage (S), Mushroom (M), and Beef (B). Their preference rankings are shown below. Which choice will the group make if they use sequential pairwise voting with agenda B, M, S?

	Number of Students				
	3	3	2	2	2
First choice	B	M	S	B	S
Second choice	M	B	M	S	B
Third choice	S	S	B	M	M

a) S   b) M   c) B   d) No winner can be chosen.

17. A group of twelve students have to decide among three types of pizza: Sausage (S), Mushroom (M), and

Beef (B). Their preference rankings are shown below. Is there a Condorcet winner among the pizza types?

	Number of Students				
	3	3	2	2	2
First choice	B	M	S	B	S
Second choice	M	B	M	S	B
Third choice	S	S	B	M	M

a) S   b) M   c) B   d) No winner can be chosen.

18. Thirty board members must vote on five candidates: X, Y, Z, U, and V. Their preference rankings are summarized in the table below. Find the winner using the Borda count.

	Number of Members		
	12	10	8
First choice	X	Y	Z
Second choice	U	Z	U
Third choice	Y	X	X
Fourth choice	Z	U	V
Fifth choice	V	V	Y

a) X   b) Y   c) Z   d) No winner is chosen.

19. Thirty board members must vote on five candidates: X, Y, Z, U, and V. Their preference rankings are summarized in the table below. Find the winner using the Hare system.

	Number of Members		
	12	10	8
First choice	X	Y	Z
Second choice	U	Z	U
Third choice	Y	X	X
Fourth choice	Z	U	V
Fifth choice	V	V	Y

a) X   b) Y   c) Z   d) No winner is chosen.

20. Thirty board members must vote on five candidates: X, Y, Z, U, and V. Their preference rankings are summarized in the table below. Find the winner using sequential pairwise voting with the agenda X, Y, Z, U, V.

	Number of Members		
	12	10	8
First choice	X	Y	Z
Second choice	U	Z	U
Third choice	Y	X	X
Fourth choice	Z	U	V
Fifth choice	V	V	Y

a) X   b) Z   c) U   d) V

21. Fifty voters who elect one of the five candidates A, B, C, D, or E have the preference schedule shown below. Which candidate will be elected using plurality voting?

	Number of Voters			
	20	14	10	6
First choice	A	B	B	C
Second choice	C	A	A	D
Third choice	E	D	C	B
Fourth choice	B	C	D	A
Fifth choice	D	E	E	E

a) A b) B c) C d) No winner is determined.

22. Fifty voters who elect one of the five candidates A, B, C, D, or E have the preference schedule shown below. Which candidate will be elected using the Borda count?

	Number of Voters			
	20	14	10	6
First choice	A	B	B	C
Second choice	C	A	A	D
Third choice	E	D	C	B
Fourth choice	B	C	D	A
Fifth choice	D	E	E	E

a) A b) B c) C d) No winner is determined.

23. Fifty voters who elect one of the five candidates A, B, C, D, or E have the preference schedule shown below. Which candidate will be elected using the Hare system?

	Number of Voters			
	20	14	10	6
First choice	A	B	B	C
Second choice	C	A	A	D
Third choice	E	D	C	B
Fourth choice	B	C	D	A
Fifth choice	D	E	E	E

a) A b) B c) C d) No winner is determined.

24. Fifty voters who elect one of the five candidates A, B, C, D, or E have the preference schedule shown below. Which candidate will be elected using sequential pairwise voting with the agenda A, B, C, D, E?

	Number of Voters			
	20	14	10	6
First choice	A	B	B	C
Second choice	C	A	A	D
Third choice	E	D	C	B
Fourth choice	B	C	D	A
Fifth choice	D	E	E	E

a) A b) B c) C d) No winner is determined.

25. Thirty voters with the preference schedules below are to elect a union spokesman from among five candidates: A, B, C, D, and E. If the Borda count is used, candidate B would win. Would there be any difference in the result if candidate C withdrew from the race before the ranking?

	Number of Voters		
	12	10	8
First choice	A	B	D
Second choice	D	C	B
Third choice	B	A	A
Fourth choice	C	D	E
Fifth choice	E	E	C

a) No, B still wins.   b) Yes, now A wins.   c) Yes, now D wins.   d) Yes, now there is no winner.

26. Consider an eleven-member committee which must choose one of three alternatives: X, Y, or Z. Their schedule of preferences is shown below. If the Hare system is used, alternative X wins. Could the voters who Z most prefer vote insincerely in some way to change the outcome in a way that would benefit them?

	Number of Voters		
	5	4	2
First choice	Z	X	Y
Second choice	Y	Y	X
Third choice	X	Z	Z

a) Yes, switch ranking of X and Y.   c) Yes, switch ranking of X and Z.
b) Yes, switch ranking of Y and Z.   d) No, X would always win.

27. Suppose that a nine-member committee needs to elect one of the four alternatives A, B, C, or D. Their preference schedule is shown below. Which alternative wins using the Borda count?

	Number of Members		
	4	3	2
First choice	A	B	C
Second choice	B	D	D
Third choice	C	A	A
Fourth choice	D	C	B

a) A   b) B   c) C   d) No winner is determined.

28. Suppose that a nine-member committee needs to elect one of the four alternatives A, B, C, or D. Their preference schedule is shown below. Which alternative wins using sequential pairwise voting with the agenda A, B, C, D?

	Number of Members		
	4	3	2
First choice	A	B	C
Second choice	B	D	D
Third choice	C	A	A
Fourth choice	D	C	B

a) A   b) B   c) C   d) D

29. Suppose that a nine-member committee needs to elect one of the four alternatives A, B, C, or D. their preference schedule is given below. Is there a Condorcet winner?

	Number of Members		
	4	3	2
First choice	A	B	C
Second choice	B	D	D
Third choice	C	A	A
Fourth choice	D	C	B

a) B wins   b) C wins   c) D wins   d) No Condorcet winner is determined.

30. Suppose that a nine-member committee needs to elect one of the four alternatives A, B, C, or D. Their preference schedule is shown below. Which alternative wins using the Hare system?

	Number of Members		
	4	3	2
First choice	A	B	C
Second choice	B	D	D
Third choice	C	A	A
Fourth choice	D	C	B

a) A   b) B   c) C   d) D

31. Consider a thirteen-person committee which is considering three applicants, A, B, and C, for an opening. The individual rankings are summarized in the table below. Which applicant would be accepted if the committee used the plurality method?

	Number of Members			
	5	4	2	2
First choice	B	C	A	A
Second choice	C	B	B	C
Third choice	A	A	C	A

a) A   b) B   c) C   d) There is no plurality winner.

32. Consider a thirteen-person committee which is considering three applicants, A, B, and C, for an opening. The individual rankings are summarized in the table below. Which applicant would be accepted if the committee used the Borda count?

	Number of Members			
	5	4	2	2
First choice	B	C	A	A
Second choice	C	B	B	C
Third choice	A	A	C	B

a) A   b) B   c) C   d) There is no Borda count winner.

33. Twenty-nine voters must choose from among three alternatives: A, B, and C. The voters preference schedules are shown below. C wins in a Borda count. Is the outcome different in a rank system which

assigns 5 points for first choice, 2 points for second, and 1 point for third?

	Number of Voters			
	12	8	6	3
First choice	B	C	A	C
Second choice	C	A	B	B
Third choice	A	B	C	A

a) No, C still wins   b) Yes, A now wins   c) Yes, B now wins   d) Yes, now there is no winner

34. Twenty-nine voters must choose from among three alternatives: A, B, and C. The voters preference schedules are shown below. C wins in a Borda count. Can the six voters in the third column change their preference list to produce an outcome they like better?

	Number of Voters			
	12	8	6	3
First choice	B	C	A	C
Second choice	C	A	B	B
Third choice	A	B	C	A

a) No, C will always win
b) Yes, they can rank A, C, B

c) Yes, they can rank B, A, C
d) Yes, they can rank C, A, B

35. Twenty-nine voters must choose from among three alternatives: A, B, and C. The voters preference schedules are shown below. Which alternative wins using the Hare system?

	Number of Voters			
	12	8	6	3
First choice	B	C	A	C
Second choice	C	A	B	B
Third choice	A	B	C	A

a) A   b) B   c) C   d) No winner is determined.

36. Twenty-nine voters must choose from among three alternatives: A, B, and C. The voters preference schedules are shown below. Using the agenda A, B, C, and sequential pairwise voting, alternative B wins. Is there an agenda which produces C as a winner?

	Number of Voters			
	12	8	6	3
First choice	B	C	A	C
Second choice	C	A	B	B
Third choice	A	B	C	A

a) No, B always wins.
b) Yes, the agenda A, C, B.

c) Yes, the agenda C, B, A.
d) Yes, the agenda B, A, C.

37. A group of twenty-two young people must decide whether to go to the beach (B), the mountain (M), or the zoo (Z) on a field trip. Their preference rankings are summarized in the table below. Which choice wins using plurality voting?

	Number of Voters		
	10	8	4
First choice	B	M	Z
Second choice	M	B	M
Third choice	Z	Z	B

a) M   b) B   c) Z   d) No winner is determined.

38. A group of twenty-two young people must decide whether to go to the beach (B), the mountain (M), or the zoo (Z) on a field trip. Their preference rankings are summarized in the table below. Which choice wins using the Borda count?

	Number of Voters		
	10	8	4
First choice	B	M	Z
Second choice	M	B	M
Third choice	Z	Z	B

a) M   b) B   c) Z   d) No winner is determined.

39. A group of twenty-two young people must decide whether to go to the beach (B), the mountain (M), or the zoo (Z) on a field trip. Their preference rankings are summarized in the table below, and the decision will be made using a Borda count. Can the 4 voters in the last column change the results of the vote by changing their preference rankings?

	Number of Voters		
	10	8	4
First choice	B	M	Z
Second choice	M	B	M
Third choice	Z	Z	B

a) No.   b) Yes.

40. A group of twenty-two young people must decide whether to go to the beach (B), the mountain (M), or the zoo (Z) on a field trip. Their preference rankings are summarized in the table below. Which choice wins using the Hare system?

	Number of Voters		
	10	8	4
First choice	B	M	Z
Second choice	M	B	M
Third choice	Z	Z	B

a) M   b) B   c) Z   d) No winner is determined.

41. A group of twenty-two young people must decide whether to go to the beach (B), the mountain (M), or the zoo (Z) on a field trip. Their preference rankings are summarized in the table below. Which choice wins using sequential pairwise voting with the agenda Z, B, M?

	Number of Voters		
	10	8	4
First choice	B	M	Z
Second choice	M	B	M
Third choice	Z	Z	B

a) M   b) B   c) Z   d) No winner is determined.

42. A group of twenty-two young people must decide whether to go to the beach (B), the mountain (M), or the zoo (Z) on a field trip. Their preference rankings are summarized in the table below. Is there a Condorcet winner?

	Number of Voters		
	10	8	4
First choice	B	M	Z
Second choice	M	B	M
Third choice	Z	Z	B

a) M   b) B   c) Z   d) No winner is determined.

43. One hundred voters are to elect one of the four candidates A, B, C, or D. Their preference schedule is shown below. Which candidate wins using the Hare system?

	Number of Voters			
	40	32	18	10
First choice	A	B	D	C
Second choice	C	C	C	D
Third choice	B	A	B	A
Fourth choice	D	D	A	B

a) A wins.   b) B wins.   c) D wins.   d) No winner is determined.

44. One hundred voters are to elect one of the four candidates A, B, C, or D. Their preference schedule is given below. Is there a Condorcet winner?

	Number of Voters			
	40	32	18	10
First choice	A	B	D	C
Second choice	C	C	C	D
Third choice	B	A	B	A
Fourth choice	D	D	A	B

a) Yes, A wins.   b) Yes, B wins.   c) Yes, C wins.   d) No winner is determined.

45. One hundred voters are to elect one of the four candidates A, B, C, or D. Their preference schedule is shown below. Which candidate wins using sequential pairwise voting with the agenda A, C, B, D?

	Number of Voters			
	40	32	18	10
First choice	A	B	D	C
Second choice	C	C	C	D
Third choice	B	A	B	A
Fourth choice	D	D	A	B

a) A wins.   b) B wins.   c) C wins.   d) D wins.

46. Eight board members vote by approval voting on four candidates, A, B, C, and D, for new positions on their board as indicated in the following table. An "X" indicates an approval vote.

	Voters							
	1	2	3	4	5	6	7	8
A	X	X	X	X		X	X	X
B		X	X		X	X		X
C		X		X	X		X	X
D	X			X	X	X	X	X

Which candidate will be chosen for the board if just one of them is to be elected?

a) A   b) B   c) C   d) D

47. Eight board members vote by approval voting on four candidates, A, B, C, and D, for new positions on their board as indicated in the following table. An "X" indicates an approval vote.

	Voters							
	1	2	3	4	5	6	7	8
A	X	X	X	X		X	X	X
B		X	X		X	X		X
C		X		X	X		X	X
D	X			X	X	X	X	X

Which candidate(s) is (are) elected if 80% approval is necessary and at most two are elected?

a) No candidates are elected.   c) Only candidate D is elected.
b) Only candidate A is elected.   d) Both candidates A and D are elected.

48. A five-member evaluating committee votes by approval voting on 10 faculty members for a promotion as indicated in the table below. An "X" indicates an approval vote.

	Voters				
Candidates	1	2	3	4	5
A	X		X	X	X
B	X	X	X	X	X
C			X		X
D		X	X	X	
E	X		X		X
F	X				X
G		X	X	X	
H		X		X	
I	X			X	X
J		X	X	X	X

Which faculty member is chosen for the promotion if just one of them is to be selected?

a) A   b) B   c) F   d) J

49. A five-member evaluating committee votes by approval voting on 10 faculty members for a promotion as indicated in the table below. An "X" indicates an approval vote.

	Voters				
Candidates	1	2	3	4	5
A	X		X	X	X
B	X	X	X	X	X
C			X		X
D		X	X	X	
E	X		X		X
F	X				X
G		X	X	X	
H		X		X	
I	X		X	X	
J		X	X	X	X

Which candidate(s) receive promotion if 80% approval is needed?

a) B only.   b) A, B, and J.   c) All except C, F and H.   d) No candidate receives promotion.

50. A five-member evaluating committee votes by approval voting on 10 faculty members for a promotion as indicated in the table below. An "X" indicates an approval vote.

	Voters				
Candidates	1	2	3	4	5
A	X		X	X	X
B	X	X	X	X	X
C			X		X
D		X	X	X	
E	X		X		X
F	X				X
G		X	X	X	
H		X		X	
I	X		X	X	
J		X	X	X	X

Which faculty member(s) is (are) chosen if 60% approval is necessary and at most three are to be selected?

a) B only.   b) A, B, and J.   c) All except C, F, and H.   d) None will be promoted.

Free-Response Questions

1. Explain why majority rule is not a good way to choose between four alternatives.

2. Arrow's Impossibility Theorem states that any voting system can give undesirable outcomes. Explain what this means.

3. Explain the Condorcet Winner Criterion.

4. Explain the difference between sincere and strategic voting.

5. Determine the number of ways it is possible to rank six candidates if no ties are allowed.

6. Which of the voting procedures, plurality, the Borda count, sequential pairwise voting, or the Hare system, satisfies the Condorcet winner criterion?

7. Which of the voting procedures, plurality, the Borda count, sequential pairwise voting, or the Hare system, satisfies the Pareto condition?

8. Which of the voting procedures, plurality, the Borda count, sequential pairwise voting, or the Hare system, satisfies monotonicity?

9. In order to choose which type of music to listen to in a student center music lounge, a Condorcet vote is held by the 15 students present. Below are the preference schedules for the students. Is there a Condorcet winner and if so, which music type?

	Number of Students		
	6	5	4
First choice	classical	rock	rock
Second choice	jazz	jazz	classical
Third choice	rock	classical	jazz

10. Given the preference schedule of 23 voters below, which candidate, if any, wins in a majority rule election?

	Number of Voters			
	8	5	6	4
First choice	A	C	B	B
Second choice	C	A	C	A
Third choice	B	B	A	C

11. Given the preference schedule of 23 voters below, if a rank method is used, which candidate, if any, wins in a straight plurality election?

	Number of Voters			
	8	5	6	4
First choice	A	C	B	B
Second choice	C	A	C	A
Third choice	B	B	A	C

12. Given the preference schedule of 23 voters below, which candidate, if any, wins if an election is held between A and C and the winner of that race runs against B? Who wins the final election?

	Number of Voters			
	8	5	6	4
First choice	A	C	B	B
Second choice	C	A	C	A
Third choice	B	B	A	C

13. Given below is the preference schedule of 23 voters. If a Borda count is used which assigns 3 points for a first place vote, 2 points for a second place vote, and 1 point for a third place vote, who wins the election?

	Number of Voters			
	8	5	6	4
First choice	A	C	B	B
Second choice	C	A	C	A
Third choice	B	B	A	C

14. Can the four voters in the last column vote strategically to change the outcome of question 13 to one they would like better? Why or why not?

15. A poll by fifteen sports announcers chooses the best basketball team from among three schools: University of Nevada at Las Vegas (LV), University of North Carolina (NC), and Indiana University (IU). If the individual rankings are as summarized below, which team wins if they use a rank method that assigns 5, 3, and 1 point(s) to each first, second, and third choice respectively?

	Number of Announcers			
	5	6	2	2
First choice	LV	NC	IU	NC
Second choice	IU	LV	NC	IU
Third choice	NC	IU	LV	LV

16. A seventeen-member committee must elect one of four candidates: R, S, T, or W. According to their preference schedule as shown below, R wins using the plurality method. Could those members who most prefer W vote strategically in some way to change the outcome in a way that will benefit them?

	Number of Members			
	6	4	3	4
First choice	R	S	T	W
Second choice	S	R	S	T
Third choice	T	T	R	S
Fourth choice	W	W	W	R

17. A seventeen-member committee must elect one of four candidates: R, S, T, or W. Their preference schedule as shown below. Which candidate wins under pairwise sequential voting with the agenda S, T,

W, R?

	Number of Members			
	6	4	3	4
First choice	R	S	T	W
Second choice	S	R	S	T
Third choice	T	T	R	S
Fourth choice	W	W	W	R

18. Seventeen board members vote on four candidates, A, B, C, or D, for a new position on their board. Their preference schedules are shown below. Which candidate will be selected if they use the Hare system?

	Number of Members		
	7	6	4
First choice	A	D	C
Second choice	B	A	B
Third choice	C	B	D
Fourth choice	D	C	A

19. Seventeen board members vote on four candidates, A, B, C, or D, for a new position on their board, using the Hare system according to the preference schedules shown below. What happens if A rejects the offer before the ranking?

	Number of Members		
	7	6	4
First choice	A	D	C
Second choice	B	A	B
Third choice	C	B	D
Fourth choice	D	C	A

20. There are 18 delegates to a political party's convention at which four people A, B, C, and D have been nominated as the party's candidate for governor. The delegates' preference schedule is shown below. What nominee would be elected if the party uses a Borda count?

	Number of Delegates		
	8	9	4
First choice	A	B	C
Second choice	B	A	B
Third choice	C	D	A
Fourth choice	D	C	D

21. There are 18 delegates to a political party's convention at which four people A, B, C, and D have been nominated as the party's candidate for governor. The delegates' preference schedule is shown below. What nominee would be elected if the party uses a rank system which assigns 5, 4, 1, and) point(s) for a first, second, third, and fourth choice, respectively? Is this result different from that which results from a Borda count?

	Number of Delegates		
	8	9	4
First choice	A	B	C
Second choice	B	A	B
Third choice	C	D	A
Fourth choice	D	C	D

22. There are 18 delegates to a political party's convention at which four people A, B, C, and D have been nominated as the party's candidate for governor. The delegates' preference schedule is shown below. If the party uses a Borda count, candidate B would be elected. Can the four voters who most prefer C vote strategically in some way to change this outcome to one they would find more favorable? Why or why not?

	Number of Delegates		
	8	9	4
First choice	A	B	C
Second choice	B	A	B
Third choice	C	D	A
Fourth choice	D	C	D

23. An eleven-member committee must choose one of the four applicants K, L, M, and N for membership on the committee. The committee members have preferences among the applicants as given below. If the committee uses pairwise sequential voting with the agenda K, L, M, N, applicant K wins. Can the three voters who least prefer K vote strategically in some way to change the outcome to one they find more favorable? Why or why not?

	Number of Members		
	6	2	3
First choice	K	M	M
Second choice	L	L	N
Third choice	N	K	L
Fourth choice	M	N	K

24. An eleven-member committee must choose one of the four applicants K, L, M, and N for membership on the committee. The committee members have preferences among the applicants as shown below. Which applicant will be given the position if the members use the Borda count to choose the new member?

	Number of Members		
	6	2	3
First choice	K	M	M
Second choice	L	L	N
Third choice	N	K	L
Fourth choice	M	N	K

25. In how many ways can one rank three candidates if ties are allowed?

Chapter 12 Multiple-Choice Questions
Weighted Voting Systems

1. What would be the quota for a voting system which has a total of 15 votes and uses a simple majority quota?
    a) 7   b) 8   c) 9   d) 15

2. What would be the quota for a voting system which has a total of 16 votes and uses a simple majority quota?
    a) 7   b) 8   c) 9   d) 16

3. What would be the quota for a voting system which has a total of 30 votes and uses a simple majority quota?
    a) 14   b) 15   c) 16   d) 30

4. Which of the following describe legitimate weighted voting systems?
    I $[q: w(A), w(B), w(C), w(D)] = [16: 13, 8, 6, 4]$
    II $[q: w(A), w(B), w(C), w(D)] = [15: 10, 8, 7, 5]$
    a) I only   b) II only   c) I and II   d) Neither I nor II

5. Which of the following describe legitimate weighted voting systems?
    I $[q: w(A), w(B), w(C), w(D)] = [27: 20, 15, 12, 5]$
    II $[q: w(A), w(B), w(C), w(D)] = [30: 20, 17, 10, 5]$
    a) I only   b) II only   c) I and II   d) Neither I nor II

6. Which of the following describe legitimate weighted voting systems?
    I $[q: w(A), w(B), w(C)] = [20: 16, 12, 8]$
    II $[q: w(A), w(B), w(C)] = [24: 20, 15, 10]$
    a) I only   b) II only   c) I and II   d) Neither I nor II

7. Which of the following describe legitimate weighted voting systems?
    I $[q: w(A), w(B), w(C)] = [20: 30, 10, 6]$
    II $[q: w(A), w(B), w(C)] = [34: 30, 18, 6]$
    a) I only   b) II only   c) I and II   d) Neither I nor II

8. In a weighted voting system, all winning coalitions would become blocking coalitions if each voter switched his/her vote from YES to NO.
    a) True   b) False

9. In a weighted voting system, all blocking coalitions would become winning coalitions if each voter switched his/her vote from NO to YES.
    a) True   b) False

10. In a weighted voting system, any voter with veto power is a dictator.
    a) True   b) False

11. A weighted voting system can have a dictator without dummy voters.
 a) True b) False

12. A weighted voting system can have dummy voters without a dictator.
 a) True b) False

13. In the weighted voting system [q: $w(A)$, $w(B)$, $w(C)$] = [9: 10, 5, 3], voter A is a dictator.
 a) True b) False

14. Which voters in the system [q: $w(A)$, $w(B)$, $w(C)$, $w(D)$] = [30: 20, 17, 10, 5] have veto power?
 a) A only b) A and B c) A, B, and C d) None

15. Which voters in the system [q: $w(A)$, $w(B)$, $w(C)$, $w(D)$] = [38: 20, 15, 12, 5] have veto power?
 a) A only b) A and B c) A, B, and C d) None

16. Given the weighted voting system [q: $w(A)$, $w(B)$, $w(C)$, $w(D)$] = [38: 20, 15, 12, 5], which is a winning coalition?
 a) {A, B} b) {B, C, D} c) {A, B, D} d) {A}

17. Given the weighted voting system [q: $w(A)$, $w(B)$, $w(C)$, $w(D)$] = [38: 20, 15, 12, 5], which of the coalitions listed is/are blocking coalitions?
      I {A}   II {C, D}   III {A, B, C}
 a) III only b) I and II only c) I, II, and III d) None

18. Given the weighted voting system [q: $w(A)$, $w(B)$, $w(C)$, $w(D)$] = [38: 20, 15, 12, 5], which voter(s) is/are dummy voters.
 a) D only b) D and C c) D, C, and B d) There are no dummy voters.

19. Given the weighted voting system [q: $w(a)$, $w(B)$, $w(C)$, $w(D)$] = [51: 45, 43, 7, 5], which of the following is a winning coalition?
 a) {A} b) {A, D} c) {A, C} d) {B, D}

20. Given the weighted voting system [q: $w(a)$, $w(B)$, $w(C)$, $w(D)$] = [52: 45, 43, 7, 5], which of the following is a minimal winning coalition?
      I {A, B}   II {A, C}   III {A, B, C}
 a) I only b) I and II c) I, II, and III d) None

21. Given the weighted voting system [q: $w(a)$, $w(B)$, $w(C)$, $w(D)$] = [51: 45, 43, 7, 5], which of the following is a blocking coalition?
      I {A}   II {B, C}   III {C}
 a) II only b) I and II c) I, II and III d) None

22. Given the weighted voting system [q: $w(A)$, $w(B)$, $w(C)$] = [9: 6, 4, 2], which of the voters are dummy voters?
 a) C only b) B and C c) B only d) None

23. Given the weighted voting system [q: $w(A)$, $w(B)$, $w(C)$] = [8: 5, 4, 3], which of the coalitions given are minimal winning coalitions?
   a) {A, B, C}   b) {A, B}   c) {B, C}   d) There are no minimal winning coalitions.

24. Given the weighted voting system [q: $w(A)$, $w(B)$, $w(C)$, $w(D)$] = [6: 4, 3, 2, 1], which of the coalitions listed are winning?
   I {A, B}   II {A, C}   III {B, C, D}
   a) I only   b) I and II   c) I and III   d) I, II, and III

25. Given the weighted voting system [q: $w(A)$, $w(B)$, $w(C)$, $w(D)$] = [6: 4, 3, 2, 1], which of the coalitions listed are minimal winning coalitions?
   I {A, B}   II {A, C}   III {B, C, D}
   a) I only   b) I and II   c) II and III   d) I, II, and III

26. Given the weighted voting system [q: $w(A)$, $w(B)$, $w(C)$, $w(D)$] = [6: 4, 3, 2, 1], which of the coalitions listed are blocking coalitions?
   I {A, B}   II {B, C}   III {C, D}
   a) I only   b) I and II   c) II and III   d) I, II, and III

27. If there are four voters in a weighted voting system, how many distinct coalitions of voters can be formed?
   a) 8   b) 16   c) 24   d) 30

28. If there are five voters in a weighted voting system, how may different combinations of YES and NO votes can there be?
   a) 10   b) 25   c) 32   d) 120

29. Calculate C^5_2
   a) 5   b) 10   c) 32   d) 25

30. Calculate C^{12}_4
   a) 48   b) 20,736   c) 495   d) 11,880

31. Calculate C^9_3
   a) 27   b) 84   c) 504   d) 729

32. In a weighted voting system with eight voters, how many coalitions would there be in which exactly five members voted YES?
   a) 32   b) 40   c) 56   d) 256

33. In a weighted voting system with 20 voters, how many distinct coalitions would there be in which exactly eight members voted YES?
   a) 12   b) 56   c) 160   d) 125,970

34. Given the weighted voting system [q: $w(A)$, $w(B)$, $w(C)$, $w(D)$] = [27: 20, 15, 12, 5], calculate the Banzhaf power index.
   a) (8, 8, 8, 0)   b) (8, 6, 6, 2)   c) (6, 6, 6, 1)   d) (8, 6, 6, 0)

35. Given the weighted voting system [q: $w(A)$, $w(B)$, $w(C)$] = [34: 30, 18, 6], calculate the Banzhaf power index.
   a) (6, 4, 2)   b) (6, 2, 2)   c) (6, 6, 6)   d) (6, 4, 0)

36. Given the weighted voting system [q: $w(A)$, $w(B)$, $w(C)$, $w(D)$] = [30: 20, 17, 10, 5], calculate the Banzhaf power index.
   a) (10, 6, 6, 0)   b) (8, 6, 6, 2)   c) (10, 6, 6, 2)   d) (8, 4, 4, 0)

37. In a weighted voting system, the Banzhaf power index of each voter is directly proportional to the weight of the vote.
   a) True   b) False

38. In a weighted voting system, the Banzhaf power index of a dummy voter is 0.
   a) True   b) False

39. In the weighted voting system [q: $w(A)$, $w(B)$, $w(C)$, $w(D)$, $w(E)$, $w(F)$] = [8: 5, 2, 2, 2, 2, 2], find the Banzhaf power index for voter A.
   a) 8   b) 10   c) 15   d) 40

40. In the weighted voting system [q: $w(A)$, $w(B)$, $w(C)$, $w(D)$, $w(E)$, $w(F)$] = [8: 5, 2, 2, 2, 2, 2], find the Banzhaf power index for voter B.
   a) 2   b) 16   c) 4   d) 20

41. In the weighted voting system [q: $w(A)$, $w(B)$, $w(C)$, $w(D)$, $w(E)$, $w(F)$,$w(G)$] = [6: 3, 1, 1, 1, 1, 1, 1], find the Banzhaf power index for voter A.
   a) 6   b) 20   c) 40   d) 82

42. Are the weighted voting systems [q: $w(A)$, $w(B)$, $w(C)$] = [8: 5,.4, 3] and [q: $w(A)$, $w(B)$, $w(C)$] = [34: 30, 18, 6] equivalent?
   a) Yes   b) No

43. Are the weighted voting systems [q: $w(A)$, $w(B)$, $w(C)$] = [8: 5, 4, 3] and [q: $w(A)$, $w(B)$, $w(C)$] = [11: 10, 9, 2] equivalent?
   a) Yes   b) No

44. Are the weighted voting systems [q: $w(A)$, $w(B)$, $w(C)$] = [18: 10, 9, 8] and [q: $w(A)$, $w(B)$, $w(C)$] = [15: 8, 7, 6] equivalent?
   a) Yes   b) No

45. Are the weighted voting systems [q: $w(A)$, $w(B)$, $w(C)$] = [11: 10, 9, 2] and [q: $w(A)$, $w(B)$, $w(C)$] = [2: 1, 1, 1] equivalent?
   a) Yes   b) No

46. How many permutations of five voters can be made?
   a) 14   b) 25   c) 32   d) 120

47. Calculate the Shapley-Shubik power index for each voter in the system [*q: w(A), w(B), w(C)*] = [8: 5, 4, 3].
  a) (4/6, 1/6, 1/6)   b) (3/6, 3/6, 0/6)   c) (2/6, 2/6, 2/6)   d) (4/6, 2/6, 2/6)

48. Calculate the Shapley-Shubik power index for each voter in the system [*q: w(A), w(B), w(C)*] = [15: 8, 7, 6].
  a) (4/6, 1/6, 1/6)   b) (3/6, 3/6, 0/6)   c) (2/6, 2/6, 2/6)   d) (4/6, 2/6, 2/6)

49. Calculate the Shapely-Shubik power index for each voter in the weighted voting system [*q: w(A), w(B), w(C), w(D), w(E), w(F)*] = [8: 5, 2, 2, 2, 2, 2].
  a) (7/12, 1/12, 1/12, 1/12, 1/12, 1/12)   c) (5/6, 1/30, 1/30, 1/30, 1/30, 1/30)
  b) (5/8, 3/40, 3/40, 3/40, 3/40, 3/40)   d) (1/3, 2/15, 2/15, 2/15, 2/15, 2/15)

50. Calculate the Shapely-Shubik power index for each voter in the weighted voting system [*q: w(A), w(B), w(C), w(D), w(E), w(F), w(G)*] = [6: 3, 1, 1, 1, 1, 1, 1].
  a) (3/7, 2/21, 2/21, 2/21, 2/21, 2/21, 2/21)   c) (1/3, 1/9, 1/9, 1/9, 1/9, 1/9, 1/9)
  b) (1/2, 1/12, 1/12, 1/12, 1/12, 1/12, 1/12)   d) (2/3, 1/18, 1/18, 1/18, 1/18, 1/18, 1/18)

Free-Response Questions

1. Give an example of a weighted voting system which has a dummy voter but no dictator.

2. Explain why the weighted voting system $[q: w(A), w(B), w(C), w(D), w(E)] = [13: 10, 6, 5, 3, 2]$ is not a legitimate weighted voting system.

3. Give an example of a weighted voting system which has a blocking coalition which would not be a winning coalition if all its members voted YES.

4. Given the weighted voting system $[q: w(A), w(B), w(C), w(D)] = [30: 20, 17, 10, 5]$, list all winning coalitions.

5. Given the weighted voting system $[q: w(A), w(B), w(C), w(D)] = [51: 45, 43, 7, 5]$, list all blocking coalitions.

6. Given the weighted voting system $[q: w(A), w(B), w(C), w(D)] = [51: 45, 43, 7, 5]$, list all minimal winning coalitions.

7. Given the weighted voting system $[q: w(A), w(B), w(C), w(D)] = [30: 20, 17, 10, 5]$, list all minimal winning coalitions.

8. Given the weighted voting system $[q: w(A), w(B), w(C), w(D)] = [30: 20, 17, 10, 5]$, list all blocking coalitions.

9. A weighted voting system has four voters, A, B, C, and D. List all possible coalitions of these voters. How many such coalitions are there?

10. In a weighted voting system, is a voter with veto power the same as a dictator? Explain why or why not.

11. A weighted voting system has five voters. How many distinct coalitions are there in which exactly three members vote YES?

12. A weighted voting system has 12 members. How many distinct coalitions are there in which exactly seven members vote YES?

13. Given the weighted voting system $[q: w(A), w(B), w(C)] = [8: 5, 4, 3]$, find the Banzhaf power index for each voter.

14. Given the weighted voting system $[q: w(A), w(B), w(C), w(D)] = [14: 10, 6, 5, 3]$, find the Banzhaf power index for each voter.

15. Given the weighted voting system $[q: w(A), w(B), w(C), w(D), w(E), w(F)] = [7: 4, 1, 1, 1, 1, 1]$, find the Banzhaf power index for each voter.

16. Suppose a weighted voting system has five members, but that voter E is a dummy voter. Can you find

the Banzhaf power index of voter E?

17. Give an example of a weighted voting which is equivalent to the system $[q: w(A), w(B), w(C)] = [8: 5, 4, 3]$.

18. Give an example of a weighted voting system which is equivalent to the system $[q: w(A), w(B), w(C)] = [15: 8, 7, 6]$.

19. Is voter C a critical voter in the coalition $\{A, B, C\}$ of the weighted voting system $[q: w(A), w(B), w(C), w(D), w(E)] = [15: 10, 6, 5, 3, 2]$? Why or why not?

20. What is the difference between a "critical" voter in a coalition and a "pivotal" voter in a permutation?

21. Evaluate C^8_3.

22. Calculate the Shapely-Shubik power index for the weighted voting system $[q: w(A), w(B), w(C), w(D)] = [30: 20, 17, 10, 5]$.

23. Calculate the Shapely-Shubik power index for the weighted voting system $[q: w(A), w(B), w(C), w(D), w(E), w(F)] = [8: 6, 1, 1, 1, 1, 1]$

24. There are five distinct three-member voting systems. Give an example of three of the five.

25. A sorority has an executive board consisting of a chair, vice chair, and three other members. Its voting rules indicate that an issue can pass in two ways: if the chair, vice chair, and one other member support the issue or if one of the chair or vice chair and two other members support the issue. Express this as a weighted voting system.

Chapter 13 Multiple-Choice Questions
Fair Division

1. In a fair-division procedure, the goal is for all participants to receive identical amounts.
   a) True   b) False

2. In a fair-division procedure, participants may receive different amounts.
   a) True   b) False

3. Which of the following fair-division procedures is not envy free?
   a) Adjusted winner procedure
   b) Knaster inheritance procedure
   c) Last-diminisher method
   d) Divide-and-choose

4. Tom and Sandy must make a fair division of three objects left by their Great Aunt Sally. They have assigned points to the objects as shown below. Using the adjusted winner procedure, who gets the car?

Object	Tom's points	Sandy's points
Painting	40	30
Jewelry	10	50
Car	50	20

   a) Tom   b) Sandy

5. Tom and Sandy must make a fair division of three objects left by their Great Aunt Sally. They have assigned points to the objects as shown below. Using the adjusted winner procedure, what does Tom end up with?

Object	Tom's points	Sandy's points
Painting	40	30
Jewelry	10	50
Car	50	20

   a) Car and painting   b) Car only   c) Painting and 1/5 car   d) Car and 3/7 painting

6. Tom and Sandy must make a fair division of three objects left by their Great Aunt Sally. They have assigned points to the objects as shown below. Using the adjusted winner procedure, how many points of value does Tom feel he ends with?

Object	Tom's points	Sandy's points
Painting	40	30
Jewelry	10	50
Car	50	20

   a) 67.14   b) 90   c) 50   d) 50.43

7. Chris and Terry must make a fair division of a stereo, television, and microwave. They place point values on the objects as shown below. Using the adjusted winner procedure, what does Terry receive?

Object	Chris' points	Terry's points
Stereo	25	45
Television	60	35
Microwave	15	20

a) Stereo and 1/4 of microwave

b) Microwave and 6/7 of television

c) Stereo and 6/7 of microwave

d) Stereo and microwave

8. Chris and Terry must make a fair division of a stereo, television, and microwave. They place point values on the objects as shown below. Using the adjusted winner procedure, what point value does Chris feel he receives in the end?

Object	Chris' points	Terry's points
Stereo	25	45
Television	60	35
Microwave	15	20

a) 60   b) 62.14   c) 50   d) 37.86

9. Andi and Toni must make fair division of a car, house, and boat. The point values they place on the objects are given below. Using the adjusted winner procedure, what does Andi end with?

Object	Andi's points	Toni's points
Car	35	45
House	40	30
Boat	25	25

a) House and boat   b) House and 2/5 of boat   c) House and 2/7 of car   d) House and 3/5 of boat

10. Andi and Toni must make fair division of a car, house, and boat. The point values they place on the objects are given below. Using the adjusted winner procedure, what point value does Andi end with?

Object	Andi's points	Toni's points
Car	35	45
House	40	30
Boat	25	25

a) 65   b) 55   c) 50   d) 60

11. At the end of the lease on their apartment, Toni and Terry decide to rent separate places and so must make a fair division of the property they purchased together. The items to be divided and the point values each person places on them are given below. If Toni and Terry use the adjusted winner procedure, who gets the microwave?

Item	Toni	Terry
CD player	15	20
Sofa	30	25
Microwave	20	25
TV	35	30

a) Toni   b) Terry

12. At the end of the lease on their apartment, Toni and Terry decide to rent separate places and so must make a fair division of the property they purchased together. The items to be divided and the point values each person places on them are given below. If Toni and Terry use the adjusted winner procedure to divide the property, what will Terry end with?

Item	Toni	Terry
CD player	15	20
Sofa	30	25
Microwave	20	25
TV	35	30

a) CD, microwave, and TV
b) CD, microwave, and 1/6 TV
c) CD and microwave only
d) CD, microwave, and 4/13 TV

13. At the end of the lease on their apartment, Toni and Terry decide to rent separate places and so must make a fair division of the property they purchased together. The items to be divided and the point values each person places on them are given below. If Toni and Terry use the adjusted winner procedure to divide the property, how many points of value will each person think they end up with?

Item	Toni	Terry
CD player	15	20
Sofa	30	25
Microwave	20	25
TV	35	30

a) 45   b) 50   c) 54.23   d) 56.5

14. Jack and Jill went up the hill and found an antique water pail. Jack and Jill must now make a fair division of the pail using the Knaster inheritance procedure. Jack bids $80 for the value of the pail and Jill bids $65. What is the outcome of the fair division?
a) Jack gets the pail and pays Jill $36.25.
b) Jack gets the pail and pays Jill $40.
c) Jack gets the pail and pays Jill $32.50.
d) Jack gets the pail and Jill gets $65.

15. Jack and Jill went up the hill and found an antique water pail. Jack and Jill must now make a fair division of the pail using the Knaster inheritance procedure. Jack bids $80 for the value of the pail and Jill bids $65. How much value does Jill think she ends with?
a) $36.25   b) $32.50   c) $40   d) $43.75

16. Jack and Jill went up the hill and found an antique water pail. Jack and Jill must now make a fair division of the pail using the Knaster inheritance procedure. Jack bids $80 for the value of the pail and Jill bids $65. How much value does Jack believe he ends with?
a) $36.25   b) $32.50   c) $40   d) $43.75

17. Andi, Chris, and Kim must make a fair division of a car left to them by their father. Using the Knaster inheritance procedure, the values they bid on the car are given below. Find the results of the fair division.

	Andi	Chris	Kim
Car	$2400	$3000	$2700

a) Chris gets the car and pays $1900; Andi gets $900, and Kim gets $1000.

b) Chris gets the car, Andi gets $800; Kim gets $900.
c) Chris gets the car and pays $1500; Andi gets $1200, and Kim gets $1350.
d) Chris gets the car and pays $2550; Andi gets $1200, and Kim gets $1350.

18. Andi, Chris, and Kim must make a fair division of a car left to them by their father. Using the Knaster inheritance procedure, the values they bid on the car are given below.

	Andi	Chris	Kim
Car	$2400	$3000	$2700

How much value does Chris think he ends up with?
a) $3000   b) $1300   c) $1100   d) $1000

19. Three children must make fair division of a painting and sculpture left them by their mother. Using the Knaster inheritance procedure, the value each child places on the objects is shown below.

Object	A	B	C
Painting	$4000	$6300	$6000
Sculpture	$2300	$1800	$2400

Who gets the sculpture?
a) A   b) B   c) C

20. Three children must make fair division of a painting and sculpture left them by their mother. Using the Knaster inheritance procedure, the value each child places on the objects is shown below.

Object	A	B	C
Painting	$4000	$6300	$6000
Sculpture	$2300	$1800	$2400

What does A end with after the fair division?
a) $2466.67   b) $2100   c) Sculpture and $166.67   d) $3150

21. Three children must make fair division of a painting and sculpture left them by their mother. Using the Knaster inheritance procedure, the value each child places on the objects is shown below.

Object	A	B	C
Painting	$4000	$6300	$6000
Sculpture	$2300	$1800	$2400

What does B get after the fair division?
a) Painting and $366.67
b) Painting and pays $3233.34
c) Painting and pays $3600
d) Painting and pays $2250

22. Ashley, Brook, Chris, and Dana must make a fair division of the estate of their uncle Bob. The estate consists of a farm house, a car, and a horse. Using the Knaster inheritance procedure, the value each person places on each item is shown below. Who gets the horse?

Item	Ashley	Brook	Chris	Dana
House	$35,000	$50,000	$48,000	$42,000
Car	$3000	$2500	$2750	$2800
Horse	$6000	$5800	$6250	$5200

a) Ashley   b) Brook   c) Chris   d) Dana

23. Ashley, Brook, Chris, and Dana must make a fair division of the estate of their uncle Bob. The estate consists of a farm house, a car, and a horse. Using the Knaster inheritance procedure, the value each person places on each item is shown below.

Item	Ashley	Brook	Chris	Dana
House	$35,000	$50,000	$48,000	$42,000
Car	$3000	$2500	$2750	$2800
Horse	$6000	$5800	$6250	$5200

What does Ashley end the fair division with?

a) Car and $18,000   b) Car and $8000   c) Car and $22,000   d) Car and $9731.25

24. Ashley, Brook, Chris, and Dana must make a fair division of the estate of their uncle Bob. The estate consists of a farm house, a car, and a horse. Using the Knaster inheritance procedure, the value each person places on each item is shown below.

Item	Ashley	Brook	Chris	Dana
House	$35,000	$50,000	$48,000	$42,000
Car	$3000	$2500	$2750	$2800
Horse	$6000	$5800	$6250	$5200

What value does Chris end the fair division with?

a) $9731   b) $14,250   c) $15,981.25   d) $1731.25

25. Suppose that Andi and Terry view a cake as shown below. They agree to divide the cake using the divide-and-choose procedure. If Andi divides the cake, where will the cut be made?

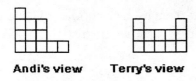

Andi's view   **Terry's view**

a) 2 columns from the left   c) 2 1/2 columns from the left
b) 1 2/3 columns from the left   d) 2 1/3 columns from the left

26. Suppose that Andi and Terry view a cake as shown below. They agree to divide the cake using the divide-and-choose procedure. If Andi divides the cake, which side will Terry choose?

Andi's view   **Terry's view**

a) The right side   b) The left side

27. Suppose that Andi and Terry view a cake as shown below. They agree to divide the cake using the divide-and-choose procedure. If Andi divides the cake and Terry chooses, how many units will Andi be left with?

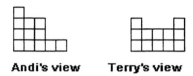

Andi's view   **Terry's view**

a) 4 1/3   b) 5   c) 6   d) 7 2/3

28. Suppose that Andi and Terry view a cake as shown below. They agree to divide the cake using the divide-and-choose procedure. If Andi divides the cake and Terry chooses, how many units of cake will Terry believe she gets?

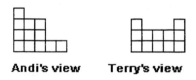

Andi's view   **Terry's view**

a) 4 1/3   b) 5   c) 6   d) 7 2/3

29. Suppose Chris and Toni each view a cake as shown below. They agree to use the divide- and-choose procedure. If Chris divides, where will the cut be made?

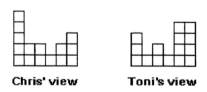

Chris' view   **Toni's view**

a) 4 columns from the left   c) 3 columns from the left
b) 3 1/2 columns from the left   d) 2 1/4 columns from the left.

30. Suppose Chris and Toni each view a cake as shown below. They agree to use the divide- and-choose procedure. If Chris divides, which side will Toni choose?

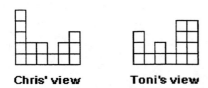

Chris' view   Toni's view

a) Right   b) Left

31. Suppose Chris and Toni each view a cake as shown below. They agree to use the divide- and-choose procedure. If Chris divides and Toni chooses, how many units will Toni believe he gets?

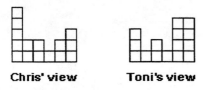

Chris' view   Toni's view

a) 4 1/2   b) 6   c) 7 1/2   d) 10 1/2

32. Suppose Chris and Toni each view a cake as shown below. They agree to use the divide- and-choose procedure. If Chris divides and Toni chooses, how much will Chris feel is left?

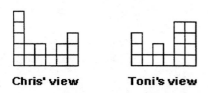

Chris' view   Toni's view

a) 4 1/2   b) 6   c) 7 1/2   d) 10 1/2

33. Alex, Betty, and Chris each view a cake as shown below. They will share the cake using the last-diminisher method with the order Alex, Betty, and Chris cutting and passing off the right side of the cake. After Alex cuts the cake, he will hand the portion on the right to Betty. Where will Alex make his cut?

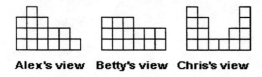

Alex's view   Betty's view   Chris's view

a) 2 columns from the right   c) 3 2/3 columns from the right
b) 3 columns from the right   d) 4 columns from the right

34. Alex, Betty, and Chris each view a cake as shown below. They will share the cake using the last-diminisher method with the order Alex, Betty, and Chris cutting and passing off the right side of the cake. After Alex cuts the cake, he will hand the portion on the right to Betty. Will Betty trim the piece before handing it to Chris?

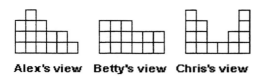

Alex's view   Betty's view   Chris's view

a) Yes   b) No

35. Alex, Betty, and Chris each view a cake as shown below. They will share the cake using the last-diminisher method with the order Alex, Betty, and Chris cutting and passing off the right side of the cake. After Alex cuts the cake, he will hand the portion on the right to Betty, who decides whether or not to trim the piece and then hands it off to Chris. Will Chris trim the piece he receives from Betty?

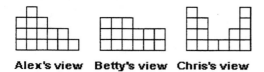

Alex's view   Betty's view   Chris's view

a) Yes   b) No

36. Alex, Betty, and Chris each view a cake as shown below. They will share the cake using the last-diminisher method with the order Alex, Betty, and Chris cutting and passing off the right side of the cake. Who will make the last cut and thus keep the first piece of cake?

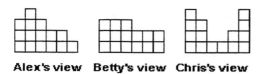

Alex's view   Betty's view   Chris's view

a) Alex   b) Betty   c) Chris

37. Dana, Kim, and Lu each view a cake as shown below. They will share the cake using the last-diminisher method with the order Dana, Kim, and Lu cutting and passing off the right side of the cake. Dana first cuts a piece off the right side of the cake and hands it to Kim. Where will Dana cut the cake?

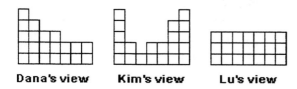

Dana's view   Kim's view   Lu's view

a) 2 1/3 columns from the right   c) 1 1/2 columns from the right
b) 3 1/3 column from the right   d) 4 columns from the right

38. Dana, Kim, and Lu each view a cake as shown below. They will share the cake using the last-diminisher method with the order Dana, Kim, and Lu cutting and passing off the right side of the cake. Dana first cuts a piece she believes is worth 7 units off the right side of the cake and hands it to Kim. How many units will Kim think this slice is worth?

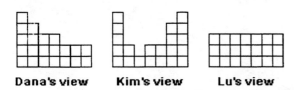

a) 7   b) 9 1/2   c) 11 2/3   d) 10 1/2

39. Dana, Kim, and Lu each view a cake as shown below. They will share the cake using the last-diminisher method with the order Dana, Kim, and Lu cutting and passing off the right side of the cake. Dana first cuts a piece she believes is worth 7 units off the right side of the cake and hands it to Kim. Will Kim trim the slice?

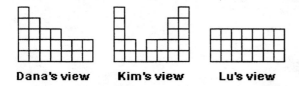

a) Yes   b) No

40. Dana, Kim, and Lu each view a cake as shown below. They will share the cake using the last-diminisher method with the order Dana, Kim, and Lu cutting and passing off the right side of the cake. Who will be the last to trim and thus keep the first piece of cake?

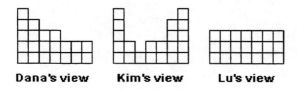

a) Dana   b) Kim   c) Lu

41. Dana, Kim, and Lu each view a cake as shown below. They will share the cake using the last-diminisher method with the order Dana, Kim, and Lu cutting and passing off the right side of the cake. How many units will Lu believe the piece handed him by Kim is worth?

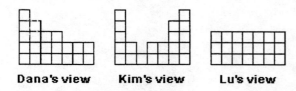

a) 7   b) 3 1/2   c) 4 1/2   d) 10

42. Dana, Chris, Kelly, and Terry each view a cake as shown below. They will divide the cake using the trimming procedure with the players ordered as listed above. Dana cuts the cake into five pieces, numbered from left to right, and hands them to Chris. Which pieces will Chris trim?

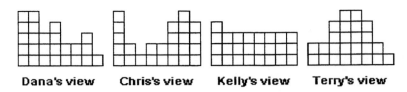

Dana's view   Chris's view   Kelly's view   Terry's view

a) None   b) #4 only   c) #1 and #4   d) #5 only

43. Kelly, Terry, Dana, and Chris each view a cake as shown below. They will divide the cake using the trimming procedure with the players ordered as listed above. Kelly cuts the cake into five pieces, numbered from left to right, and hands them to Terry. Which pieces will Terry trim?

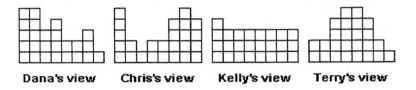

Dana's view   Chris's view   Kelly's view   Terry's view

a) None   b) #3 only   c) #3 and #4   d) #4 only

44. Four heirs need to make a fair division of the property left in an estate. The objects and the point values assigned to them are given below. If the heirs want to use the trimming procedure, with the order Chris, Kelly, Dana, and Kim, would the house need to be sold?

Object	Chris's points	Kelly's points	Dana's points	Kim's points
House	20	15	18	20
Car	10	12	10	5
Painting	10	8	12	15
Furniture	8	10	10	5
Money	52	55	50	55

a) Yes   b) No

45. Four heirs need to make a fair division of the property left in an estate. The objects and the point values assigned to them are given below. If the heirs want to use the trimming procedure, with the order Chris, Kelly, Dana, and Kim, would the house need to be sold?

Object	Chris's points	Kelly's points	Dana's points	Kim's points
House	20	25	18	25
Car	10	12	10	5
Painting	10	8	12	15
Furniture	8	10	10	5
Money	52	45	50	50

a) Yes   b) No

46. Four heirs need to make a fair division of the property left in an estate. The objects and the point values assigned to them are given below. The heirs want to use the trimming procedure, with the order Chris, Kelly, Dana, and Kim. Chris divides the estate into the following parts: (1) house, (2) car and 10 points from money, (3) painting and 10 points from money, (4) furniture and 15 points from money, and (5)

remaining 20 points from money. Which parts will Kelly trim?

Object	Chris's points	Kelly's points	Dana's points	Kim's points
House	20	25	18	25
Car	10	12	10	5
Painting	10	8	12	15
Furniture	8	10	10	5
Money	52	45	50	50

a) Part #4 only   b) Parts #2, #3, and #4   c) Parts #2 and #4   d) None

47. Tom and Huck need to paint a fence and agree to use a modification of the divide-and- choose procedure to make a fair division of the chore. The boys' views of the fence are shown below. If Tom divides, will Huck choose the piece he believes is larger or smaller in modifying the procedure?

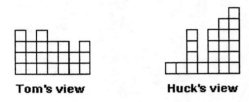

a) Huck chooses the part he feels is smaller.   b) Huck chooses the part he feels is larger.

48. Tom and Huck need to paint a fence and agree to use a modification of the divide-and- choose procedure to make a fair division of the chore. The boys' views of the fence are shown below. If Tom divides and Huck chooses, how many units of fence will Tom think each boy is painting?

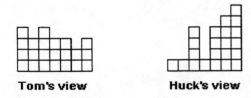

a) Tom paints 11 and Huck paints 11.   c) Tom paints 16 and Huck paints 6.
b) Tom paints 6 and Huck paints 16.   d) Tom paints 12 and Huck paints 10.

49. Tom and Huck need to paint a fence and agree to use a modification of the divide-and- choose procedure to make a fair division of the chore. The boys' views of the fence are shown below. If Tom divides and Huck chooses, how many units of fence will Huck think each boy is painting?

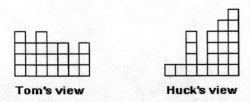

a) Tom paints 11 and Huck paints 11.   c) Tom paints 16 and Huck paints 6.
b) Tom paints 6 and Huck paints 16.   d) Tom paints 12 and Huck paints 10.

50. Andi and Terry need to make a fair division of a sofa they bought when sharing an apartment. They agree that Andi is entitled to 2/3 of the sofa and Terry is entitled to 1/3 of the sofa. They agree to use a modification of the Knaster inheritance procedure to divide the sofa. Andi believes the sofa is worth $360 and Terry believes the sofa is worth $315. Using the Knaster inheritance procedure, how much will Andi pay Terry for the sofa?
 a) $105   b) $110   c) $120   d) $315

Free-Response Questions

1. After having been roommates for four years at college, Alex and Bob are moving on. Several items they have accumulated belong jointly to the pair, but now must be divided between the two. They assign points to the items as follows:

Object	Alex's points	Bob's points
Bicycle	10	12
Textbooks	20	16
Barbells	5	2
Rowing machine	7	10
Music collection	8	11
Computer	15	17
Novels	20	22
Desk	15	10

    Use the adjusted winner procedure to determine a fair division of the property.

2. In recent labor-management negotiations, several issues were identified, and points assigned to them indicating relative importance to each side, as follows:

Issue	Management's points	Labor's points
Base pay	20	23
Incentive pay	10	5
Health care benefits	6	12
Worker safety	8	15
Opportunity for promotion	20	13
Retirement package	20	20
Employee accountability	16	12

    Use the adjusted winner procedure to determine a fair resolution between labor and management.

3. A husband and wife are getting divorced. The property to be divided, and the relative value of the items to each, are as follows:

Object	Husband's points	Wife's points
House	30	15
Car	25	25
Cabin	20	40
Boat	16	15
Television	5	3
Stereo	4	2

    Use the adjusted winner procedure to determine a fair division of the property.

4. The administration and the student body at a local college are at odds over several issues. The relative importance of each issue to each group is as follows:

Issue	Administration's points	Student's points
Mandatory meal plan	40	15
Mandatory campus living	5	30
Cars on campus	5	20
Campus curfew	10	15
Weekday fraternity parties	40	20

Use the adjusted winner procedure to determine a fair resolution.

5. Henry and Lisa inherit a house. If their monetary bids on the house are $135,000 and $114,000, respectively, what is the fair division arrived at by the Knaster inheritance procedure?

6. Two people inherit a painting. If their monetary bids on the painting are $12,560 and $9750, what is the fair distribution arrived at by the Knaster inheritance procedure?

7. John, Ken, and Linda inherit a painting. If their monetary bids on the painting are $25,200, $21,600, and $18,000 respectively, what is the fair distribution arrived at by the Knaster inheritance procedure?

8. John, Ken, and Linda inherit a painting. Their monetary bids on the painting are $25,200, $21,600, and $18,000 respectively. If Linda had known of John and Ken's evaluations in advance, should she have changed her own evaluation?

9. A parent leaves a house, a farm, and a piece of property to be divided equally among four children who submit dollar bids on these objects as follows:

		Children		
Objects	First	Second	Third	Fourth
House	120,000	125,000	100,000	90,000
Farm	80,000	60,000	70,000	75,000
Property	40,000	30,000	25,000	45,000

What is the fair division arrived at by the Knaster inheritance procedure?

10. Three indivisible objects A, B, and C are to be shared equally among four people. Assume that the objects have monetary values to the four people as follows:

		People		
Object	First	Second	Third	Fourth
A	8600	3500	2300	4800
B	5500	4200	4400	2700
C	3600	5100	3400	2300

What is the fair distribution arrived at by the Knaster inheritance procedure?

11. Suppose that Bob and Carol view a cake as shown below:

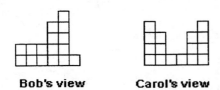

Bob's view   **Carol's view**

Assume that Bob and Carol use divide-and-choose to divide the cake between them, and that all cuts are made corresponding to vertical lines. If Bob is the divider, how many units of value will Bob and Carol think he or she is receiving?

12. Suppose that Bob and Carol view a cake as shown below:

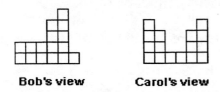

Bob's view   **Carol's view**

Bob and Carol will use divide-and-choose to divide the cake between them, and all cuts made correspond to vertical lines. Will Bob like the results better if he is the divider or the chooser? Explain your answer.

13. Suppose that Bob and Carol view a cake as shown below:

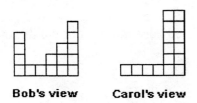

Bob's view   **Carol's view**

Assume that Bob and Carol use divide-and-choose to divide the cake between them and that all cuts are vertical. If Bob is the divider, how many units of value will Bob and Carol think he or she is receiving? Is this different if Carol is the divider? Explain.

14. Suppose that Bob and Carol view a cake as shown below:

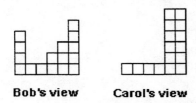

Bob's view   **Carol's view**

Assume that Bob and Carol know how each other values the cake (and that neither is spiteful). Suppose they are to divide the cake using the rules of divide-and-choose but not necessarily the strategies. If Bob is the divider, where will he cut the cake and how many units of value will Bob and Carol think he or she is receiving?

15. Suppose that Bob, Carol, and Ted view a cake as shown below:

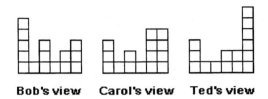

Bob's view   Carol's view   Ted's view

Assume that each player regards a piece as acceptable if and only if it is at least five square units of value. Assume all cuts are vertical. Provide a total of three drawings to show how each player views a division of the cake, by Bob, into three pieces he or she considers to be the same size or value.

16. Suppose that Bob, Carol, and Ted view a cake as shown below:

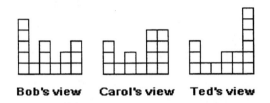

Bob's view   Carol's view   Ted's view

Assume that each player regards a piece as acceptable if and only if it is at least five square units of value. Assume all cuts are vertical. Provide a total of three drawings to show how each player views a division of the cake by Bob into three pieces he considers to be the same size or value. Now use the Steinhaus lone-divider method to get a proportional allocation, indicating who approves of which piece and how large a piece each player thinks he or she is receiving.

17. Assume that Bob, Carol, Ted, and Alice view a cake as shown below:

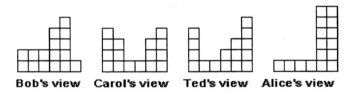

Bob's view   Carol's view   Ted's view   Alice's view

Notice that each player views the cake as having 16 units of value. Assume that the four players use the last diminisher method to divide the cake among themselves. Give a step-by-step description of the cuts made and the pieces with which each player exits assuming that the order in which they proceed is Bob, then Carol, then Ted, and then Alice.

18. Assume that Bob, Carol, Ted, and Alice view a cake as shown below:

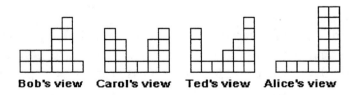

Bob's view   Carol's view   Ted's view   Alice's view

Notice that each player views the cake as having 16 units of value. Assume that the four players use the last diminisher method to divide the cake among themselves. Give a step-by-step description of the cuts made and the pieces with which each player exits assuming that the order in which they proceed is Alice, then Ted, then Carol, and then Bob.

19. Suppose players 1, 2, and 3 view a cake as shown below, and that all cuts are vertical.

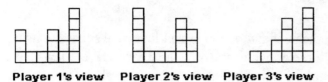

Player 1's view   Player 2's view   Player 3's view

Describe the steps in using the last-diminisher method to divide the cake. Assume players will use the order of player 1, then player 2, and then player 3 and that all pieces will be cut from the left side of the cake. Use drawings to clarify your description.

20. Suppose players 1, 2, and 3 view a cake as shown below and that all cuts are vertical.

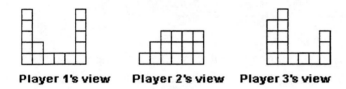

Player 1's view   Player 2's view   Player 3's view

Illustrate the envy-free procedure for $n = 3$ (yielding an allocation of part of the cake) by following steps a-c below:
a) Provide a total of three drawings to show how each player views a division of the cake by player 1 into three pieces he or she considers to be the same size or value. Label the pieces A, B, and C.
b) Redraw the picture from player 2's view and illustrate the trimmings of piece B that he or she would do. Label the trimmed piece b' and the actual trimmings T.
c) Indicate which piece each player would choose (and what he or she thinks its size is) if the players choose in the following order: player 3, player 2, player 1 according to the rules of the procedure.

21. Apply the remainder of the Selfridge-Conway procedure to what was obtained in question 20 by completing a-c below:
a) Draw a picture of T from each player's view.
b) The procedure calls for the player (other that player 1) who did not receive the trimmed piece to divide T into three pieces he or she considers to be the same size. Illustrate this division, and label the pieces X, Y, and Z.
c) Indicate which parts of T (and the sizes or values) the players will choose when they go in the order: player 2, player 1, player 3.

22. Suppose Chris and Terry need to make a fair division of a stereo they jointly purchased. Suppose also, that both agree Chris is entitled to 2/3 of the stereo and Terry to 1/3. Chris and Terry place monetary bids on the value of the stereo of $500 and $450 respectively. Modify the Knaster inheritance procedure to make a fair division of the stereo.

23. Aunt Sally dies and leaves her estate to be shared between Ariel, Binky, and Chris. The estate consists of

a painting and a sculpture by a modern artist. Aunt Sally had decreed that Ariel was to receive half her estate and that Binky and Chris were to share equally the remaining half. The values that each heir placed on the painting and sculpture are given below. Modify the Knaster inheritance procedure to make a fair division of the estate.

Object	Ariel	Binky	Chris
Painting	4000	6300	6000
Sculpture	2300	1800	2400

24. Explain why the divide-and-choose method of cake division is considered an envy-free procedure for dividing a cake between two participants.

25. Tom and Jerry must rake all the leaves in a yard. They each view the yard as shown below and agree to divide the chore by the divide-and-choose method. Tom will divide the yard in two parts and Jerry will choose the side he has to rake. Describe the results of this fair division.

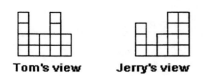

Tom's view   **Jerry's view**

Chapter 14 Multiple-Choice Questions
Apportionment

1. The Hamilton method of apportionment can display the population paradox.
   a) True   b) False

2. The Jefferson method of apportionment can display the population paradox.
   a) True   b) False

3. The Webster method of apportionment can display the population paradox.
   a) True   b) False

4. The Jefferson method of apportionment can display the Alabama paradox
   a) True   b) False

5. An apportionment method exists which satisfies the quota condition and is free from both the population paradox and the Alabama paradox.
   a) True   b) False

6. Which method of apportionment always satisfies the quota condition?
   a) Hamilton   b) Hill-Huntington   c) Jefferson   d) Webster

7. For a given set of populations and house sizes, different methods of apportionment may lead to different apportionments.
   a) True   b) False

8. For a given set of populations and house sizes, different methods of apportionment may lead to the same apportionment.
   a) True   b) False

9. A county is supposed to apportion 25 seats on a county council using Jefferson's method. When using 4300 as a divisor, 23 seats are given out. The critical divisor for a district would be
   a) 4300.
   b) bigger than 4300.
   c) smaller than 4300.
   d) No decision can be made from the given information.

10. A county is divided into three districts with the populations shown below. There are 10 seats on the county council which need to be apportioned. Find the quota for the Applewood district.

District	Population
Applewood	8280
Boxwood	4600
Central	5220

    a) 4.57   b) 4   c) 5   d) 8.28

11. We are scheduling seven course sections for a total of 217 students. Enrollments are: 109 in Calculus I, 79 in Calculus II, and 29 in Advanced Calculus. Find the quota of sections for Calculus II.
a) 2   b) 2.55   c) 3.64   d) 3

12. A small county has populations in three districts as shown below. They are to apportion 10 seats on the county council. Find the quota for Riverdale.

District	Population
Parkview	43,000
Hillside	32,800
Riverdale	24,200

a) 4.13   b) 2   c) 4   d) 2.42

13. A county is divided into three districts with the populations shown below. There are 10 seats on the county council which need to be apportioned, using the Hamilton method. Find the apportionment for the Applewood district.

District	Population
Applewood	8280
Boxwood	4600
Central	5220

a) 4   b) 3   c) 5   d) 2

14. We are scheduling seven course sections for a total of 217 students. Enrollments are: 109 in Calculus I, 79 in Calculus II, 29 in Advanced Calculus. Find the apportionment for Advanced Calculus using the Hamilton method.
a) 0   b) 1   c) 2   d) 3

15. A county is divided into three districts with the populations shown below. There are 10 seats on the county council which need to be apportioned, using the Hamilton method. Find the apportionment for the Boxwood district.

District	Population
Applewood	8280
Boxwood	4600
Central	5220

a) 2   b) 3   c) 1   d) 4

16. A county is divided into three districts with the populations shown below. There are 10 seats on the county council which need to be apportioned. If the county uses the Jefferson method, what would be the first critical divisor for the Applewood district?

District	Population
Applewood	8280
Boxwood	4600
Central	5220

a) 1800   b) 2070   c) 1656   d) 4570

17. A county has three districts with the populations shown below. The 11 seats on the county council are to be apportioned using the Jefferson method. Find the apportionment for each district.

District	Population
A	43,000
B	32,800
C	24,200

a) 5, 3, 3   b) 5, 4, 2   c) 6, 3, 2   d) 4, 4, 3

18. A state has four districts with the populations shown below. The House of Representatives has 20 seats which are to be apportioned using the Jefferson method. Find the first critical divisor for district A.

District	Population
A	87,000
B	56,000
C	72,000
D	35,000

a) 12,428   b) 17,500   c) 14,500   d) 10,875

19. A county is divided into three districts with the populations shown below. There are 10 seats on the county council which need to be apportioned. If the county uses the Jefferson method, what would be the initial divisor used?

District	Population
Applewood	8280
Boxwood	4600
Central	5220

a) 828   b) 18,100   c) 6033   d) 1810

20. A county has three districts with the populations shown below. The 11 seats on the county council are to be apportioned using the Jefferson method. Find the initial divisor which would be used.

District	Population
A	43,000
B	32,800
C	24,200

a) 100,000   b) 3909   c) 2558   d) 9091

21. A county has three districts with the populations shown below. The 11 seats on the county council are to be apportioned using the   Webster method. Find the first critical divisor for district A.

District	Population
A	43,000
B	32,800
C	24,200

a) 10750   b) 8600   c) 7818   d) 9556

22. A county has three districts with the populations shown below. The 11 seats on the county council are to be apportioned using the Webster method. Find the apportionment for each district.

District	Population
A	43,000
B	32,800
C	24,200

a) 5, 4, 2   b) 5, 3, 3   c) 4, 4, 3   d) 6, 3, 2

23. A state has four districts with the populations shown below. The House of Representatives has 20 seats which are to be apportioned using the Jefferson method. Find the apportionment for each district.

District	Population
A	87,000
B	56,000
C	72,000
D	35,000

a) 6, 5, 6, 3   b) 7, 4, 5, 4   c) 6, 4, 6, 4   d) 7, 4, 6, 3

24. A country has four states with the populations shown below. The House of Representatives is to have 15 members. Use the Webster method of apportionment to find the number of seats for each state.

State	Population
A	52,600
B	39,900
C	34,000
D	23,500

a) 6, 4, 3, 2   b) 5, 4, 4, 2   c) 6, 3, 3, 3   d) 5, 4, 3, 3

25. A small county has populations in three districts as shown below. They are to apportion 15 seats on the county council using the Webster method. Find the apportionment for each district.

District	Population
Parkview	43,000
Hillside	32,800
Riverdale	24,200

a) 7, 5, 3   b) 6, 6, 3   c) 6, 5, 4   d) 7, 4, 4

26. A small county has populations in three districts as shown below. They are to apportion 15 seats on the county council using the Hill-Huntington method. Find the apportionment for each district.

District	Population
Parkview	43,000
Hillside	32,800
Riverdale	24,200

a) 7, 5, 3   b) 6, 6, 3   c) 6, 5, 4   d) 7, 4, 4

27. A country has four states with the populations shown below. The House of Representatives is to have 15 members, apportioned by the Hill-Huntington method. Find the first critical divisor for district A.

State	Population
A	52,600
B	39,900
C	34,000
D	23,500

a) 9,603   b) 10,520   c) 11,761   d) 8,767

28. A country has four states with the populations shown below. The House of Representatives is to have 15

members. Use the Hill-Huntington method of apportionment to find the number of seats for each state.

State	Population
A	52,600
B	39,900
C	34,000
D	23,500

a) 5, 4, 4, 2   b) 6, 4, 3, 2   c) 5, 4, 3, 3   d) 6, 3, 3, 3

29. A county has four districts with the populations shown below. They are to use the Hill- Huntington method of apportionment to distribute 20 seats on a county council. Find the first critical divisor for district B.

District	Population
A	87,000
B	56,000
C	72,000
D	35,000

a) 11,200   b) 10,224   c) 14,000   d) 12,522

30. Given three states with the populations shown below, and a national senate with 10 seats, use the Hill-Huntington method of apportionment to distribute the seats to the states.

State	Population
Apathy	69,000
Bliss	43,500
Confusion	37,500

a) 4, 3, 3   b) 4, 4, 2   c) 5, 4, 1   d) 5, 3, 2

31. Find the geometric mean of 5 and 6.
a) 5.5   b) 5.48   c) 4.69   d) 3.32

32. Find the geometric mean of 8 and 9.
a) 5.83   b) 8.5   c) 8.74   d) 8.49

33. Find the geometric mean of 3 and 7.
a) 4.38   b) 5.00   c) 4.58   d) 3.16

34. We are scheduling seven course sections for a total of 217 students. Enrollments are: 109 in Calculus I, 79 in Calculus II, and 29 in Advanced Calculus. Find the apportionment for each course using the Jefferson method.
a) 4, 2, 1   b) 3, 3, 1   c) 4, 3, 0   d) 3, 2, 2

35. We are scheduling seven course sections for a total of 217 students. Enrollments are: 109 in Calculus I, 79 in Calculus II, and 29 in Advanced Calculus. Find the apportionment for each course using the Hill-Huntington method.
a) 4, 2, 1   b) 4, 3, 0   c) 3, 3, 1   d) 3, 2, 2

36. Suppose a country has four states with the populations shown below and a parliament with 30 seats. Use

the Jefferson method of apportionment to apportion the seats between the states.

State	Population
A	182,575
B	243,170
C	322,115
D	252,140

a) 5, 7, 10, 8   b) 6, 7, 9, 8   c) 5, 7, 11, 7   d) 6, 8, 8, 8

37. A state has a population of 24,000 and holds 3 of 28 seats in a parliament. What is the district population of the state?

a) 857   b) 2571   c) 4320   d) 8000

38. A county council has 15 seats on its county council which are apportioned among four regions. The population of the West region is 3560 and the West region holds 4 seats on the council. What is the district population for the West region?

a) 949   b) 890   c) 237   d) 59

39. A county council has 15 seats that are apportioned among four regions. The population of the West region is 3560 and the West region holds 4 seats on the council. What is the representative share for the West region?

a) 0.004213   b) 0.001123   c) 0.2667   d) 0.01685

40. A small country has four states and a parliament with 23 seats. One state has a population of 4277 and holds five seats in the parliament. Find the representative share for the state.

a) 0.001167   b) 0.2174   c) 0.005378   d) 0.02689

41. A country has three states and a national senate with 10 seats. The state populations and the apportionment of the senate seats are shown below. Find the difference in representative shares of states A and B.

State	Population	Seats
A	69,000	5
B	43,500	3
C	37,500	2

a) 0.2   b) 0.00000349   c) 0.00000125   d) 0.0000725

42. A country has three states and a national senate with 10 seats. The state populations and the apportionment of the senate seats are shown below. Find the difference in district population of states A and B.

State	Population	Seats
A	69,000	5
B	43,500	3
C	37,500	2

a) 25,500   b) 20,000   c) 1400   d) 700

43. A small county has populations in three districts as shown below. They have apportioned 15 seats on the county council and obtained the apportionment for each district shown. Find the difference in

representative share between the Parkview and Hillside districts.

District	Population	Apportionment
Parkview	43,000	6
Hillside	32,800	5
Riverdale	24,200	4

a) 0.06667   b) 0.00004237   c) 0.00001294   d) 0.0000008522

44. A small county has populations in three regions as shown below. They have apportioned 15 seats on the county council and obtained the apportionment for each region shown. Find the difference in district population between the Parkview and Hillside regions.

District	Population	Apportionment
Parkview	43,000	6
Hillside	32,800	5
Riverdale	24,200	4

a) 10,200   b) 607   c) 6267   d) 2867

45. Find the relative difference of 7 and 9.
   a) 28.57%   b) 2%   c) 22.22%   d) 43.75%

46. Find the relative difference of 12 and 17.
   a) 41.67%   b) 70.58%   c) 29.41%   d) 17.24%

47. A country has three states and a national senate with 10 seats. The state populations and the apportionment of the senate seats are shown below. Find the relative difference in representative shares of states A and B.

State	Population	Seats
A	69,000	5
B	43,500	3
C	37,500	2

a) 66.7%   b) 4.97%   c) 5.06%   d) 6.70%

48. A country has three states and a national senate with 10 seats. The state populations and the apportionment of the senate seats are shown below. Find the relative difference in district population of states A and B.

State	Population	Seats
A	69,000	5
B	43,500	3
C	37,500	2

a) 4.83%   b) 1.61%   c) 1.01%   d) 5.07%

49. A small county has populations in three regions as shown below. They have apportioned 15 seats on the county council and obtained the apportionment for each region shown. Find the relative difference in district population between the Parkview and Hillside regions.

Region	Population	Apportionment
Parkview	43,000	6
Hillside	32,800	5
Riverdale	24,200	4

a) 9.25%   b) 8.47%   c) 1.85%   d) 1.41%

50. A small county has populations in three regions as shown below. They have apportioned 15 seats on the county council and obtained the apportionment for each region shown. Find the relative difference in representative share between the Parkview and Hillside regions.

Region	Population	Apportionment
Parkview	43,000	6
Hillside	32,800	5
Riverdale	24,200	4

a) 9.2%   b) 8.5%   c) 16.7%   d) 20.0%

Free-Response Questions

1. Explain the Alabama paradox.

2. Explain the population paradox.

3. The Hamilton method of apportionment always satisfies what is called the "quota condition." What does this mean?

4. Find the geometric mean of 4 and 9.

5. Round the following numbers by the method used in the Hill-Huntington apportionment procedure: 3.67, 9.42, 2.46, and 6.49

6. Given the cities and the populations below, use the Hamilton method of apportionment to distribute 25 seats on a regional board.

City	Population
Greenville	34,569
Riverdale	27,943
Oceanside	21,350
Parkview	16,138

7. Use the Hamilton method of apportionment to distribute 15 representatives to the three states with the populations shown below.

State	Population
A	253,000
B	182,000
C	85,000

8. Use the Hamilton method of apportionment to distribute 12 seats on a city council to three districts with the populations shown below.

District	Population
North	30,000
Central	10,100
South	34,900

9. Given the cities and the populations below, use the Jefferson method of apportionment to distribute 25 seats on a regional board.

City	Population
Greenville	34,569
Riverdale	27,943
Oceanside	21,350
Parkview	16,138

10. Use the Jefferson method of apportionment to distribute 15 representatives to the three states with the populations shown below.

State	Population
A	253,000
B	182,000
C	85,000

11. Use the Jefferson method of apportionment to distribute 12 seats on a city council to three districts with the populations shown below.

District	Population
North	30,000
Central	10,100
South	34,900

12. Given the cities and the populations below, use the Webster method of apportionment to distribute 25 seats on a regional board.

City	Population
Greenville	34,569
Riverdale	27,943
Oceanside	21,350
Parkview	16,138

13. Use the Webster method of apportionment to distribute 15 representatives to the three states with the populations shown below.

State	Population
A	253,000
B	182,000
C	85,000

14. Use the Webster method of apportionment to distribute 12 seats on a city council to three districts with the populations shown below.

District	Population
North	30,000
Central	10,100
South	34,900

15. Given the cities and the populations below, use the Hill-Huntington method of apportionment to distribute 25 seats on a regional board.

City	Population
Greenville	34,569
Riverdale	27,943
Oceanside	21,350
Parkview	16,138

16. Use the Hill-Huntington method of apportionment to distribute 15 representatives to the three states with the populations shown below.

State	Population
A	253,000
B	182,000
C	85,000

17. Use the Hill-Huntington method of apportionment to distribute 12 seats on a city council to three districts with the populations shown below.

District	Population
North	30,000
Central	10,100
South	34,900

18. A city is divided into four regions for distributing the 20 representatives on a public utility board. The regions and their populations are shown below. The board uses the Hamilton method of apportionment to distribute seats. Find the district population for each region based on this apportionment.

Region	Population
North	8700
South	5600
East	7200
West	3500

19. A country has three states with the populations shown below. The House of Representatives for the country is to have 15 members. Find the district population for each state if the country uses the Jefferson method of apportionment.

State	Population
A	245,000
B	320,000
C	155,000

20. A city is divided into four regions for distributing the 20 representatives on a public utility board. The regions and their populations are shown below. The board uses the Hamilton method of apportionment to distribute seats. Find the representative share for each region based on this apportionment.

Region	Population
North	8700
South	5600
East	7200
West	3500

21. A country has three states with the populations shown below. The House of Representatives for the country is to have 15 members. Find the representative share for each state if the country uses the Jefferson method of apportionment.

State	Population
A	245,000
B	320,000
C	155,000

22. A town board has 10 members, divided among three regions of the town using the Hamilton method of apportionment. The regions and their populations are shown below. Find the difference in district population for the North and South region.

Region	Population
North	13,400
Central	21,900
South	8700

23. A small country has four states and a House of Representatives with 20 seats. Given the states, populations, and apportionment below, find the relative difference in district population between states A and C.

State	Population	Apportionment
A	234,000	5
B	124,000	3
C	346,500	7
D	268,500	5

24. A town board has 10 members, divided among three regions of the town using the Hamilton method of apportionment. The regions and their populations are given below. Find the difference in representative share for the North and South region.

Region	Population
North	13,400
Central	21,900
South	8700

25. A small country has four states and a House of Representatives with 20 seats. Given the states, populations and apportionment below, find the relative difference in representative share between states A and C.

State	Population	Apportionment
A	234,000	5
B	124,000	3
C	346,500	7
D	268,500	5

Chapter 15 Multiple-Choice Questions
Game Theory: The Mathematics of Competition

1. In the following two-person zero-sum game, the payoffs represent gains to the row Player I and losses to column Player II.

    $$\begin{bmatrix} 1 & 3 \\ 4 & 2 \end{bmatrix}$$

    Which of the following statements is true?
    a) The game has no saddle point.
    b) The game has a saddle point; the value of the game is 3.
    c) The game has a saddle point; the value of the game is 2.
    d) The game has a saddle point; the value of the game is 2.5.

2. In the following two-person zero-sum game, the payoffs represent gains to the row Player I and losses to column Player II.

    $$\begin{bmatrix} 3 & 5 \\ 4 & 2 \end{bmatrix}$$

    Which of the following statements is true?
    a) The game has no saddle point.
    b) The game has a saddle point; the value of the game is 3.
    c) The game has a saddle point; the value of the game is 4.
    d) The game has a saddle point; the value of the game is 3.5.

3. In the following two-person zero-sum game, the payoffs represent gains to the row Player I and losses to column Player II.

    $$\begin{bmatrix} 1 & 4 & 3 \\ 8 & 2 & 6 \\ 5 & 9 & 7 \end{bmatrix}$$

    Which of the following statements is true?
    a) The game has no saddle point.
    b) The game has a saddle point; the value of the game is 3.
    c) The game has a saddle point; the value of the game is 4.
    d) The game has a saddle point; the value of the game is 5.

4. In the following two-person zero-sum game, the payoffs represent gains to the row Player I and losses to column Player II.

$$\begin{bmatrix} 4 & 3 & 6 \\ 2 & 8 & 1 \\ 9 & 7 & 5 \end{bmatrix}$$

Which of the following statements is true?
a) The game has no saddle point.
b) The game has a saddle point; the value of the game is 2.
c) The game has a saddle point; the value of the game is 5.
d) The game has a saddle point; the value of the game is 6.

5. In the following two-person zero-sum game, the payoffs represent gains to the row Player I and losses to column Player II.

$$\begin{bmatrix} 3 & 7 & 2 \\ 1 & 4 & 6 \\ 9 & 5 & 8 \end{bmatrix}$$

Which of the following statements is true?
a) The game has no saddle point.
b) The game has a saddle point; the value of the game is 4.
c) The game has a saddle point; the value of the game is 5.
d) The game has a saddle point; the value of the game is 6.

6. In the following two-person zero-sum game, the payoffs represent gains to the row Player I and losses to column Player II.

$$\begin{bmatrix} 1 & 5 & 7 & 3 \\ 6 & 2 & 14 & 12 \\ 15 & 9 & 16 & 4 \\ 10 & 11 & 8 & 13 \end{bmatrix}$$

Which of the following statements is true?
a) The game has no saddle point.
b) The game has a saddle point; the value of the game is 8.
c) The game has a saddle point; the value of the game is 9.
d) The game has a saddle point; the value of the game is 11.

7. In the following two-person zero-sum game, the payoffs represent gains to the row Player I and losses to column Player II.

$$\begin{bmatrix} 6 & 7 & 11 & 8 \\ 2 & 5 & 4 & 12 \\ 1 & 16 & 3 & 15 \\ 9 & 14 & 13 & 10 \end{bmatrix}$$

Which of the following statements is true?
a) The game has no saddle point.
b) The game has a saddle point; the value of the game is 8.
c) The game has a saddle point; the value of the game is 9.
d) The game has a saddle point; the value of the game is 11.

8. In the following two-person zero-sum game, the payoffs represent gains to the row Player I and losses to column Player II.

$$\begin{bmatrix} 1 & 3 \\ 4 & 2 \end{bmatrix}$$

Which of the following statements is true?
a) The maximin strategy of Player I is to always play the first row; the minimax strategy of Player II is to always play the first column.
b) The maximin strategy of Player I is to always play the second row; the minimax strategy of Player II is to always play the first column.
c) The maximin strategy of Player I is to always play the first row; the minimax strategy of Player II is to always play the second column.
d) The maximin strategy of Player I is to always play the second row; the minimax strategy of Player II is to always play the second column.

9. In the following two-person zero-sum game, the payoffs represent gains to the row Player I and losses to column Player II.

$$\begin{bmatrix} 3 & 5 \\ 4 & 2 \end{bmatrix}$$

Which of the following statements is true?
a) The maximin strategy of Player I is to always play the first row; the minimax strategy of Player II is to always play the first column.
b) The maximin strategy of Player I is to always play the second row; the minimax strategy of Player II is to always play the first column.
c) The maximin strategy of Player I is to always play the first row; the minimax strategy of Player II is to always play the second column.
d) The maximin strategy of Player I is to always play the second row; the minimax strategy of Player II is to always play the second column.

10. In the following two-person zero-sum game, the payoffs represent gains to the row Player I and losses to column Player II.

$$\begin{bmatrix} 1 & 4 & 3 \\ 8 & 2 & 6 \\ 5 & 9 & 7 \end{bmatrix}$$

The maximin strategy of Player I is
a) to always play the first row.
b) to always play the second row.
c) to always play the third row.
d) to play two or more of the rows.

11. In the following two-person zero-sum game, the payoffs represent gains to the row Player I and losses to column Player II.

$$\begin{bmatrix} 1 & 4 & 3 \\ 8 & 2 & 6 \\ 5 & 9 & 7 \end{bmatrix}$$

The minimax strategy of Player II is
a) to always play the first column.
b) to always play the second column.
c) to always play the third column.
d) to play two or more of the columns.

12. In the following two-person zero-sum game, the payoffs represent gains to the row Player I and losses to column Player II.

$$\begin{bmatrix} 4 & 3 & 6 \\ 2 & 8 & 1 \\ 9 & 7 & 5 \end{bmatrix}$$

The maximin strategy of Player I is
a) to always play the first row.
b) to always play the second row.
c) to always play the third row.
d) to play two or more of the rows.

13. In the following two-person zero-sum game, the payoffs represent gains to the row Player I and losses to column Player II.

$$\begin{bmatrix} 4 & 3 & 6 \\ 2 & 8 & 1 \\ 9 & 7 & 5 \end{bmatrix}$$

The minimax strategy of Player II is
a) to always play the first column.
b) to always play the second column.
c) to always play the third column.
d) to play two or more of the columns.

14. In the following two-person zero-sum game, the payoffs represent gains to the row Player I and losses to column Player II.

$$\begin{bmatrix} 3 & 7 & 2 \\ 1 & 4 & 6 \\ 9 & 5 & 8 \end{bmatrix}$$

The maximin strategy of Player I is
a) to always play the first row.
b) to always play the second row.
c) to always play the third row.
d) to play two or more of the rows.

15. In the following two-person zero-sum game, the payoffs represent gains to the row Player I and losses to column Player II.

$$\begin{bmatrix} 3 & 7 & 2 \\ 1 & 4 & 6 \\ 9 & 5 & 8 \end{bmatrix}$$

The minimax strategy of Player II is
a) to always play the first column.
b) to always play the second column.
c) to always play the third column.
d) to play two or more of the columns.

16. In the following two-person zero-sum game, the payoffs represent gains to the row Player I and losses to column Player II.

$$\begin{bmatrix} 1 & 5 & 7 & 3 \\ 6 & 2 & 14 & 12 \\ 15 & 9 & 16 & 4 \\ 10 & 11 & 8 & 13 \end{bmatrix}$$

The maximin strategy of Player I is
a) to always play the first row.
b) to always play the second row.
c) to always play the third row.
d) to always play the fourth row.

17. In the following two-person zero-sum game, the payoffs represent gains to the row Player I and losses to column Player II.

$$\begin{bmatrix} 1 & 5 & 7 & 3 \\ 6 & 2 & 14 & 12 \\ 15 & 9 & 16 & 4 \\ 10 & 11 & 8 & 13 \end{bmatrix}$$

The minimax strategy of Player II is
a) to always play the first column.
b) to always play the second column.
c) to always play the third column.
d) to always play the fourth column.

18. In the following two-person zero-sum game, the payoffs represent gains to the row Player I and losses to column Player II.

$$\begin{bmatrix} 6 & 7 & 11 & 8 \\ 2 & 5 & 4 & 12 \\ 1 & 16 & 3 & 15 \\ 9 & 14 & 13 & 10 \end{bmatrix}$$

The maximin strategy of Player I is
a) to always play the first row.
b) to always play the second row.
c) to always play the third row.
d) to always play the fourth row.

19. In the following two-person zero-sum game, the payoffs represent gains to the row Player I and losses to column Player II.

$$\begin{bmatrix} 6 & 7 & 11 & 8 \\ 2 & 5 & 4 & 12 \\ 1 & 16 & 3 & 15 \\ 9 & 14 & 13 & 10 \end{bmatrix}$$

The minimax strategy of Player II is
a) to always play the first column.
b) to always play the second column.
c) to always play the third column.
d) to always play the fourth column.

20. In the following game of batter-versus-pitcher in baseball, the batter's batting averages are shown in the game matrix.

		Pitcher Fastball	Curve
Batter	Fastball	.300	.100
	Curve	.200	.400

Which of the following statements is true?
a) The game has no saddle point.
b) The game has a saddle point; the value of the game is .200.
c) The game has a saddle point; the value of the game is .300.
d) The game has a saddle point; the value of the game is .400.

21. In the following game of batter-versus-pitcher in baseball, the batter's batting averages are shown in the game matrix.

		Pitcher	
		Fastball	Curve
Batter	Fastball	.400	.100
	Curve	.200	.300

Which of the following statements is true?
a) The game has no saddle point.
b) The game has a saddle point; the value of the game is .200.
c) The game has a saddle point; the value of the game is .300.
d) The game has a saddle point; the value of the game is .400.

22. In the following game of batter-versus-pitcher in baseball, the batter's batting averages are shown in the game matrix.

		Pitcher	
		Fastball	Curve
Batter	Fastball	.300	.100
	Curve	.200	.400

What is the pitcher's optimal strategy?
a) Pitch more fastballs than curves.
b) Pitch more curves than fastballs.
c) Pitch fastballs and curves equally.

23. In the following game of batter-versus-pitcher in baseball, the batter's batting averages are shown in the game matrix.

		Pitcher	
		Fastball	Curve
Batter	Fastball	.300	.100
	Curve	.200	.400

What is the batter's optimal strategy?
a) Expect more fastballs than curves.
b) Expect more curves than fastballs.
c) Expect equal numbers of curves and fastballs.

24. In the following game of batter-versus-pitcher in baseball, the batter's batting averages are shown in the game matrix.

		Pitcher Fastball	Curve
Batter	Fastball	.400	.100
	Curve	.200	.300

What is the pitcher's optimal strategy?
a) Pitch more fastballs than curves.
b) Pitch more curves than fastballs.
c) Pitch fastballs and curves equally.

25. In the following game of batter-versus-pitcher in baseball, the batter's batting averages are shown in the game matrix.

		Pitcher Fastball	Curve
Batter	Fastball	.400	.100
	Curve	.200	.300

What is the batter's optimal strategy?
a) Expect more fastballs than curves.
b) Expect more curves than fastballs.
c) Expect equal numbers of curves and fastballs.

26. You can choose to buy an extended warranty for your computer for $200. During this period, you will experience either a minor ($100) or major ($500) repair bill. If you buy the warranty, you will not have to pay the repair bill. Assume the company wants to make as much money as possible, and you wish to spend as little as possible.

Which of the following is a true statement?
a) This game has no saddle point.
b) This game has a saddle point; the value of the game is $100.
c) This game has a saddle point; the value of the game is $200.
d) This game has a saddle point; the value of the game is $500.

27. You can choose to buy an extended warranty for your computer for $200. During this period, you will experience either a minor ($100) or major ($500) repair bill. If you buy the warranty, you pay 50% of any repair bill: that is, you will pay either $50 or $250 for the subsequent repair. Assume the company wants to make as much money as possible, and you wish to spend as little as possible.

Which of the following is a true statement?
a) This game has no saddle point.

b) This game has a saddle point; the value of the game is $200.
c) This game has a saddle point; the value of the game is $250.
d) This game has a saddle point; the value of the game is $450.

28. As the buyer for your business, you can choose to buy an extended warranty for each new computer for $200 each. During this period, each computer will experience either a minor ($100) or major ($500) repair bill. Repairs for each warranted computer are reduced by 50% to $50 or $250. Assume the computer company wants to make as much money as possible, and you wish to spend as little as possible.

What is your optimal strategy?
a) Never buy the warranty.
b) Always buy the warranty.
c) Buy the warranty for less than half of the computers.
d) Buy the warranty for more than half of the computers.

29. As the buyer for your business, you can choose to buy an extended warranty for each new computer for $200 each. During this period, each computer will experience either a minor ($100) or major ($500) repair bill. Repairs for each warranted computer are reduced by 50% to $50 or $250. Assume the computer company wants to make as much money as possible, and you wish to spend as little as possible.

What is the computer company's optimal strategy?
a) Always sell the warranty.
b) Never sell the warranty.
c) Sell the warranty for less than half of the computers.
d) Sell the warranty for more than half of the computers.

30. You are considering cheating on your income tax return. If you cheat you will pay $1000 in taxes; if you don't cheat you will pay $2000. If you are audited and you didn't cheat, your auditor will be kind and reduce your taxes from $2000 to $1500. If you are audited and you did cheat, you will be caught and have to pay a total of $2500, including penalties.

Statistically, which is the best option for you to choose?
a) Definitely cheat.   b) Probably cheat.   c) Probably don't cheat.   d) Definitely don't cheat.

31. If you cheat on your income tax return you will pay $1000 in taxes; if you don't cheat you will pay $2000. If you are audited and you didn't cheat, your auditor will be kind and reduce your taxes from $2000 to $1500. If you are audited and you did cheat, you will be caught and have to pay a total of $2500, including penalties.

Assuming the government wants to receive as much money as possible, statistically, which is the best option for the government to choose?
a) Always audit.   b) Usually audit.   c) Occasionally audit.   d) Never audit.

32. In American football the "third down and short" situation occurs often. The probabilities of obtaining a first down shown below, are dependent on the choice of the offense and the anticipated choice of the defense.

		Defense	
		Run	Pass
Offense	Run	0.4	0.8
	Pass	0.6	0.2

In such situations, what is the optimal solution for the defense?

a) Always anticipate a run.
b) Always anticipate a pass.
c) Anticipate a run more often than a pass.
d) Anticipate a pass more often than a run.

33. In American football the "third down and short" situation occurs often. Tthe probabilities of obtaining a first down shown below, are dependent on the choice of the offense and the anticipated choice of the defense.

		Defense	
		Run	Pass
Offense	Run	0.4	0.8
	Pass	0.6	0.2

In such situations, what is the optimal solution for the offense?
a) Always choose to run.
b) Always choose to pass.
c) Choose to run more often than pass.
d) Choose to pass more often than run.

34. Consider the following partial-conflict game played in a non-cooperative manner.

		Player II	
		Choice A	Choice B
Player I	Choice A	(3,3)	(5,1)
	Choice B	(1,5)	(2,2)

What outcomes constitute a Nash equilibrium?
a) Only when both players select choice A
b) Only when both players select choice B
c) Only when one player selects choice A; the other selects choice B.
d) Only when both players select choice A or both players select choice B.

35. Consider the following partial-conflict game played in a non-cooperative manner.

		Player II	
		Choice A	Choice B
Player I	Choice A	(3,3)	(5,1)
	Choice B	(1,5)	(2,2)

Which of the following statements is true?
a) The dominant strategy for Player I is to select choice A.
b) The dominant strategy for Player I is to select choice B.
c) Player I has no dominant strategy.

36. Consider the following partial-conflict game played in a non-cooperative manner.

		Player II	
		Choice A	Choice B
Player I	Choice A	(4,1)	(3,2)
	Choice B	(2,3)	(1,4)

Which of the following statements is true?
a) Both Player I and Player II has a dominant strategy.
b) Neither Player I nor II has a dominant strategy.
c) Only Player I has a dominant strategy.
d) Only Player II has a dominant strategy.

37. Consider the following partial-conflict game played in a non-cooperative manner.

		Player II	
		Choice A	Choice B
Player I	Choice A	(4,1)	(3,2)
	Choice B	(2,3)	(1,4)

Which of the following is a Nash equilibrium?
a) Player I selects choice A; Player II selects choice A.
b) Player I selects choice A; Player II selects choice B.
c) Player I selects choice B; Player II selects choice A.
d) Player I selects choice B; Player II selects choice B.

38. Consider the following partial-conflict game played in a non-cooperative manner.

		Player II	
		Choice A	Choice B
Player I	Choice A	(4,1)	(3,2)
	Choice B	(2,3)	(1,4)

Assume that the game is played continually, and players can change their choices at noon each day. If the game begins with both players selecting Choice B, what should happen at the first opportunity to change?
a) Nothing.
b) Player I switches to choice A.
c) Player II switches to choice A.
d) Both players switch to choice A.

39. Consider the following partial-conflict game played in a non-cooperative manner.

		Player II	
		Choice A	Choice B
Player I	Choice A	(4,1)	(3,2)
	Choice B	(2,3)	(1,4)

Assume that the game is played continually, and players can change their choices at noon each day. If the game begins with both players selecting choice A, what should happen at the first opportunity to change?
a) Nothing.
b) Player I switches to choice B.
c) Player II switches to choice B.
d) Both players switch to choice B.

40. Suppose a committee of three people(the chair), Chris, and Terry each have one vote, but Kim breaks any tie. In attempting to elect someone to host the summer picnic, each person has a priority list:

	Kim's Priorities	Chris's Priorities	Terry's Priorities
1st choice	Kim	Chris	Terry
2nd choice	Terry	Kim	Chris
3rd choice	Chris	Terry	Kim

Which of the following are Nash equilibria?

I: Every person votes for his/her first choice.
II: Every person votes for his/her second choice.

a) I only   b) II only   c) Both I and II   d) Neither I nor II

41. Suppose a committee of three people(the chair), Chris, and Terry each have one vote, but Kim breaks any tie. In attempting to elect someone to host the summer picnic, each person has a priority list:

	Kim's Priorities	Chris's Priorities	Terry's Priorities
1st choice	Kim	Chris	Terry
2nd choice	Terry	Kim	Chris
3rd choice	Chris	Terry	Kim

Which of the following are Nash equilibria?

    I: Every person votes for Kim.
    II: Every person votes for Chris.

a) I only   b) II only   c) Both I and II   d) Neither I nor II

42. Suppose a committee of three people(the chair), Chris, and Terry each have one vote, but Kim breaks any tie. In attempting to elect someone to drive the van, each person has a priority list:

	Kim's Priorities	Chris's Priorities	Terry's Priorities
1st choice	Chris	Kim	Terry
2nd choice	Kim	Chris	Chris
3rd choice	Terry	Terry	Kim

Which of the following are Nash equilibria?

    I: Every person votes for his/her 1st choice.
    II: Kim and Chris vote for Chris; Terry votes for Terry.

a) I only   b) II only   c) Both I and II   d) Neither I nor II

43. Suppose a committee of three people(the chair), Chris, and Terry each have one vote, but Kim breaks any tie. In attempting to elect someone to drive the van, each person has a priority list:

	Kim's Priorities	Chris's Priorities	Terry's Priorities
1st choice	Chris	Kim	Terry
2nd choice	Kim	Chris	Chris
3rd choice	Terry	Terry	Kim

Which of the following are Nash equilibria?

    I: Every person votes for Chris.
    II: Every person votes for his/her 2nd choice.

a) I only   b) II only   c) Both I and II   d) Neither I nor II

44. The game of Chicken is an example of

I: a variable-sum game.

II: a partial-conflict game.

a) I only   b) II only   c) Both I and II   d) Neither I nor II

45. The game of Prisoner's Dilemma is an example of

I: a variable-sum game.

II: a partial-conflict game.

a) I only   b) II only   c) Both I and II   d) Neither I nor II

46. The "paradox of the chair's position"

I: doesn't really happen.

II: can be alleviated by deception strategies.

a) I only   b) II only   c) Both I and II   d) Neither I nor II

47. In a pure strategy game, each player consistently selects one particular option.

a) True   b) False

48. In a symmetrical game, both players will always choose the same particular option.

a) True   b) False

49. Every "zero-sum" game is a "fair" game.

a) True   b) False

50. Game theory is used by intelligence services to check for security violations.

a) True   b) False

Free-Response Questions

1. Create a two-by-two matrix that represents a two-person zero-sum game in which each player has two options and the game has a saddle point.

2. Create a two-by-two matrix that represents a two-person zero-sum game in which each player has two options and the game has no saddle point.

3. Create a two-by-two matrix that represents a two-person zero-sum game in which each player has two options and at least one player has a dominated strategy.

4. Create a three-by-three matrix that represents a two-person zero-sum game in which each player has three options and the game has a saddle point.

5. Create a three-by-three matrix that represents a two-person zero-sum game in which each player has three options and the game has no saddle point.

6. Create a three-by-three matrix that represents a two-person zero-sum game in which each player has three options and at least one player has a dominated strategy.

7. In the following two-person zero-sum game, the payoffs represent gains to the row Player I and losses to column Player II.

$$\begin{bmatrix} 4 & 9 \\ 2 & 6 \end{bmatrix}$$

Does this game have a saddle point? What is each player's minimax or maximin strategy? Justify your response.

8. In the following two-person zero-sum game, the payoffs represent gains to the row Player I and losses to column Player II.

$$\begin{bmatrix} 2 & 7 \\ 5 & 9 \end{bmatrix}$$

Does this game have a saddle point? What is each player's minimax or maximin strategy? Justify your response.

9. In the following two-person zero-sum game, the payoffs represent gains to the row Player I and losses to column Player II.

$$\begin{bmatrix} 2 & 9 & 6 \\ 5 & 7 & 3 \end{bmatrix}$$

Does this game have a saddlepoint? What is each player's minimax or maximin strategy? Justify your response.

10. In the following two-person zero-sum game, the payoffs represent gains to the row Player I and losses to column Player II.

$$\begin{bmatrix} 4 & 7 & 5 \\ 2 & 8 & 6 \end{bmatrix}$$

Does this game have a saddlepoint? What is each player's minimax or maximin strategy? Justify your response.

11. In the following two-person zero-sum game, the payoffs represent gains to the row Player I and losses to column Player II.

$$\begin{bmatrix} 2 & 7 & 4 \\ 1 & 9 & 5 \\ 3 & 8 & 6 \end{bmatrix}$$

Does this game have a saddlepoint? What is each player's minimax or maximin strategy? Justify your response.

12. In the following two-person zero-sum game, the payoffs represent gains to the row Player I and losses to column Player II.

$$\begin{bmatrix} 3 & 6 & 7 \\ 1 & 8 & 5 \\ 4 & 2 & 9 \end{bmatrix}$$

Does this game have a saddlepoint? What is each player's minimax or maximin strategy? Justify your response.

13. In the following game of batter-versus-pitcher in baseball, the batter's batting averages are shown in the game matrix:

		Pitcher Fastball	Knuckleball
Batter	Fastball	.400	.200
	Knuckleball	.100	.300

Solve the game determining the best mix of selections for both batter and pitcher.

14. In the following game of batter-versus-pitcher in baseball, the batter's batting averages are shown in the game matrix:

		Pitcher Fastball	Knuckleball
Batter	Fastball	.500	.400
	Knuckleball	.300	.200

Solve the game determining the best mix of selections for both batter and pitcher.

15. In the following game of batter-versus-pitcher in baseball, the batter's batting averages are shown in the game matrix:

		Pitcher Fastball	Knuckleball
Batter	Fastball	.500	.200
	Knuckleball	.200	.300

Solve the game, determining the best mix of selections for both batter and pitcher.

16. In the game of matching pennies, Player I wins a penny if the coins match and Player II wins if the coins do not match. Present this game as a two-by-two matrix, where each player has two outcomes from which to select.

17. In the game of matching pennies, Player I wins a penny if the coins match and Player II wins if the coins do not match. Is this a zero-sum game? Is this a fair game?

18. In a game, each player chooses one of three coinspenny, nickel, or dime. If both players choose the same coin, both players loose their coin. Otherwise, the player with the more valuable coin wins the less valuable coin from the other player. Represent this game as a three-by-three matrix of ordered pairs.

19. In a game, each player chooses one of three coinspenny, nickel, or dime. If both players choose the same coin, both players loose their coin. Otherwise, the player with the more valuable coin wins the less valuable coin from the other player. Is this a symmetric game? Is there a dominated strategy?

20. You want to carry insurance for your small business. The annual policy costs $1000 this year. If you are sued and you have no insurance, you will pay $5000. If you have insurance and are sued you pay nothing, and your partner gives you $500 for your wise foresight, so that the policy costs you only $500. Represent this game as a two-by-two matrix.

21. If you cheat on your income tax return you will pay $1000 in taxes; if you don't cheat you will pay $2000. If you are audited and you didn't cheat, your auditor will be kind and reduce your taxes from $2000 to $1500. If you are audited and you did cheat, you will be caught and have to pay a total of $2500, including penalties. Statistically, how often should you cheat?

22. If you cheat on your income tax return you will pay $1000 in taxes; if you don't cheat you will pay $2000. If you are audited and you didn't cheat, your auditor will be kind and reduce your taxes from $2000 to $1500. If you are audited and you did cheat, you will be caught and have to pay a total of $2500, including penalties. Statistically, how often should the government audit you?

23. Consider the following partial-conflict game played in a non-cooperative manner. The first payoff is to Player I; the second to Player II.

		Player II	
		Choice A	Choice B
Player I	Choice A	(4,1)	(3,2)
	Choice B	(2,3)	(1,4)

Discuss the players' possible strategy when this game is played.

24. Set up an example of a situation in which the paradox of the chair's position occurs.

25. How can the chair use deception to minimize the paradox of the chair's position? Set up an example to illustrate your comments.

Chapter 16 Multiple-Choice Questions
Theory of Moves: A Dynamic Approach to Games

1. For the total-conflict game shown below, what is the dominant strategy for the row player?

(1,2)	(4,3)
(2,4)	(3,1)

   a) Select the first row.   b) Select the second row.   c) The row player has no dominant strategy.

2. For the total-conflict game shown below, what is the dominant strategy for the column player?

(1,2)	(4,3)
(2,4)	(3,1)

   a) Select the first column.   c) The column player has no dominant strategy.
   b) Select the second column.

3. For the total-conflict game shown below, what is/are the Nash equilibria?

(1,2)	(4,3)
(2,4)	(3,1)

   a) (2,4) only   b) (4,3) only   c) (2,4) and (4,3)   d) There are no Nash equilibria.

4. For the total-conflict game shown below, if play begins at (3,1), who can benefit by moving?

(1,2)	(4,3)
(2,4)	(3,1)

   a) The row player   b) The column player   c) Neither player   d) Both players

5. For the total-conflict game shown below, if play begins at (1,2), who can benefit by moving?

(1,2)	(4,3)
(2,4)	(3,1)

   a) The row player   b) The column player   c) Neither player   d) Both players

6. The rules of the theory of moves (TOM) and the termination rule (5.) apply for the total- conflict game shown below. If (1,2) is the initial state and the row player moves first, what is the survivor for this state?

$$\begin{array}{ll} (1,2) & (4,3) \\ (2,4) & (3,1) \end{array}$$

a) (1,2)   b) (4,3)   c) (2,4)   d) (3,1)

7. The rules of TOM and the termination rule (5.) apply for the total-conflict game shown below. If (1,2) is the initial state and the column player moves first, what is the survivor for this state?

$$\begin{array}{ll} (1,2) & (4,3) \\ (2,4) & (3,1) \end{array}$$

a) (1,2)   b) (4,3)   c) (2,4)   d) (3,1)

8. The rules of TOM and the termination rule (5.) apply for the total-conflict game shown below. If (4,3) is the initial state and the row player moves first, what is the survivor for this state?

$$\begin{array}{ll} (1,2) & (4,3) \\ (2,4) & (3,1) \end{array}$$

a) (1,2)   b) (4,3)   c) (2,4)   d) (3,1)

9. The rules of TOM and the termination rule (5.) apply for the total-conflict game shown below. If (4,3) is the initial state and the column player moves first, what is the survivor for this state?

$$\begin{array}{ll} (1,2) & (4,3) \\ (2,4) & (3,1) \end{array}$$

a) (1,2)   b) (4,3)   c) (2,4)   d) (3,1)

10. The rules of TOM and the termination rule (5.) apply for the total-conflict game shown below. If (2,4) is the initial state and the row player moves first, what is the survivor for this state?

$$\begin{array}{ll} (1,2) & (4,3) \\ (2,4) & (3,1) \end{array}$$

a) (1,2)   b) (4,3)   c) (2,4)   d) (3,1)

11. The rules of TOM and the termination rule (5.) apply for the total-conflict game shown below. If (2,4) is the initial state and the column player moves first, what is the survivor for this state?

$$\begin{array}{ll} (1,2) & (4,3) \\ (2,4) & (3,1) \end{array}$$

a) (1,2)   b) (4,3)   c) (2,4)   d) (3,1)

12. The rules of TOM and the termination rule (5.) apply for the total-conflict game shown below. If (3,1) is the initial state and the row player moves first, what is the survivor for this state?

(1,2)	(4,3)
(2,4)	(3,1)

a) (1,2) b) (4,3) c) (2,4) d) (3,1)

13. The rules of TOM and the termination rule (5.) apply for the total-conflict game shown below. If (3,1) is the initial state and the column player moves first, what is the survivor for this state?

(1,2)	(4,3)
(2,4)	(3,1)

a) (1,2) b) (4,3) c) (2,4) d) (3,1)

14. For the total-conflict game shown below, what is the dominant strategy for the row player?

(1,3)	(4,2)
(2,4)	(3,1)

a) Select the first row.   b) Select the second row.   c) The row player has no dominant strategy.

15. For the total-conflict game shown below, what is the dominant strategy for the column player?

(1,3)	(4,2)
(2,4)	(3,1)

a) Select the first column.   c) The column player has no dominant strategy.
b) Select the second column.

16. For the total-conflict game shown below, what is/are the Nash equilibria?

(1,3)	(4,2)
(2,4)	(3,1)

a) (2,4) only b) (4,2) only c) (2,4) and (4,2) d) There are no Nash equilibria.

17. For the total-conflict game shown below, if play begins at (3,1), who can benefit by moving?

(1,3)	(4,2)
(2,4)	(3,1)

a) The row player   b) The column player   c) Neither player   d) Both players

18. For the total-conflict game shown below, if play begins at (1,3), who can benefit by moving?

```
| (1,3)   (4,2)
| (2,4)   (3,1)
```

a) The row player   b) The column player   c) Neither player   d) Both players

19. The rules of TOM and the termination rule (5.) apply for the total-conflict game shown below. If (1,3) is the initial state and the row player moves first, what is the survivor for this state?

```
| (1,3)   (4,2)
| (2,4)   (3,1)
```

a) (1,3)   b) (4,2)   c) (2,4)   d) (3,1)

20. The rules of TOM and the termination rule (5.) apply for the total-conflict game shown below. If (1,3) is the initial state and the column player moves first, what is the survivor for this state?

```
| (1,3)   (4,2)
| (2,4)   (3,1)
```

a) (1,3)   b) (4,2)   c) (2,4)   d) (3,1)

21. The rules of TOM and the termination rule (5.) apply for the total-conflict game shown below. If (4,2) is the initial state and the row player moves first, what is the survivor for this state?

```
| (1,3)   (4,2)
| (2,4)   (3,1)
```

a) (1,3)   b) (4,2)   c) (2,4)   d) (3,1)

22. The rules of TOM and the termination rule (5.) apply for the total-conflict game shown below. If (4,2) is the initial state and the column player moves first, what is the survivor for this state?

```
| (1,3)   (4,2)
| (2,4)   (3,1)
```

a) (1,3)   b) (4,2)   c) (2,4)   d) (3,1)

23. The rules of TOM and the termination rule (5.) apply for the total-conflict game shown below. If (2,4) is the initial state and the row player moves first, what is the survivor for this state?

$$\begin{array}{|cc} (1,3) & (4,2) \\ (2,4) & (3,1) \end{array}$$

a) $(1,3)$ b) $(4,2)$ c) $(2,4)$ d) $(3,1)$

24. The rules of TOM and the termination rule (5.) apply for the total-conflict game shown below. If $(2,4)$ is the initial state and the column player moves first, what is the survivor for this state?

$$\begin{array}{|cc} (1,3) & (4,2) \\ (2,4) & (3,1) \end{array}$$

a) $(1,3)$ b) $(4,2)$ c) $(2,4)$ d) $(3,1)$

25. The rules of TOM and the termination rule (5.) apply for the total-conflict game shown below. If $(3,1)$ is the initial state and the row player moves first, what is the survivor for this state?

$$\begin{array}{|cc} (1,3) & (4,2) \\ (2,4) & (3,1) \end{array}$$

a) $(1,3)$ b) $(4,2)$ c) $(2,4)$ d) $(3,1)$

26. The rules of TOM and the termination rule (5.) apply for the total-conflict game shown below. If $(3,1)$ is the initial state and the column player moves first, what is the survivor for this state?

$$\begin{array}{|cc} (1,3) & (4,2) \\ (2,4) & (3,1) \end{array}$$

a) $(1,3)$ b) $(4,2)$ c) $(2,4)$ d) $(3,1)$

27. The rules of TOM and the termination rule (5.) apply for the total-conflict game shown below. If $(1,2)$ is the initial state and the row player moves first, what is the survivor for this state?

$$\begin{array}{|cc} (1,2) & (3,3) \\ (4,1) & (2,4) \end{array}$$

a) $(1,2)$ b) $(3,3)$ c) $(4,1)$ d) $(2,4)$

28. The rules of TOM and the termination rule (5.) apply for the total-conflict game shown below. If $(1,2)$ is the initial state and the column player moves first, what is the survivor for this state?

$$\begin{array}{|cc} (1,2) & (3,3) \\ (4,1) & (2,4) \end{array}$$

a) $(1,2)$ b) $(3,3)$ c) $(4,1)$ d) $(2,4)$

29. The rules of TOM and the termination rule (5.) apply for the total-conflict game shown below. If (3,3) is the initial state and the row player moves first, what is the survivor for this state?

(1,2)	(3,3)
(4,1)	(2,4)

a) (1,2)   b) (3,3)   c) (4,1)   d) (2,4)

30. The rules of TOM and the termination rule (5.) apply for the total-conflict game shown below. If (3,3) is the initial state and the column player moves first, what is the survivor for this state?

(1,2)	(3,3)
(4,1)	(2,4)

a) (1,2)   b) (3,3)   c) (4,1)   d) (2,4)

31. The rules of TOM and the termination rule (5.) apply for the total-conflict game shown below. If (4,1) is the initial state and the row player moves first, what is the survivor for this state?

(1,2)	(3,3)
(4,1)	(2,4)

a) (1,2)   b) (3,3)   c) (4,1)   d) (2,4)

32. The rules of TOM and the termination rule (5.) apply for the total-conflict game shown below. If (4,1) is the initial state and the column player moves first, what is the survivor for this state?

(1,2)	(3,3)
(4,1)	(2,4)

a) (1,2)   b) (3,3)   c) (4,1)   d) (2,4)

33. The rules of TOM and the termination rule (5.) apply for the total-conflict game shown below. If (2,4) is the initial state and the row player moves first, what is the survivor for this state?

(1,2)	(3,3)
(4,1)	(2,4)

a) (1,2)   b) (3,3)   c) (4,1)   d) (2,4)

34. The rules of TOM and the termination rule (5.) apply for the total-conflict game shown below. If (2,4) is the initial state and the column player moves first, what is the survivor for this state?

$$\begin{vmatrix} (1,2) & (3,3) \\ (4,1) & (2,4) \end{vmatrix}$$

a) (1,2)   b) (3,3)   c) (4,1)   d) (2,4)

35. The rules of TOM apply for the total-conflict game shown below. What is/are the nonmyopic equilibrium (NMEs) for this game?

$$\begin{vmatrix} (4,4) & (2,3) \\ (3,2) & (1,1) \end{vmatrix}$$

a) (4,4) only   b) (2,3) only   c) (2,3) and (3,2) only   d) (2,3) (3,2) and (4,4)

36. The rules of TOM apply for the total-conflict game shown below. What is/are the NMEs for this game?

$$\begin{vmatrix} (2,3) & (4,4) \\ (1,1) & (3,2) \end{vmatrix}$$

a) (4,4) only   b) (2,3) only   c) (2,3) and (3,2) only   d) (2,3) (3,2) and (4,4)

37. The rules of TOM apply for the total-conflict game shown below. What is/are the NMEs for this game?

$$\begin{vmatrix} (2,3) & (1,1) \\ (4,4) & (3,2) \end{vmatrix}$$

a) (4,4) only   b) (2,3) only   c) (2,3) and (3,2) only   d) (2,3) (3,2) and (4,4)

38. Consider the cyclicity of the total-conflict game shown below. Which statement is true?

$$\begin{vmatrix} (3,4) & (4,1) \\ (2,2) & (1,3) \end{vmatrix}$$

a) The game is cyclic only in the clockwise direction.
b) The game is cyclic only in the counter-clockwise direction.
c) The game is cyclic in both directions.
d) The game is not cyclic in either direction.

39. Consider the cyclicity of the total-conflict game shown below. Which statement is true?

$$\begin{vmatrix} (4,2) & (1,3) \\ (2,4) & (3,1) \end{vmatrix}$$

a) The game is cyclic only in the clockwise direction.
b) The game is cyclic only in the counter-clockwise direction.

c) The game is cyclic in both directions.
d) The game is not cyclic in either direction.

40. Consider the cyclicity of the total-conflict game shown below. Which statement is true?

$$\begin{vmatrix} (3,3) & (4,2) \\ (2,1) & (1,4) \end{vmatrix}$$

a) The game is cyclic only in the clockwise direction.
b) The game is cyclic only in the counter-clockwise direction.
c) The game is cyclic in both directions.
d) The game is not cyclic in either direction.

41. Consider the cyclicity of the total-conflict game shown below. Is moving power effective in this game?

$$\begin{vmatrix} (3,4) & (4,1) \\ (2,2) & (1,3) \end{vmatrix}$$

a) Yes, for the row player only.
b) Yes, for the column player only.
c) Yes, for either the row or the column player.
d) No, not for either player.

42. Consider the cyclicity of the total-conflict game shown below. Is moving power effective in this game?

$$\begin{vmatrix} (4,2) & (1,3) \\ (2,4) & (3,1) \end{vmatrix}$$

a) Yes, for the row player only.
b) Yes, for the column player only.
c) Yes, for either the row or the column player.
d) No, not for either player.

43. Consider the cyclicity of the total-conflict game shown below. Is moving power effective in this game?

$$\begin{vmatrix} (3,3) & (4,2) \\ (2,1) & (1,4) \end{vmatrix}$$

a) Yes, for the row player only.
b) Yes, for the column player only.
c) Yes, for either the row or the column player.
d) No, not for either player.

44. The game of duel is extended to four players, A,B,C,D, in which each of the four players simultaneously randomly select another player, shoot, and kill this person. What is the probability that player A is shot by player B?
a) 1/4   b) 1/3   c) 2/3   d) 3/4

45. The game of duel is extended to four players, A,B,C,D, in which each of the four players simultaneously randomly select another player, shoot, and kill this person. What is the probability that player A survives; that is, A is not shot by B, C, or D?

a) 1/27   b) 1/8   c) 6/27   d) 8/27

46. The game of duel is extended to four players, A,B,C,D, in which each of the four players can decide when and if to shoot and kill another player. What is the best strategy for each player?
a) Immediately shoot someone.   b) Wait, and hope no one shoots.

47. The TOM uses mixed strategies to determine selections.
a) True   b) False

48. The TOM weigh the relative values of outcomes to derive expected-value calculations.
a) True   b) False

49. The Biblical game of Samson and Delilah can be modeled by
a) Success.   b) Chicken.   c) Prisoners' Dilemma.   d) Variation.

50. Two people are bidding for an old chest. Each person wants to buy the chest, prevent the other from buying the chest, and pay as little as possible. However, as long as they continue to bid and counterbid, the price increases. This game can be modeled by
a) Success.   b) Chicken.   c) Prisoners' Dilemma.   d) Variation.

51. Two people robbed the bank. The police offer leniency to either person if he will incriminate the other. This game can be modeled by
a) Success.   b) Chicken.   c) Prisoners' Dilemma.   d) Variation.

52. If the first player has moving power, the first player can always determine the eventual outcome of the game.
a) True   b) False

53. If the first player has possession of order power, the first player can always determine the eventual outcome of the game.
a) True   b) False

Free-Response Questions

1. Find the dominant strategies (if any) for the total-conflict game shown below.

$$\begin{array}{|cc}\hline (4,3) & (1,2) \\ (2,4) & (3,1) \end{array}$$

2. Find the Nash equilibria (if any) for the total-conflict game shown below.

$$\begin{array}{|cc}\hline (4,3) & (1,2) \\ (2,4) & (3,1) \end{array}$$

3. Find the NMEs (if any) for the total-conflict game shown below.

$$\begin{array}{|cc}\hline (4,3) & (1,2) \\ (2,4) & (3,1) \end{array}$$

4. Find the dominant strategies (if any) for the total-conflict game shown below.

$$\begin{array}{|cc}\hline (2,3) & (1,2) \\ (3,4) & (4,1) \end{array}$$

5. Find the Nash equilibria (if any) for the total-conflict game shown below.

$$\begin{array}{|cc}\hline (2,3) & (1,2) \\ (3,4) & (4,1) \end{array}$$

6. Find the NMEs (if any) for the total-conflict game shown below.

$$\begin{array}{|cc}\hline (2,3) & (1,2) \\ (3,4) & (4,1) \end{array}$$

7. Find the dominant strategies (if any) for the total-conflict game shown below.

$$\begin{array}{|cc}\hline (2,2) & (1,3) \\ (3,4) & (4,1) \end{array}$$

8. Find the Nash equilibria (if any) for the total-conflict game shown below.

$$\begin{vmatrix} (2,2) & (1,3) \\ (3,4) & (4,1) \end{vmatrix}$$

9. Find the NMEs (if any) for the total-conflict game shown below.

$$\begin{vmatrix} (2,2) & (1,3) \\ (3,4) & (4,1) \end{vmatrix}$$

10. The rules of TOM and the termination rule (5.) apply for the total-conflict game shown below. If the row player moves first, what are the survivors for each state?

$$\begin{vmatrix} (4,3) & (1,2) \\ (2,4) & (3,1) \end{vmatrix}$$

11. The rules of TOM and the termination rule (5.) apply for the total-conflict game shown below. If the row player moves first, what are the survivors for each state?

$$\begin{vmatrix} (2,3) & (1,2) \\ (3,4) & (4,1) \end{vmatrix}$$

12. The rules of TOM and the termination rule (5.) apply for the total-conflict game shown below. If the row player moves first, what are the survivors for each state?

$$\begin{vmatrix} (2,2) & (1,3) \\ (3,4) & (4,1) \end{vmatrix}$$

13. The rules of TOM and the termination rule (5.) apply for the total-conflict game shown below. If the column player moves first, what are the survivors for each state?

$$\begin{vmatrix} (4,3) & (1,2) \\ (2,4) & (3,1) \end{vmatrix}$$

14. The rules of TOM and the termination rule (5.) apply for the total-conflict game shown below. If the column player moves first, what are the survivors for each state?

$$\begin{vmatrix} (2,3) & (1,2) \\ (3,4) & (4,1) \end{vmatrix}$$

15. The rules of TOM and the termination rule (5.) apply for the total-conflict game shown below. If the column player moves first, what are the survivors for each state?

(2,2)	(1,3)
(3,4)	(4,1)

16. Is the total-conflict game shown below cyclic? If, so, in which direction(s)?

(4,3)	(1,2)
(2,4)	(3,1)

17. Is the total-conflict game shown below cyclic? If, so, in which direction(s)?

(2,3)	(1,2)
(3,4)	(4,1)

18. Is the total-conflict game shown below cyclic? If, so, in which direction(s)?

(2,2)	(1,3)
(3,4)	(4,1)

19. Is moving power effective for either player in the game shown below?

(4,3)	(1,2)
(2,4)	(3,1)

20. Is moving power effective for either player in the game shown below?

(2,3)	(1,2)
(3,4)	(4,1)

21. Is moving power effective for either player in the game shown below?

(2,2)	(1,3)
(3,4)	(4,1)

22. Describe a situation which can be modeled by Success.

23. Describe a situation which can be modeled by Chicken.

24. Describe a situation which can be modeled by Prisoners' Dilemma.

25. Describe a situation which can be modeled by Variation.

26. Describe a situation which can be modeled by truel.

Chapter 17 Multiple-Choice Questions
Growth and Form

1. You own a painting whose dimensions are 24 inches by 30 inches. If you create a slide of this work so that the longest side of the image is 1 inch, what is the scaling factor for the slide?
a) 1 / 24   b) 1 / 30   c) 1 / 720   d) 4 / 5

2. You own a painting whose dimensions are 24 inches by 30 inches. If you create a slide of this work so that the longest side of the image is 1 inch, what is the length of the smaller side of the slide image?
a) 1 inch   b) 4 / 5 inch   c) 16 / 25 inch   d) 1 / 5 inch

3. You own a painting whose dimensions are 24 inches by 30 inches. If you create a slide of this work so that the longest side of the image is 1 inch, what is the area of the slide image?
a) 1 square inch   b) 4 / 5 square inch   c) 16 / 25 square inch   d) 5 / 4 square inches

4. You own a painting whose dimensions are 24 inches by 30 inches. If you create a full-size copy of this painting as a poster, what is the scaling factor for the poster?
a) 1   b) 4 / 5   c) 1 / 24   d) 1 / 30

5. You own a painting whose dimensions are 24 inches by 30 inches. If you create a postcard-sized reproduction of the painting whose area is 20 square inches, what is the scaling factor for the reproduction?
a) 1 / 4   b) 1 / 6   c) 1 / 36   d) 2 / 3

6. The cost of photographic paper is nearly proportional to the area of the paper. You own a painting whose dimensions are 24 inches by 30 inches. You create a small photographic reproduction whose smaller side is 5 inches. What is the scaling factor for this reproduction?
a) 0.2083   b) 0.1667   c) 0.0434   d) 0.0278

7. The cost of photographic paper is nearly proportional to the area of the paper. You own a painting whose dimensions are 24 inches by 30 inches. You create a large photographic reproduction whose smaller side is 8 inches. How does its area compare with that of the original painting?
a) 0.3333   b) 0.2667   c) 0.1111   d) 0.0711

8. The cost of photographic paper is nearly proportional to the area of the paper. You own a painting whose dimensions are 24 inches by 30 inches. You create a small photographic reproduction whose smaller side is 5 inches, and a large photographic reproduction whose smaller side is 8 inches. If the paper required for the small reproduction costs $1.50, how much will the paper required for the large reproduction cost?
a) $1.90   b) $2.40   c) $3.84   d) $4.50

9. A scale model of a truck is 1.5 inches high. If the actual truck is 9 feet high, what is the scaling factor of the model?
a) 1 to 6   b) 1 to 18   c) 1 to 36   d) 1 to 72

10. A scale model of a truck is 5 inches long. If the model is built to a scale of 1 to 54, what is the length of the actual truck?

a) 270 feet   b) 101 feet   c) 36.7 feet   d) 22.5 feet

11. A model of a truck is built to a scale of 1 to 54. If the model will hold 7 cubic inches, how much will the actual truck hold?

a) 378 cubic feet   b) 638 cubic feet   c) 1544 cubic feet   d) 4536 cubic feet

12. A model of a truck is built to a scale of 1 to 54. If the model casts a shadow of 8 square inches, how large a shadow will the actual truck cast?

a) 36 square feet   b) 162 square feet   c) 288 square feet   d) 729 square feet

13. Last summer you grew a giant squash that was 6 feet long and proportionally similar to your other squash. These squash tend to be about 1.5 feet long and weigh about a pound. About how much do you think the giant squash weighs?

a) Less than 10 pounds   c) Between 20 and 50 pounds
b) Between 10 and 20 pounds   d) More than 50 pounds

14. Last summer you grew a giant squash that was 4.5 feet long and proportionally similar to your other squash. These squash tend to be about 1.5 feet long and weigh about a pound. About how much do you think the giant squash weighs?

a) Less than 10 pounds   c) Between 20 and 50 pounds
b) Between 10 and 20 pounds   d) More than 50 pounds

15. Artificial Christmas trees tend to be proportional in shape. If a 4-foot tree needs approximately 60 ornaments to cover the outer limbs of the tree, how many ornaments will a 6-foot tree need?

a) Approximately 90 ornaments   c) Approximately 135 ornaments
b) Approximately 120 ornaments   d) Approximately 150 ornaments

16. Artificial Christmas trees tend to be proportional in shape. If a 4-foot tree needs about two strings of lights, what size tree would need five strings of lights?

a) A tree shorter than 6 feet   c) A tree between 8 and 9 feet tall
b) A tree between 6 and 8 feet tall   d) A tree taller than 9 feet

17. Christmas trees tend to be proportional in shape. You have a tree skirt which is circular and with diameter 3 feet, which you bought for a 7-foot tree. If you have a 5-foot tree this year, what size tree skirt will you need? (Round to the nearest size.)

a) A skirt whose diameter is 2.5 feet   c) A skirt whose diameter is 1.5 feet
b) A skirt whose diameter is 2 feet   d) A skirt whose diameter is 1 foot

18. In 1965 powdered gelatine cost 10 cents per box at the grocery store. If the 1965 CPI is 31.5 and the 1997 CPI is 160.5, compute this cost in 1997 dollars.

a) 13 cents   b) 19 cents   c) 48 cents   d) 51 cents

19. In 1976 a roast beef sandwich cost 89 cents at a local fast food shop. If the 1976 CPI is 56.9 and the 1997 CPI is 160.5, compute this cost in 1997 dollars.

a) 92 cents   b) $1.43   c) $1.93   d) $2.51

20. In 1997 a compact car can cost approximately $14,000. What is this cost in 1990 dollars, the year that you bought your last car? (Assume the 1997 CPI is 160.5 and the 1990 CPI is 130.7.)
a) Approximately $9,300
b) Approximately $9,800
c) Approximately $11,400
d) Approximately $12,700

21. You bought a house for $130,000 in 1997. The previous owner paid $50,000 for the house in 1980. Comparing the converted cost, who paid more for the house? (Assume the 1997 CPI is 160.5 and the 1980 CPI is 82.4.)
a) You paid much more.
b) The previous owner paid much more.
c) You both paid approximately the same amount.

22. The minimum wage in 1996 is $4.50. What is the equivalent amount in 1942 dollars? (Assume the 1996 CPI is 156.3 and the 1942 CPI is 16.3.)
a) About 41 cents   b) About 43 cents   c) About 47 cents   d) About 50 cents

23. Bananas cost about $1.25 Australian dollars per kilogram in Australia. If an Australian dollar exchanges for 80 US cents and a kilogram is about 2.2 pounds, what is the equivalent cost in US dollars?
a) 45 US cents per pound
b) 71 US cents per pound
c) $2.20 US per pound
d) $3.44 US per pound

24. Apples cost about $1.75 Canadian dollars per kilogram in Canada. If a Canadian dollar exchanges for 75 US cents and a kilogram is about 2.2 pounds, what is the equivalent cost in US dollars?
a) $0.60 US per pound   b) $1.06 US per pound   c) $2.89 US per pound   d) $5.13 US per pound

25. Ground steak costs about $2.50 per pound in the US. If an Australian dollar exchanges for 80 US cents and a kilogram is about 2.2 pounds, what is the equivalent cost in Australian dollars?
a) $0.91 per kilogram   b) $1.42 per kilogram   c) $4.40 per kilogram   d) $6.88 per kilogram

26. Trout costs about $6.50 per pound in the US. If a Canadian dollar exchanges for 75 US cents and a kilogram is about 2.2 pounds, what is the equivalent cost in Canadian dollars?
a) $2.22 per kilogram   b) $3.94 per kilogram   c) $10.73 per kilogram   d) $19.07 per kilogram

27. The weight of a block of granite 1 ft × 2 ft × 4 ft is 1320 lbs. If it stands on a small face (1 ft × 2 ft), what is the pressure on the bottom face?
a) 1.15 lb/in^2 b) 2.29 lb/in^2 c) 4.58 lb/in^2 d) 9.17 lb/in^2

28. The weight of a block of granite 1 ft × 2 ft × 4 ft is 1320 lbs. If it stands on a large face (4 ft × 2 ft), what is the pressure on the bottom face?
a) 1.15 lb/in^2 b) 2.29 lb/in^2 c) 4.58 lb/in^2 d) 9.17 lb/in^2

29. The weight of a block of granite 1 ft × 2 ft × 4 ft is 1320 lbs. If twelve blocks are used to build a wall 8 ft high, 12 ft long, and 1 ft wide, what is the pressure on the bottom faces?
a) 4.58 lb/in^2 b) 9.17 lb/in^2 c) 18.3 lb/in^2 d) 36.7 lb/in^2

30. A granite sculpture weighs approximately 4500 lbs. If a smaller version 2/3 the height of the original is created from granite, how much will it weigh?
a) Approximately 3675 lbs.
b) Approximately 3000 lbs.
c) Approximately 2000 lbs.
d) Approximately 1300 lbs.

31. A granite sculpture weighs approximately 4500 lbs. If a smaller version 3/4 the height of the original is created from granite, how much will it weigh?
a) Approximately 3900 lbs.
b) Approximately 3475 lbs.
c) Approximately 2500 lbs.
d) Approximately 1900 lbs.

32. A wooden carving of an eagle stands 2 inches high and weighs approximately 3 ounces. If a larger carving made from the same material stands 5 feet high, how much will it weigh?
a) Approximately 50 lbs.
b) Approximately 70 lbs.
c) Approximately 170 lbs.
d) Approximately 5000 lbs.

33. A small steel spoon is 6 inches long and weighs approximately 4 ounces. If it is used as a model for a large steel spoon 4 feet long to be installed at the local cafe, how much would it weigh?
a) Approximately 16 lbs.
b) Approximately 32 lbs.
c) Approximately 128 lbs.
d) Approximately 2048 lbs.

34. A small steel spoon is 6 inches long and weighs approximately 4 ounces. If it is used as a model for a large steel spoon to be constructed from melting approximately 200 lbs. of steel spoons, how long will the large spoon be?
a) Approximately 4.6 ft   b) Approximately 7.4 ft   c) Approximately 10 ft   d) Approximately 14 ft

35. An artist wishes to melt 2000 copper pennies to create a large penny proportional to an ordinary penny. The diameter of a penny is approximately 3/4 in. What will be the diameter of the large penny?
a) Approximately 0.78 ft   b) Approximately 2.2 ft   c) Approximately 5 ft   d) Approximately 9.4 ft

36. An artist wishes to melt copper pennies to create a large penny proportional to an ordinary penny and with diameter 5 inches. An ordinary penny has diameter 3/4 in. How many pennies will be needed?
a) Approximately 10   b) Approximately 50   c) Approximately 150   d) Approximately 300

37. A sparrow has a minimum speed of about 20 miles per hour. If a robin is twice as long as a sparrow and proportional in shape, what is the minimum speed of a robin?
a) 40 miles per hour   b) 28 miles per hour   c) 14 miles per hour   d) 10 miles per hour

38. A sparrow has a minimum speed of about 20 miles per hour. If a blue jay is five times as long as a sparrow and proportional in shape, what is the minimum speed of a blue jay?
a) 100 miles per hour   b) 45 miles per hour   c) 9 miles per hour   d) 4 miles per hour

39. A spherical balloon has a circumference of 10 inches. If it expands to twice the volume, what happens to its surface area?
a) Its surface area more than doubles.
b) Its surface area doubles.
c) Its surface area increases but does not double.

40. A spherical balloon has a circumference of 10 inches. If it expands so that its surface area is doubled, what happens to its volume?
   a) Its volume more than doubles.   b) Its volume doubles.   c) Its volume increases but does not double.

41. A spherical balloon has a circumference of 10 inches. If it expands to twice the volume, what happens to its circumference?
   a) Its circumference more than doubles.
   b) Its circumference doubles.
   c) Its circumference increases but does not double.

42. Assuming that the sail of the *Dimetrodon* developed to dissipate heat when an individual doubled in weight, how much did the sail grow?
   a) It more than doubled in surface area.   c) It grew, but did not double in surface area.
   b) It doubled in surface area.

43. When a bird doubles its weight, how much do its wings grow?
   a) They more than double in surface area.   c) They grow, but do not double in surface area.
   b) They double in surface area.

44. A baby's head is about 1/3 its length; an adult's head is about 1/7 its length. This type of growth is called
   a) Allometric growth.   b) Proportional growth.   c) Geometric growth.   d) Isometric growth.

45. What is the value of the following fraction?
$$\frac{\log 24 - \log 15}{\log 43 - \log 24}$$
   a) 0.806 b 0.558   b) 0.474   c) 0.325

46. What is the value of the following fraction?
$$\frac{\log 73 - \log 15}{\log 15 - \log 6}$$
   a) 4.827   b) 1.947   c) 1.727   d) 0.809

47. If points (1,23) and (3,38) lie on the graph of $y = bx^a$, solve for a.
   a) $a = 0.200$ b) $a = 0.457$ c) $a = 0.810$ d) $a = 1.235$

48. If points (1,32) and (3,75) lie on the graph of $\log y = bx^a$, solve for a.
   a) $a = 0.775$ b) $a = 0.929$ c) $a = 1.077$ d) $a = 1.156$

49. If points (0.4, 26) and (1.2, 41) lie on the graph of
$$\log y = B + a \log x$$
   solve for a.
   a) $a = 0.415$ b) $a = 0.664$ c) $a = 0.846$ d) $a = 1.273$

50. If points (0.4, 25) and (1.2, 53) lie on the graph of

$$y = B + a \log x$$

solve for a.

a) $a = 0.684$ b) $a = 0.916$ c) $a = 1.182$ d) $a = 1.544$

Free-Response Questions

1. You want to copy a poster whose dimensions are 24 inches by 30 inches onto a piece of paper 8.5 inches by 11 inches. You want the image to be as large as possible, but maintain the proportions of the original poster. What scaling factor will you use?

2. You want to copy a poster whose dimensions are 24 inches by 30 inches onto a piece of paper 8.5 inches by 11 inches. You want the image to be as large as possible, but maintain the proportions of the original poster. What are the dimensions of the image?

3. You want to copy a poster whose dimensions are 24 inches by 30 inches onto a piece of paper 11 inches by 17 inches. You want the image to be as large as possible, but maintain the proportions of the original poster. What scaling factor will you use?

4. You want to copy a poster whose dimensions are 24 inches by 30 inches onto a piece of paper 11 inches by 17 inches. You want the image to be as large as possible, but maintain the proportions of the original poster. What are the dimensions of the image?

5. When comparing prices for pizzas, you discover that the large pizza has twice as much surface area of a medium pizza and costs less than two medium pizzas. However, your group decides to order two medium pizzas anyway. What additional factors could be omitted in the mathematical model?

6. When comparing the relative dimensions of model trains you discover that their wheels are larger than they should be. Why might they be scaled incorrectly?

7. The cost of photographic paper is nearly proportional to the area of the paper. But some shops charge extra for "nonstandard" sizes. Why would they feel the need to do this?

8. Each year, the area's largest tomatoes and pumpkins are showcased at the county fair. If there is a maximum size for such produce, how can larger and larger specimens be grown each year?

9. Other than the crushing strength considerations, what other factors limit the size of trees?

10. How does a whale's size impact the depth to which it can descend?

11. Are all rectangles similar? Why or why not?

12. Are all circles similar? Why or why not?

13. Are all pentagons similar? Why or why not?

14. One of the famous problems of Greek antiquity was the *duplication of the cube*; that is, creating a cube similar to but double the volume of an existing cube. What if you instead wish to *triplicate the cube*, building a cube with three times the volume of an existing cube. What would be the scaling factor? Assuming the original cube was 1 cubic unit, what would be the dimensions of the larger cube?

15. Create an example of an advertisement which misuses proportional change through its use of percent growth.

16. Create an example of an advertisement which misuses proportional change through its use of graphics.

17. Use the Consumer Price Index table to estimate when a loaf of bread, 50 cents in 1970, doubled in price.

18. In 1997 a bottle of soda costs about 75 cents. Use the CPI table to estimate when this soda would have cost 5 cents.

19. In the Consumer Price Index table, the index numbers tend to grow, but the numbers for the 1930s are less than those for the 1920s. Can you explain this?

20. A miniature model for a sculpture weighs about 10 ounces and stands 8 inches high. The actual model is to be 3 feet high and weigh about 25 pounds. Can it be made from the same material as the model? If not, how should its weight per cubic inch compare to that of the model material?

21. Why do spike heels cause more damage to hardwood floors than loafers?

22. Large trucks often have multiple wheels on an axle. How would multiple wheels allow trucks to carry heavier loads?

23. Why is allometric growth an appropriate model when the National Center for Missing and Exploited Children create sketches of missing people?

24. Find the values of a and b so that the points (0.5, 21) and (1.4, 56) lie on the curve $y = bx^a$.

25. Find the values of a and b so that the points (1.1, 14) and (1.4, 38) lie on the curve $y = bx^a$.

Chapter 18 Multiple-Choice Questions
Geometric Growth

1. If you deposit $2000 at 7% simple interest, what is the balance after 2 years?
   a) $2280.00   b) $2289.80   c) $2295.05   d) $2300.52

2. If you deposit $2000 at 7% compounded quarterly, what is the balance after 2 years?
   a) $2280.00   b) $2289.80   c) $2297.76   d) $2300.52

3. If you deposit $2000 at 7% compounded annually, what is the balance after 2 years?
   a) $2280.00   b) $2289.80   c) $2297.76   d) $2300.52

4. If you deposit $2000 at 7% compounded daily, what is the balance after 2 years?
   a) $2280.00   b) $2289.80   c) $2297.76   d) $2300.52

5. What is the annual percentage yield (APY) for 7.5% compounded monthly?
   a) Less than 7.6%   c) At least 7.7%, less than 7.8%
   b) At least 7.6%, less than 7.7%   d) At least 7.8%

6. What is the APY for 7.2% compounded quarterly?
   a) Less than 7.3%   c) At least 7.4%, less than 7.5%
   b) At least 7.3%, less than 7.4%   d) At least 7.5%

7. What is the APY for 6.8% compounded daily?
   a) Less than 6.9%   c) At least 7.0%, less than 7.1%
   b) At least 6.9%, less than 7.0%   d) At least 7.1%

8. Which has the higher APY: 8% compounded annually or 7.75% compounded daily?
   a) 8% compounded annually   b) 7.75% compounded daily   c) The two have exactly the same APY

9. Which has the higher APY: 6% compounded annually or 5.85% compounded quarterly?
   a) 6% compounded annually   b) 5.85% compounded quarterly   c) The two have exactly the same APY

10. If the interest rate in the economy is 6% compounded daily, what is the fair value today for a bond that will mature in 4 years and pay $5000?
    a) $3875.97   b) $3933.22   c) $3960.47   d) $4032.26

11. If the interest rate in the economy has an annual percentage rate (APR) of 5.7%, what is the fair value today for a bond that will mature in 3 years and pay $5000?
    a) $4214.16   b) $4233.94   c) $4269.85   d) $4730.37

12. If the interest rate in the economy has an interest rate of 4.9% compounded annually, what is the fair value today for a bond that will mature in 2 years and pay $5000?
    a) $4510.00   b) $4533.27   c) $4543.80   d) $4553.73

13. Suppose that your credit union savings account for some 30-day period shows an old balance of $211.15 and a new balance of $211.72 after interest is added. This is the only activity in your account. What was the effective APY for this account?
    a) Less than 3.20%
    b) At least 3.20%, less than 3.25%
    c) At least 3.25%, less than 3.30%
    d) At least 3.30%

14. Suppose your money market account increases from $1732.30 to $1753.80 during a 30- day period. What is the effective APY for this account?
    a) Less than 15% b) At least 15%, less than 16% c) At least 16%, less than 17% d) At least 17%

15. Suppose you invest $1000 for two years at 6% compounded interest, but you do not know the frequency of compounding. Which of the following statements is/are true?

    I: You will definitely earn at least $120 in interest.
    II: You could possibly earn $125 in interest.
    a) I only b) II only c) Both I and II are true d) Neither I nor II is true

16. Suppose you invest $1000 for three years at 7% compounded interest, but you do not know the frequency of compounding. Which of the following statements is/are true?

    I: You will definitely earn at least $210 in interest.
    II: You could possibly earn $235 in interest.
    a) I only b) II only c) Both I and II are true d) Neither I nor II is true

17. If your accountant claims that you can earn 12% compounded annually on your investment, how long should it take for your investment to double in size?
    a) At least 8 years, less than 9 years
    b) At least 7 years, less than 8 years
    c) At least 6 years, less than 7 years
    d) Less than 6 years

18. US Savings Bonds are purchased at half their face value. If they pay 6% compounded annually, how long should you have to wait for the bond to mature (that is, be worth its face value)?
    a) At least 16 years
    b) At least 14 years, less than 16 years
    c) At least 12 years, less than 14 years
    d) Less than 12 years

19. Christmas Club accounts used to be quite popular. You deposited a fixed amount in your account each of 50 weeks, and the bank would return to you a check equal to 51 payments when you make the last payment. Which would be better: Making weekly payments into a Christmas Club account or into a savings account which pays 2% compounded weekly?
    a) Payments into a Christmas Club account
    b) Payments into a savings account
    c) The two accounts are exactly equivalent

20. Suppose you deposit $100 each month into an account which pays 2.25% compounded monthly. After two years of payments, how much will you find in your account as you make your 24th payment?
    a) $2452.47 b) $2504.94 c) $2508.00 d) $2509.22

21. Suppose you deposit $100 each month into an account which pays 2.5% compounded monthly. After

three years of payments, how much will you find in your account as you make your 36th payment?
a) $3645.00   b) $3734.40   c) $3870.00   d) $3876.81

22. Suppose you buy a home by taking a 30-year mortgage for $80,000 at an interest rate of 7% compounded monthly. How much will the monthly payments be?
a) $654.75   b) $609.99   c) $601.22   d) $532.24

23. Suppose you buy a home by taking a 30-year mortgage for $60,000 at an interest rate of 8% compounded monthly. How much will the monthly payments be?
a) $455.66   b) $444.14   c) $440.26   d) $402.59

24. Suppose you furnish your home by purchasing $3000 of items and agree to pay your bill off in 2 years of monthly payments at an interest rate of 12% compounded monthly. How much will the monthly payments be?
a) $126.87   b) $140.00   c) $141.22   d) $155.00

25. Suppose you buy $2500 in new appliances for your home and agree to pay your bill off in 18 months of monthly payments at an interest rate of 18% compounded monthly. How much will the monthly payments be?
a) $245.83   b) $184.38   c) $163.89   d) $159.51

26. Suppose you buy a new car for $18,000 and arrange a car loan at an interest rate of 8.5% compounded monthly, to be paid off in 48 monthly payments. How much will the monthly payments be?
a) Less than $450   b) At least $450, less than $500   c) At least $500, less than $550   d) At least $550

27. Suppose you buy a new car for $18,000 and arrange a car loan at an interest rate of 8.5% compounded monthly, to be paid off in 72 monthly payments. How much will the monthly payments be?
a) Less than $300   b) At least $300, less than $350   c) At least $350, less than $400   d) At least $400

28. Suppose your parents started saving $10 per month when you were born into an account which pays 9% compounded monthly. At your 18th birthday they present you a check for your college expenses. What will be the amount of this check?
a) Less than $4000
b) At least $4000, less than $5000
c) At least $5000, less than $6000
d) At least $6000

29. Suppose your parents started saving $10 per month when you were born into an account which pays 8% compounded monthly. At your 18th birthday they present you a check for your college expenses. What will be the amount of this check?
a) Less than $4000
b) At least $4000, less than $4500
c) At least $4500, less than $5000
d) At least $5000

30. Suppose you buy a new tractor for $50,000. It depreciates steadily at 8% per year. When will it be worth approximately $10,000?
a) After 10 years   b) After 15 years   c) After 20 years   d) After 25 years

31. Suppose you buy a new duplicator for $12,000. It depreciates steadily at 11% per year. When will it be

worth approximately $2000?

a) After 8 years   b) After 12 years   c) After 15 years   d) After 21 years

32. Suppose you buy a new truck for $17,000. It depreciates steadily for 10 years until you trade it in. When you trade it in it is valued at $3000. What was the annual depreciation rate?

a) Less than 9%   b) At least 9%, less than 12%   c) At least 12%, less than 15%   d) At least 15%

33. You buy a new computer $5000 that depreciates steadily for 5 years until you determine that it has little value (less than $100). What was the annual depreciation rate?

a) Less than 40%   b) At least 40%, less than 45%   c) At least 45%, less than 50%   d) At least 50%

34. Radioactive radon-222 has a half-life of 3.82 days. If 2 grams of this isotope become exposed today, how much will remain 2 weeks from now?

a) 0.08 grams   b) 0.16 grams   c) 0.27 grams   d) 0.54 grams

35. Radioactive radon-222 has a half-life of 3.82 days. If 2 grams are detected today, how much of this isotope existed here 2 weeks ago?

a) 25 grams   b) 12.5 grams   c) 7.3 grams   d) 6.3 grams

36. Carbon-14 has a half-life of 5730 years. If a body is found which is decaying at a rate of 790 atoms per hour per gram of carbon, how long has the body been dead?

a) Less than 25 years   c) At least 100 years, less than 200 years
b) At least 25 years, less than 100 years   d) At least 200 years

37. Carbon-14 has a half-life of 5730 years. If a body is found which is decaying at a rate of 800 atoms per hour per gram of carbon, how long has the body been dead?

a) Less than 25 years   c) At least 100 years, less than 200 years
b) At least 25 years, less than 100 years   d) At least 200 years

38. The population of the US was 266 million at the beginning of 1997. Assuming an average growth rate of 0.6% per year, what will be the population of the US at the beginning of 2001?

a) 272.38 million   b) 272.44 million   c) 273.98 million   d) 274.08 million

39. The population of the US was 266 million at the beginning of 1997. Assuming an average growth rate of 0.55% per year, what will be the population of the US at the beginning of 2001?

a) 271.85 million   b) 271.90 million   c) 273.32 million   d) 273.40 million

40. Suppose an island's wolf population grows by the logistic model, where the carrying capacity M = 200, the current population is 20, and the natural rate of increase is r = 4% per year. What is the current annual growth rate?

a) 3.6%   b) 4%   c) 10%   d) 14%

41. Suppose an island's cat population grows by the logistic model, where the carrying capacity M = 500, the current population is 100, and the natural rate of increase is r = 7% per year. What is the current annual growth rate?

a) 1.4%   b) 5.6%   c) 6%   d) 20%

42. Suppose that in 1996 the world's current demand for a certain commodity is 5 tons. Consumption rises 1.5% each year and the known resources include 800 tons. What is the static reserve for this commodity in 1996?
    a) About 160 years   b) About 120 years   c) About 82 years   d) About 67 years

43. Suppose that in 1996 the world's current demand for a certain commodity is 5 tons. Consumption rises 1.5% each year and the known resources include 800 tons. Assuming that consumption continues to increase by 1.5% each year, what is the exponential reserve for this commodity in 1996?
    a) About 160 years   b) About 120 years   c) About 82 years   d) About 67 years

44. Suppose the reproduction curve for a certain creature is the graph $y = g(x)$. Suppose this curve intersects the line $y = x$ at the point (300, 300). If this year's population is 300, what will next year's population be?
    a) 300   b) More than 300   c) Less than 300

45. Suppose the reproduction curve for a certain creature is the graph $y = g(x)$. Suppose this curve lies above the line $y = x$ for x values between 0 and 500, and below the line $y = x$ for all x-values greater than 500. If this year's population is 400, what will next year's population be?
    a) 400   b) More than 400   c) Less than 400

46. Suppose the reproduction curve for a certain creature is the graph $y = g(x)$. Suppose this curve rises, falls, and drifts toward the x-axis for large values of x. If this year's population is unusually large, what will next year's population be?
    a) About the same   b) Even larger   c) Smaller

47. Suppose the reproduction curve for a certain creature is the graph $y = g(x)$. For this graph, how would you find an equilibrium population size?
    a) The x-value of the intersection of $y = g(x)$ and $y = 100$
    b) The y-value of the intersection of $y = g(x)$ and $x = 100$
    c) The x-value of the intersection of $y = g(x)$ and $y = x$
    d) None of these

48. Suppose the reproduction curve for a certain creature is the graph $y = g(x)$. If the curve never crosses the line $y = x$ (except at $x = 0$), what can you say about the population throughout several years?
    a) It will sometimes increase and sometimes decrease.
    b) It will always increase each year.
    c) It will always decrease each year.
    d) It will either always increase each year, or always decrease each year.

49. In the logistic model, when population increases, the growth rate
    a) always increases.
    b) always decreases.
    c) sometimes increases and sometimes decreases.
    d) stays constant.

50. In the logistic model, if the carrying capacity suddenly increases, the growth rate
    a) always increases.
    b) always decreases.
    c) sometimes increases and sometimes decreases.
    d) stays constant.

Free-Response Questions

1. You can choose between an account which pays 6.5% simple interest, or another which pays 6.25% compounded quarterly. Which account will pay more interest on a deposit of $2000 for 2 years?

2. You can choose between an account which pays 6.8% simple interest, or another which pays 6.5% compounded monthly. Which account will pay more interest on a deposit of $2000 for 2 years?

3. You can choose between an account which pays 6.6% compounded annually, or another which pays 6.4% compounded daily. Which account will pay more interest on a deposit of $2000 for 2 years?

4. You can choose between an account which pays 6.5% compounded quarterly, or another which pays 6.4% compounded daily. Which account will pay more interest on a deposit of $2000 for 2 years?

5. A new company offers a bond which will pay $5000 two years from now and an additional $5000 five years from now. If the interest rate in the economy is 6% compounded annually, what is a fair price for the bond today?

6. A new company offers a bond which will pay $1000 per year for ten years, starting one year from today. If the interest rate in the economy is 6% compounded annually, what is a fair price for the bond today?

7. Suppose you invested $2500 in a stock account five months ago. Today the account has a value of $2660. What is the effective annual percentage yield (APY) for this account?

8. Suppose you invested $500 in silver coins 10 months ago. Today the coins have been valued at $540. What is the effective APY for this investment?

9. If you compare the APY of 10% interest compounded at various frequencies, what strict upper bound exists for these values? Why?

10. Is the *rule of 72* an effective estimate for doubling time for all interest rates? Why?

11. Savings bonds are typically sold at half their face value. If a bond will mature (be worth its face value) in 10 years, what is the effective annual percentage rate (APR) for the bond?

12. Mortgages sometimes are scheduled for biweekly payments (26 payments per year). How would the payments for a biweekly-pay mortgage compare to a traditional monthly-pay mortgage with the same APR?

13. You have a mortgage with required monthly payments of $370 per month for 30 years and an interest rate of 8% compounded monthly. If you instead pay $400 each month, when will you pay off the mortgage?

14. You have a mortgage with required monthly payments of $520 per month for 30 year and an interest rate of 9% compounded monthly. If you instead pay $550 each month, when will you pay off the mortgage?

15. Your local appliance store offers to defer your payment 6 months by selling your account to a finance company. The store pays a 2% fee to the company for this service. What is the APR paid by the store for this service?

16. You want to pay at most $250 per month for your new car. The price of the car is $15,000, and the interest rate is 7.9% compounded monthly. How many months will you have to pay?

17. If you set the monthly payment, the price, and the interest rate for a new car loan, is it possible that the loan would *never* be paid off? Justify your response.

18. You have monthly payments of $200, paying off a 12% (compounded monthly) loan, and you owe six more payments. Suppose you renegotiate your terms so that you instead pay one payment 6 months from now. How much will it be?

19. Some cars depreciate more when newer than when older. Suppose your new car will depreciate 15% (compounded annually) the first year, 10% the second year, and 5% each year thereafter. When will it be worth 20% of the original value?

20. Some cars appreciate after several years. Suppose your car will depreciate by 7% (compounded annually) for the next 10 years, and then appreciate by 10% each year thereafter. When will its value exceed today's value?

21. An unknown radioactive substance is discovered. How can you determine its half-life?

22. What aspects of population change are captured by the logistic model?

23. What is the difference between the static reserve and the exponential reserve?

24. What happens if the harvest of a product exceeds the *maximum sustainable yield*?

25. How could it be realistic that a very large population in one season could be followed by a very small population?

Chapter 19 Multiple-Choice Questions
New Geometries for a New Universe

1. Suppose the triangle ABC in the Euclidean Plane is constructed so that the measure of $\angle A$ is equal to the measure of $\angle B$ and two times the measure of $\angle C$. What is the measure of the smallest angle?
   a) 30° b) 36° c) 45° d) 72°

2. Suppose the triangle ABC in the Euclidean Plane is constructed so that the measure of $\angle A$ is twice the measure of $\angle B$ and three times the measure of $\angle C$. What is the measure of the smallest angle?
   a) Less than 30° b) At least 30°, less than 45° c) At least 45°, less than 60° d) At least 60°

3. Suppose the triangle ABC in the Euclidean Plane is constructed so that the measure of $\angle A$ is three times the measure of $\angle B$ and six times the measure of $\angle C$. What is the measure of the smallest angle?
   a) 18° b) 20° c) 30° d) 60°

4. Suppose the triangle ABC in the hyperbolic plane is constructed so that the measures of the angles are all equal. What is the measure of each angle?
   a) 60° b) Less than 60° c) More than 60°

5. Suppose the triangle ABC in the hyperbolic plane is constructed so that the measure of $\angle A$ is two times the measure of $\angle B$ and five times the measure of $\angle C$. Then the largest angle
   a) always has a measure of 100°.
   b) always has a measure greater than 100°.
   c) always has a measure less than 100°.
   d) sometimes has a measure greater than 100° and sometimes has a measure less than 100°.

6. Suppose the triangle ABC in the elliptic plane is constructed so that the measures of the angles are all equal. What is the measure of each angle?
   a) 60° b) Less than 60° c) More than 60°

7. Suppose the triangle ABC in the elliptic plane is constructed so that the measure of $\angle A$ is two times the measure of $\angle B$ and five times the measure of $\angle C$. Then the largest angle
   a) always has a measure of 100°.
   b) always has a measure greater than 100°.
   c) always has a measure less than 100°.
   d) sometimes has a measure greater than 100° and sometimes has a measure less than 100°.

8. Suppose a quadrilateral ABCD is constructed in the elliptic plane. If the measures of angles A, B, and C are all equal to 90°, what is the measure of the remaining angle?
   a) 90 ° b) Less than 90° c) More than 90°

9. Suppose a quadrilateral ABCD is constructed in the Euclidean plane. If the measures of angles A, B, and C are all equal to 90°, what is the measure of the remaining angle?
   a) 90 ° b) Less than 90° c) More than 90°

10. Suppose a quadrilateral ABCD is constructed in the hyperbolic plane. If the measures of angles A, B, and C are all equal to 90°, what is the measure of the remaining angle?
a) 90 °   b) Less than 90°   c) More than 90°

11. Suppose a quadrilateral ABCD is constructed in the Euclidean plane. Suppose the measures of angles A and C are equal and the measures of angles B and D are equal. If the measure of angle A is twice that of angle B, what is the measure of angle A?
a) 45°   b) 60°   c) 90°   d) 120°

12. Suppose a quadrilateral ABCD is constructed in the Euclidean plane. Suppose the measures of angles A and C are equal and the measures of angles B and D are equal. If the measure of angle A is three times that of angle B, what is the measure of angle B?
a) 45°   b) 60°   c) 120°   d) 135°

13. Suppose a pentagon ABCDE is constructed in the Euclidean plane. What is the sum of the measures of angles A, B, C, D, and E?
a) 360°   b) 540°   c) 720°   d) The sum will vary.

14. Which of the following is larger:

I: The sum of the measures of the angles of a pentagon in the Euclidean plane.
II: The sum of the measures of the angles of a pentagon in the hyperbolic plane.
a) I   b) II   c) I and II are equal.   d) I is sometimes larger; II is sometimes larger.

15. Which of the following is larger:

I: The sum of the measures of the angles of a pentagon in the Euclidean plane.
II: The sum of the measures of the angles of a pentagon in the elliptic plane.
a) I   b) II   c) I and II are equal.   d) I is sometimes larger; II is sometimes larger.

16. In the hyperbolic plane, parallel lines
a) never exist.   b) always intersect.   c) sometimes intersect.   d) never intersect.

17. In the elliptic plane, parallel lines
a) never exist.   b) always intersect.   c) sometimes intersect.   d) never intersect.

18. In the hyperbolic plane, parallelograms (quadrilaterals whose opposite faces are parallel)
a) never exist.   c) cannot have an arbitrarily small area.
b) can have any area.   d) cannot have an arbitrarily large area.

19. In the hyperbolic plane, rectangles
a) never exist.   b) are always squares.   c) are never squares.   d) could possibly be squares.

20. In the hyperbolic plane, right triangles
a) never exist.   b) can have three right angles.   c) can have any area.   d) are always isosceles.

21. Suppose the following collection of axioms are satisfied:
    A: Every line contains exactly two points.
    B: Any pair of points has exactly one line in common.
    C: There are exactly four points.

    How many lines are there?
    a) 4   b) 5   c) 6   d) More than 6

22. Suppose the following collection of axioms are satisfied:
    A: Every line contains exactly two points.
    B: Any pair of points has exactly one line in common.
    C: There are exactly three lines.

    How many points are there?
    a) Less than 4   b) 4   c) 5   d) 6

23. Suppose the following collection of axioms are satisfied:
    A: Every line contains *at least* two points.
    B: Any pair of points has exactly one line in common.
    C: There are exactly four points.

    What is the smallest number of lines possible?
    a) 1   b) 2   c) 3   d) 4

24. Suppose the following collection of axioms are satisfied:
    A: Every line contains exactly two points.
    B: Any pair of points has *at most one* line in common.
    C: There are exactly three lines.

    What is the largest number of points possible?
    a) Less than 4   b) 4   c) 5   d) 6

25. Suppose the following collection of axioms are satisfied:
    A: Every line contains exactly two points.
    B: Any pair of points has *at most one* line in common.
    C: There are exactly four points.

    What is the smallest number of lines possible?
    a) Less than 4   b) 4   c) 5   d) 6

26. Is the following axiomatic system possible?
    A: Every line contains exactly two points.
    B: Every point is on exactly two lines.
    C: There are exactly four points.
    a) No.   c) Yes. There are exactly three lines.

b) Yes. There are exactly two lines.

d) Yes. There are at least four lines.

27. Is the following axiomatic system possible?
    A: Every line contains exactly two points.
    B: Every point is on exactly two lines.
    C: There are exactly five points.

a) No.

b) Yes. There are less than five lines.

c) Yes. There are exactly five lines.

d) Yes. There are at least six lines.

28. Is the following axiomatic system possible?
    A: Every line contains exactly two points.
    B: Every point is on exactly three lines.
    C: There are exactly four points.

a) No.

b) Yes. There are less than six lines.

c) Yes. There are between six and nine lines.

d) Yes. There are more than nine lines.

29. Is the following axiomatic system possible?
    A: Every line contains exactly three points.
    B: Every point is on exactly two lines.
    C: There are exactly six points.

a) No.

b) Yes. There are less than four lines.

c) Yes. There are between four and six lines.

d) Yes. There are more than six lines.

30. In the following axiomatic system, how many triangles exist?
    A: Every line contains exactly two points.
    B: Every point lies on exactly three lines.
    C: There are exactly four points and exactly six lines.

a) 0   b) 4   c) 6   d) 12

31. In the following axiomatic system, how many triangles exist?
    A: Every line contains exactly two points.
    B: Every point lies on exactly four lines.
    C: There are exactly five points and exactly ten lines.

a) 0   b) 5   c) 10   d) 25

32. In the following axiomatic system, are there any parallel lines?
    A: Every line contains exactly two points.
    B: Every point lies on exactly three lines.
    C: There are exactly four points and exactly six lines.

a) No.

b) Yes, exactly one pair of parallel lines.

c) Yes, exactly three pairs of parallel lines.

d) Yes, more than three pairs of parallel lines.

33. In the following axiomatic system, are there any parallel lines?
    A: Every line contains exactly two points.
    B: Every point lies on exactly four lines.
    C: There are exactly five points and exactly ten lines.

a) No.

c) Yes, exactly five pairs of parallel lines.

b) Yes, exactly one pair of parallel lines.

d) Yes, more than five pairs of parallel lines.

34. In the following axiomatic system, are there any parallel lines?
    A: Every line contains exactly two points.
    B: Every point lies on exactly two lines.
    C: There are exactly four points and exactly four lines.

a) No

c) Yes, exactly two pairs of parallel lines.

b) Yes, exactly one pair of parallel lines.

d) Yes, more than two pairs of parallel lines.

35. In the following axiomatic system, does Euclid's parallel postulate hold?
    A: Every line contains exactly two points.
    B: Every point lies on exactly two lines.
    C: There are exactly three points and exactly three lines.

a) No   b) Yes

36. In the following axiomatic system, does Euclid's parallel postulate hold?
    A: Every line contains exactly two points.
    B: Every point lies on exactly four lines.
    C: There are exactly five points and exactly ten lines.

a) No   b) Yes

37. In the following axiomatic system, does Euclid's parallel postulate hold?
    A: Every line contains exactly two points.
    B: Every point lies on exactly two lines.
    C: There are exactly four points and exactly four lines.

a) No   b) Yes

38. Suppose your spaceship moves with a speed of 20 miles/second. Recall that the speed of light is 186,000 miles/second. What is the Lorentz-Fitzgerald factor γ for this situation?

a) Approximately 0.99989248

c) Approximately 1.00000001

b) Approximately 0.99999998

d) Approximately 1.00000006

39. Suppose your spaceship moves with a speed of 2000 miles/second. Recall that the speed of light is 186,000 miles/second. What is the Lorentz-Fitzgerald factor γ for this situation?

a) Approximately 0.98924731

c) Approximately 1.00002891

b) Approximately 0.99994219

d) Approximately 1.00005782

40. Suppose an object is traveling at 95% of the speed of light. What is the Lorentz- Fitzgerald factor γ for this situation?

a) Approximately 0.3122

c) Approximately 14.337

b) Approximately 3.2026

d) Approximately 20.000

41. Suppose an object is traveling at 98% of the speed of light. What is the Lorentz- Fitzgerald factor γ for this situation?

a) Approximately 0.9996

c) Approximately 5.0252

b) Approximately 2.2417   d) Approximately 25.253

42. The Poincaré Disk Model is a model for
a) Euclidean geometry.   b) hyperbolic geometry.   c) elliptic geometry.

43. In the Poincaré Disk Model, "lines" are
a) circular arcs that pass through the center point.
b) circular arcs that meet the boundary at right angles.
c) circular arcs that never intersect.
d) chords through the disk.

44. The Klein Disk Model is a model for
a) Euclidean geometry.   b) hyperbolic geometry.   c) elliptic geometry.

45. In the Klein Disk Model, "lines" are
a) chords that pass through the center point.   c) circular arcs that pass through the center point.
b) chords that meet the boundary at right angles.   d) chords through the disk.

46. The Upper Half-Plane Model is a model for
a) Euclidean geometry.   b) hyperbolic geometry.   c) elliptic geometry.

47. In the Upper Half-Plane Model, "lines" are
a) vertical rays.
b) open semicircles that are perpendicular to the bounding line.
c) both vertical rays and open semicircles that are perpendicular to the bounding line.
d) both vertical rays and open parabolas that are perpendicular to the bounding line.

48. The spherical model is a model for
a) Euclidean geometry.   b) hyperbolic geometry.   c) elliptic geometry.

49. In the spherical model, geodesics
a) never lie along great circles.   b) sometimes lie along great circles.   c) always lie along great circles.

50. In the spherical model, the plane of a great circle
a) always includes the center point of the sphere.
b) sometimes includes the center point of the sphere.
c) never includes the center point of the sphere.

Free-Response Questions

1. How do the angle sums of a Euclidean triangle, a hyperbolic triangle, and an elliptic triangle compare?

2. How do the angle sums of a Euclidean hexagon, a hyperbolic hexagon, and an elliptic hexagon compare?

3. Why is it impossible to construct a square in hyperbolic geometry?

4. Why is it impossible to construct a square in elliptic geometry?

5. Why does hyperbolic geometry violate Euclid's parallel postulate?

6. Why does elliptic geometry violate Euclid's parallel postulate?

7. Is it possible to construct a rhombus (with four equal-length sides) in hyperbolic geometry?

8. Is it possible to construct a rhombus (with four equal-length sides) in elliptic geometry?

9. Is it possible to construct a right triangle in hyperbolic geometry?

10. Is it possible to construct a right triangle in elliptic geometry?

11. Create a finite geometry which satisfies Euclid's parallel postulate.

12. Create a finite geometry which does not satisfy Euclid's parallel postulate.

13. Create a finite geometry which has no triangles.

14. Create a finite geometry which has six points and four lines, and for which every point lies on exactly two lines.

15. Create a finite geometry which has four points and six lines, and for which every line contains exactly two points.

16. Create a "real-world" situation where points represent stores and lines represent products.

17. Create a "real-world" situation where points represent products and lines represent stores.

18. Create an axiomatic system which has no model.

19. Why do airplanes flying from New York to London generally fly near the arctic circle?

20. Are the earth's latitudes or longitudes geodesics?

21. How do the models for hyperbolic geometry differ?

22. What is Minkowskian geometry?

23. Why does the general theory of relativity suggest a non-Euclidean geometry model?

24. How fast must you be moving in order to have a Lorentz-Fitzgerald factor γ of at least 10?

25. How could you (hypothetically) use the locations of three mountain peaks to determine the geometry of space?

Chapter 20 Multiple-Choice Questions
Symmetry and Patterns

1. The numbers 8 and 13 are consecutive Fibonacci numbers. What is the next Fibonacci number in the sequence?
   a) 16   b) 18   c) 21   d) 26

2. The numbers 21 and 34 are consecutive Fibonacci numbers. What is the next Fibonacci number in the sequence?
   a) 42   b) 47   c) 55   d) 68

3. Suppose a sequence begins with 1, 3, and continues by adding the previous two numbers to get the next number in the sequence. In this sequence, 7 and 11 are consecutive numbers. What is the next number in this sequence?
   a) 18   b) 17   c) 15   d) 14

4. Suppose a sequence begins with 1, 3, and continues by adding the previous two numbers to get the next number in the sequence. In this sequence, 18 and 29 are consecutive numbers. What is the next number in this sequence?
   a) 47   b) 41   c) 40   d) 32

5. The value of the golden ratio is
   a) less than 1.   b) between 1 and 1.5.   c) between 1.5 and 2.   d) greater than 2.

6. What is the value of the product of the golden ratio ϕ and $(1 - \phi)$?
   a) 1   b) -1   c) ϕ d) Another answer

7. What is the geometric mean of 4 and 16?
   a) 8   b) 10   c) 12   d) Another answer

8. What is the geometric mean of 9 and 81?
   a) 27   b) 36   c) 45   d) Another answer

9. The geometric mean of 10 and 16 is
   a) 13.   b) less than 13.   c) more than 13.

10. The geometric mean of 25 and 45 is
    a) 35.   b) more than 35.   c) less than 35.

11. Which of these letters: S A E has a shape which is preserved by a reflection isometry?
    a) S only   b) A only   c) E only   d) A and E only

12. Which of these letters: S A E has a shape which is preserved by a rotation isometry?
    a) S only   b) A only   c) E only   d) A and E only

13. Assume the following patterns continue in both directions. Which of these patterns has a translation isometry?
AAAAAAAAA   ZZZZZZZZZ
a) AAAAAAAAA only
b) ZZZZZZZZZ only
c) Both AAAAAAAAA and ZZZZZZZZZ
d) Neither pattern

14. Assume the following patterns continue in both directions. Which of these patterns has a rotation isometry?
AAAAAAAAA   ZZZZZZZZZ
a) AAAAAAAAA only
b) ZZZZZZZZZ only
c) Both AAAAAAAAA and ZZZZZZZZZ
d) Neither pattern

15. Assume the following patterns continue in both directions. Which of these patterns has a reflection isometry?
AAAAAAAAA   ZZZZZZZZZ
a) AAAAAAAAA only
b) ZZZZZZZZZ only
c) Both AAAAAAAAA and ZZZZZZZZZ
d) Neither pattern

16. Assume the following patterns continue in both directions. Which of these patterns has a rotation isometry?

I PЬPЬPЬPЬ II ЭЄЭЄЭЄЭЄ

a) I only   b) II only   c) Both I and II   d) Neither pattern

17. Assume the following patterns continue in both directions. Which of these patterns has a translation isometry?

I PЬPЬPЬPЬ II ЭЄЭЄЭЄЭЄ

a) I only   b) II only   c) Both I and II   d) Neither pattern

18. Assume the following patterns continue in both directions. Which of these patterns has a reflection isometry?

I PЬPЬPЬPЬ II ЭЄЭЄЭЄЭЄ

a) I only   b) II only   c) Both I and II   d) Neither pattern

19. Assume the following patterns continue in both directions. Which of these patterns has a glide reflection isometry?

I PЬPЬPЬPЬ II AAAAAAAAA

a) I only   b) II only   c) Both I and II   d) Neither pattern

20. Assume the following pattern continues in both directions. What isometries preserve the pattern?

ᖇ Ψ ᖇ Ψ ᖇ Ψ ᖇ Ψ

a) Translation and rotation only
b) Translation and horizontal reflection only
c) Translation, rotation, and vertical reflection only
d) Translation, rotation, glide reflection, and vertical reflection only

21. Assume the following pattern continues in both directions. What isometries preserve the pattern?

⊓ ⊔ ⊓ ⊔ ⊓ ⊔ ⊓ ⊔

a) Translation and rotation only
b) Translation and vertical reflection only
c) Translation, rotation, and vertical reflection only
d) Translation, rotation, glide reflection, and vertical reflection only

22. Assume the following pattern continues in both directions. What isometries preserve the pattern?

Γ L Γ L Γ L Γ L

a) Translation only
b) Translation and horizontal reflection only
c) Translation and glide reflection only
d) Translation, glide reflection, and vertical reflection only

23. Assume the following pattern continues in both directions. What isometries preserve the pattern?

⊣ ⊣ ⊣ ⊣ ⊣ ⊣

a) Translation and rotation only
b) Translation and horizontal reflection only
c) Translation and glide reflection only
d) Translation, horizontal reflection, and vertical reflection only

24. Assume the following pattern continues in both directions. What isometries preserve the pattern?

⊔⊔ ⊓⊓ ⊔⊔ ⊓⊓ ⊔⊔ ⊓⊓

a) Translation only   c) Translation and rotation only

b) Translation and glide reflection only   d) Translation, glide reflection, and rotation only

25. Consider the following statement: "If three points are collinear, their images after an isometry are also collinear." This statement is
a) always true.   b) sometimes true, depending on the isometry.   c) never true.

26. Consider the following statement: "If three numbered points are placed in a circle so that they increase from smallest to largest in clockwise order, their images after an isometry will also lie on a circle and increase from smallest to largest in clockwise order." This statement is
a) always true.   b) sometimes true, depending on the isometry.   c) never true.

27. Consider the following statement: "If four points form the corners of a square, their images after an isometry will also form a square." This statement is
a) always true.   b) sometimes true, depending on the isometry.   c) never true.

28. Consider the following statement: "The image of a right-side print after an isometry is a left-side print." This statement is
a) always true.   b) sometimes true, depending on the isometry.   c) never true.

29. How many symmetry lines can a square have?
a) 2   b) 4   c) 8   d) Infinitely many

30. How many symmetry lines can a perfect five-point have?
a) 5   b) 10   c) 20   d) Infinitely many

31. How many symmetry lines can a non-square rectangle have?
a) None   b) Infinitely many   c) 2   d) 4

32. How many different strip patterns exist?
a) 4   b) 7   c) 17 d 24

33. How many different wallpaper patterns exist?
a) 7   b) 14   c) 17   d) 24

34. How many elements are in the symmetry group of a square?
a) 2   b) 3   c) 4   d) 8

35. How many elements are in the symmetry group of an equilateral triangle?
a) 3   b) 4   c) 6   d) 7

36. How many elements are in the symmetry group of a rectangle?
a) 2   b) 3   c) 4   d) 8

37. How many elements are in the symmetry group of a non-rectangle parallelogram?
a) 1   b) 2   c) 4   d) None

38. Assume the pattern continues in all directions. What are the isometries of the pattern?

a) Translations only
b) Translations and reflections only

c) Translations and rotations only
d) Translations, reflections, and rotations

39. Assume the pattern continues in all directions. What are the isometries of the pattern?

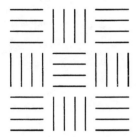

a) Translations only
b) Translations and reflections only

c) Translations and rotations only
d) Translations, reflections, and rotations

40. Assume the pattern continues in all directions. What are the isometries of the pattern?

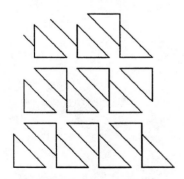

a) Translations only
b) Translations and reflections only

c) Translations and rotations only
d) Translations, reflections, and rotations

41. Assume the pattern continues in all directions. What are the isometries of the pattern?

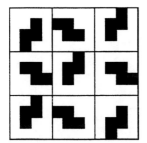

a) Translations only

b) Translations and reflections only

c) Translations and rotations only

d) Translations, reflections, and rotations

42. Assume the pattern continues in all directions. What are the isometries of the pattern?

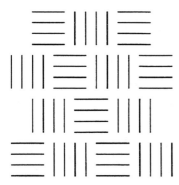

a) Translations only

b) Translations and reflections only

c) Translations and rotations only

d) Translations, reflections, and rotations

43. Suppose a wallpaper pattern has no rotations and no reflections, but has a glide reflection. Use the flowchart in the textbook to find the standard notation for the pattern.

a) pg   b) cm   c) pm   d) pgg

44. Suppose a wallpaper pattern whose smallest rotation is 90°, and has reflection lines which intersect at 90° angles.   Use the flowchart in the textbook to find the standard notation for the pattern.

a) p4m   b) p4g   c) p4   d) pmm

45. Suppose a wallpaper pattern with only a 180° rotation, and reflection lines which always intersect at a rotational center.   Use the flowchart in the textbook to find the standard notation for the pattern.

a) pmm   b) cmm   c) pmg   d) p2

46. Is it possible for a wallpaper pattern to have a translation and glide reflection isometries but no reflection isometry?

a) Yes   b) No

47. Is it possible for a wallpaper pattern to have translation, rotation, and glide reflection isometries, but no reflection isometry?

a) Yes   b) No

48. The symmetry group of a pattern always has
    I: the identity element.
    II: an even number of elements.
    a) I only   b) II only   c) I and II   d) Neither I nor II

49. If a figure has two reflection symmetries across perpendicular lines, it
    a) always has a rotation symmetry.   c) never has a rotation symmetry.
    b) sometimes has a rotation symmetry.

50. If a figure has translation symmetry and reflection symmetry across the translation line, it
    a) always has a glide reflection.   b) sometimes has a glide reflection.   c) never has a glide reflection.

Free-Response Questions

1. Starting with 1,1, determine the next five Fibonacci numbers.

2. Suppose a sequence begins 1, 4, and continues by adding the previous two numbers to determine the next number. Determine the next five numbers in this sequence.

3. Suppose a sequence begins 2, 1, and continues by adding the previous two numbers to determine the next number. Determine the next five numbers in this sequence.

4. Suppose a sequence begins 1, 4, and continues by adding the previous two numbers to determine the next number. What do the quotients of consecutive numbers drift toward?

5. Suppose a sequence begins 2, 1, and continues by adding the previous two numbers to determine the next number. What do the quotients of consecutive numbers drift toward?

6. Show that the difference between the golden mean ϕ and its reciprocal is 1.

7. How does the geometric mean of two numbers compare to their arithmetic mean?

8. Construct a rectangle with area 1 whose ratio of dimensions is the golden mean.

9. Draw a figure which has rotational symmetry but no reflectional symmetry.

10. Draw a figure which has reflectional symmetry but no rotational symmetry.

11. Draw a figure which has both reflectional and rotational symmetry.

12. Draw a strip pattern which has only translation and rotation symmetries.

13. Draw a strip pattern which has only translation and glide reflection symmetries.

14. Draw a strip pattern which has all possible symmetries.

15. Draw a wallpaper pattern which has only translation symmetries.

16. Draw a wallpaper pattern which has only translation and rotation symmetries.

17. Draw a wallpaper pattern which has only translation and reflection symmetries.

18. Draw a wallpaper pattern which has only translation and glide reflection symmetries.

19. Draw a wallpaper pattern which has translation, rotation, and reflection symmetries.

20. Identify the elements of the symmetry group of a square.

21. Identify the elements of the symmetry group of a non-equilateral isosceles triangle.

22. Why do imperfect patterns sometimes pose a challenge to the classification scheme?

23. How do pattern classification schemes aid anthropologists?

24. What are some of the isometries of a cube?

25. What are the isometries of a circle?

Chapter 21 Multiple-Choice Questions
Tilings

1. Which of the following polygons can tile the plane?
   I: Regular pentagon
   II: Regular hexagon
   a) I only   b) II only   c) Both I and II   d) Neither

2. Which of the following polygons can tile the plane?
   I: Regular octagon
   II: Non-rectangle parallelogram
   a) I only   b) II only   c) Both I and II   d) Neither

3. Which of the following polygons can tile the plane?
   I: Non-square rhombus
   II: Non-equilateral isosceles triangle
   a) I only   b) II only   c) Both I and II   d) Neither

4. Which of the following polygons can tile the plane?
   I: Scalene triangle
   II: Equilateral triangle
   a) I only   b) II only   c) Both I and II   d) Neither

5. The exterior angle of a regular hexagon has a measure of
   a) 18°   b) 30°   c) 45°   d) 60°

6. The exterior angle of a regular pentagon has a measure of
   a) 18°   b) 30°   c) 60°   d) 72°

7. The exterior angle of a regular octagon (8-gon) has a measure of
   a) 18°   b) 30°   c) 45°   d) 60°

8. The exterior angle of a regular decagon (10-gon) has a measure of
   a) 18°   b) 36°   c) 45°   d) 54°

9. Choose the correct word.
   . . . pentagons can form a tiling of the plane.
   a) All . . .   b) Some . . .   c) No . . .

10. Choose the correct word.
    . . . hexagons can form a tiling of the plane.
    a) All . . .   b) Some . . .   c) No . . .

11. Choose the correct word.
    . . . non-convex quadrilaterals can form a tiling of the plane.

a) All . . .   b) Some . . .   c) No . . .

12. Choose the correct word.
     . . . convex quadrilaterals can form a tiling of the plane.
     a) All . . .   b) Some . . .   c) No . . .

13. Semiregular tilings can tile with
     I: Three different regular polygons.
     II: Three different vertex combinations.
     a) I only   b) II only   c) Both I and II   d) Neither

14. Squares and equilateral triangles can form a tiling which has at every vertex
     a) three squares and two triangles.   c) one square and four triangles.
     b) two squares and three triangles.   d) one square and five triangles.

15. Regular hexagons and equilateral triangles can form a tiling of the plane which has at every vertex
     a) three hexagons and one triangle.   c) two hexagons and three triangles
     b) two hexagons and two triangles.   d) one hexagon and five triangles

16. Regular octagons and squares can form a tiling of the plane which has at every vertex
     a) two octagons and two squares.   c) one octagon and two squares.
     b) two octagons and one square.   d) one octagon and three squares.

17. Regular dodecagons (12-gons) and equilateral triangles can form a tiling of the plane which has at every vertex
     a) two dodecagons and two triangles.   c) one dodecagon and two triangles.
     b) two dodecagons and one triangle.   d) one dodecagon and three triangles.

18. A semiregular tiling has one equilateral triangle and two regular p-gons at each vertex. What is p?
     a) 8   b) 9   c) 10   d) 12

19. A semiregular tiling has one square, one regular hexagon, and one regular p-gon at each vertex. What is p?
     a) 8   b) 9   c) 10   d) 12

20. A semiregular tiling has two regular octagons and one regular p-gon at each vertex. What is p?
     a) 3   b) 4   c) 5   d) 6

21. A semiregular tiling has four equilateral triangles and one p-gon at each vertex. What is p?
     a) 3   b) 4   c) 5   d) 6

22. A semiregular tiling has one square and two regular p-gons at each vertex. What is p?
     a) 5   b) 6   c) 8   d) 10

23. A scalene triangle ABC tiles the plane. What is a possible configuration of the angles at the vertices?
     I: Three types of vertices: 6 As, or 6 Bs, or 6 Cs

I: One type of vertex: with 2As, 2 Bs, and 2Cs
a) I only   b) II only   c) Both I and II   d) Neither

24. A non-convex quadrilateral ABCD tiles the plane. What is a possible configuration of the angles at the vertices?
I: Two types of vertices: 2 As and 2 Cs; 2 Bs and 2 Ds
I: One type of vertex: with an A, B, C, D
a) I only   b) II only   c) Both I and II   d) Neither

25. Which of the following form the faces of a regular polyhedron?
I: Eight squares
II: Four equilateral triangles
a) I only   b) II only   c) Both I and II   d) Neither

26. Which of the following form the faces of a regular polyhedron?
I: Six equilateral triangles
II: Eight equilateral triangles
a) I only   b) II only   c) Both I and II   d) Neither

27. Which of the following form the faces of a regular polyhedron?
I: Six squares
II: Ten pentagons
a) I only   b) II only   c) Both I and II   d) Neither

28. A regular polyhedron with 12 faces has what regular polygon as faces?
a) Triangle   b) Square   c) Pentagon   d) Hexagon

29. A regular polyhedron with 20 faces has what regular polygon as faces?
a) Triangle   b) Square   c) Pentagon   d) Hexagon

30. A regular polyhedron with six faces has what regular polygon as faces?
a) Triangle   b) Square   c) Pentagon   d) Hexagon

31. What is a possible way to tile the plane with a right triangle?
I: Six at every vertex
II: Four or eight at every vertex
a) I only   b) II only   c) Both I and II   d) Neither

32. What is a possible way to tile the plane with a general isosceles triangle?
I: Six at a vertex
II: Four or eight at a vertex
a) I only   b) II only   c) Both I and II   d) Neither

33. What is a possible way to tile the plane with a parallelogram with 60° and 120° angles?
I: Four at a vertex
II: Three or six at a vertex

a) I only   b) II only   c) Both I and II   d) Neither

34. What is a possible way to tile the plane with a pentagon with three 90° angles and two equal obtuse angles?
I: Three at a vertex
II: Three or four at a vertex
a) I only   b) II only   c) Both I and II   d) Neither

35. What is a possible way to tile the plane with a pentagon with two 90° angles and three equal obtuse angles?
I: Three at a vertex
II: Three or four at a vertex
a) I only   b) II only   c) Both I and II   d) Neither

36. Can the tile below be used to tile the plane?

a) No.
b) Yes, with translations only.

c) Yes, with translations and half-turns only.
d) Yes, but reflections must be included.

37. Can the tile below be used to tile the plane?

a) No.
b) Yes, with translations only.

c) Yes, with translations and half-turns only.
d) Yes, but reflections must be included.

38. Can the tile below be used to tile the plane?

a) No.
b) Yes, with translations only.

c) Yes, with translations and half-turns only.
d) Yes, but reflections must be included.

39. Can the tile below be used to tile the plane?

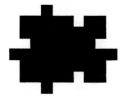

a) No.
b) Yes, with translations only.

c) Yes, with translations and half-turns only.
d) Yes, but reflections must be included.

40. Can the tile below be used to tile the plane?

a) No.
b) Yes, with translations only.

c) Yes, with translations and half-turns only.
d) Yes, but reflections must be included.

41. Penrose Tilings are non-periodic.
a) True   b) False

42. Portions of Penrose Tilings can have rotational symmetry.
a) True   b) False

43. Most Penrose Tilings require at least 10 differently shaped tiles.
a) True   b) False

44. Any finite portion of a Penrose Tiling can be found in another Penrose Tiling.
a) True   b) False

45. Escher No. 128 [*Bird*], Figure 21.10 in the textbook, tiles by
a) Translations only.
b) Translations and half-turns only.

c) Translations and reflections only.
d) Translations, half-turns, and reflections.

46. Escher No. 67 [*Horseman*], Figure 21.11a in the textbook, tiles by
a) Translations only.
b) Translations and half-turns only.

c) Translations and reflections only.
d) Translations, half-turns, and reflections.

47. Escher No. 6 [*Camel*], Figure 21.12 in the textbook, tiles by
a) Translations only.
b) Translations and half-turns only.

c) Translations and reflections only.
d) Translations, half-turns, and reflections.

48. Escher No. 88 [*Sea Horse*], Figure 21.13 in the textbook, tiles by
a) Translations only.
b) Translations and half-turns only.

c) Translations and reflections only.
d) Translations, half-turns, and reflections.

49. If you attempt to tile a non-Euclidean surface with eight triangles meeting at each vertex,
   a) you will find your efforts to be impossible.
   b) you will be tiling a surface with elliptic geometry.
   c) you will be tiling a surface with hyperbolic geometry.

50. If you attempt to tile a non-Euclidean surface with five squares meeting at each vertex,
   a) you will find your efforts to be impossible.
   b) you will be tiling a surface with elliptic geometry.
   c) you will be tiling a surface with hyperbolic geometry.

Free-Response Questions

1. Tile the plane with a scalene triangle.

2. Tile the plane with a non-square rhombus.

3. Tile the plane with a (tileable) pentagon.

4. Tile the plane with a (tileable) hexagon.

5. Create a non-regular tiling with a right triangle tile.

6. Create a non-regular tiling with pentagon.

7. Create a non-regular tiling with octagons and squares.

8. Create a tiling with a parallelogram. Is it regular?

9. Create a tiling with a non-convex quadrilateral. Is it regular?

10. Use the figure below to tile the plane, if possible.

11. Use the figure below to tile the plane, if possible.

12. Use the figure below to tile the plane, if possible.

13. Choose one of Marjorie Rice's pentagon tiles, and use it to tile the plane.

14. Why are regular pentagons not usable to tile the plane?

15. Why are regular octagons not useable to tile the plane?

16. Create a tiling of the plane using squares and hexagons, if possible.

17. Create a tiling of the plane using triangles and octagons, if possible.

18. Create an Escher-like tiling which uses only translations.

19. Create an Escher-like tiling which uses only translations and half-turns.

20. Create an Escher-like tiling which uses only translations and reflections.

21. Create an Escher-like tiling with uses translations, rotations, and reflections.

22. Why are Penrose tilings of interest to chemists?

23. If a tiling has only translations, how could it be classified in wallpaper pattern notation?

24. How can you "tile" three dimensions using cubes?

25. How can you "tile" three dimensions using non-cube solid "tiles?"

Chapter 1 Multiple-Choice Answers

1.	c	26.	d
2.	b	27.	c
3.	d	28.	b
4.	a	29.	a
5.	b	30.	b
6.	b	31.	c
7.	a	32.	d
8.	c	33.	d
9.	b	34.	b
10.	b	35.	c
11.	b	36.	d
12.	a	37.	b
13.	a	38.	c
14.	b	39.	b
15.	c	40.	d
16.	a	41.	b
17.	b	42.	c
18.	a	43.	c
19.	b	44.	d
20.	a	45.	c
21.	b	46.	a
22.	a	47.	a
23.	a	48.	b
24.	b	49.	a
25.	b	50.	d

1. If the valence of vertex A is four, it means there are four roads which lead to town A.
2. If the graph that represents 6 cities and the roads between them, is not connected, it means that it is not possible to travel between all cities. More specifically, it means at least one pair of cities has no connecting path of roads.
3.

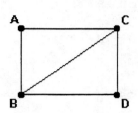

4.

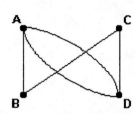

5.

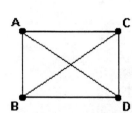

6. The path is not an Euler circuit because it does not start and stop at the same vertex.
7. The path is not an Euler circuit because it does not cover every edge of the graph.
8. Answers may vary. One solution is:

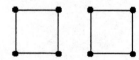

9. The graph does not have an Euler circuit because the valences of vertex B and vertex D are odd.
10. The graph does not have an Euler circuit because it is not connected.
11. Answers may vary. One solution is:

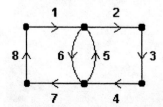

12. Answers may vary. One solution is:

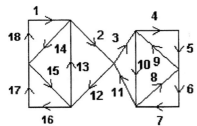

13. Answers may vary. One solution is:

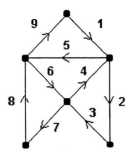

14. Answers may vary. One solution is:

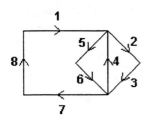

15. f1Answers may vary. One solution is:

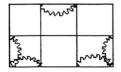

16. Answers may vary. One solution is:

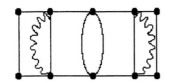

17. Answers may vary. One solution is:

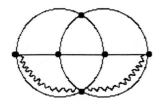

18. Answers may vary. One solution is:

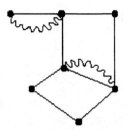

19.

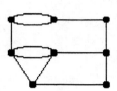

20.

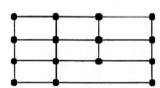

21. Answers may vary. One solution is:

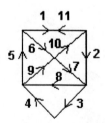

22. Answers may vary. One solution is:

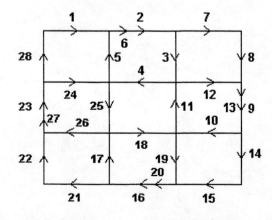

23. Answers may vary. One solution is:

24. If the snow plow operator followed an Euler circuit, he would end his route at the city garage where he started. Also, no time or gas would be wasted traveling down streets that were already plowed.

25. Answers may vary. Some situations include:
Plowing snow
Painting lines down the center of streets

Trash collection
Checking gutters on the corners of all streets
Checking parking meters along the edge of all streets
Delivering mail to all houses on all streets

1.	d	28.	a
2.	c	29.	b
3.	b	30.	a
4.	b	31.	a
5.	d	32.	b
6.	b	33.	a
7.	c	34.	b
8.	a	35.	a
9.	b	36.	c
10.	c	37.	b
11.	b	38.	b
12.	b	39.	c
13.	a	40.	b
14.	d	41.	a
15.	c	42.	b
16.	b	43.	c
17.	c	44.	a
18.	c	45.	b
19.	b	46.	c
20.	c	47.	b
21.	d	48.	c
22.	b	49.	c
23.	b	50.	b
24.	d	51.	a
25.	a	52.	c
26.	b	53.	a
27.	b		

1.

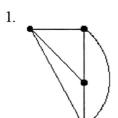

2.

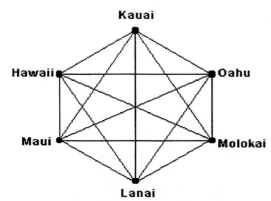

3.

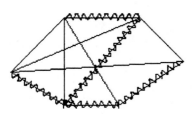

4.

5.

Permit ⟶ Foundation ⟶ Walls ⟶ Wiring ⟶ Final Inspection

⟶ Doghouse ⟶

6.

Slice bread ⟶ Mayo on bread ⟶ Meat and Cheese on bread ⟶ Cut Sandwich

Slice Meat ⟶

Slice Cheese ⟶

7.

Pack food ↘
　　　　　　Go to site ⟶ Unpack ⟶ Clean up
Pack chairs ↗
↗
Pack umbrella

8. Route ABCDA and ACBDA have cost 155. Route ABDCA has (minimum) cost 120.
9. Route PQRSP and PQSRP have (minimum) cost 1200. Route PRQSP has cost 1400.
10. Only one route, with cost 594.
11. $(11!/2)(1/2) = 9979200$ minutes, approximately 19 years.
12. $(9!/2)(1/3) = 60480$ minutes, or 42 days.
13. $(50)(49)/2 = 1225$
14. $(10)(9)/2 = 45$
15. 120
16. 93
17. $26^3 \, 10^3 = 17{,}576{,}000$
18. $26^4 \, 10^2 = 6{,}760{,}000$
19. Fast.
20. Not always optimal.
21. It requires the critical or essential amount of time required to complete the project.
22.

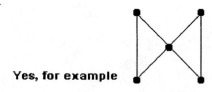

Yes, for example

23.

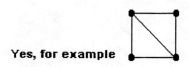

Yes, for example

24. Yes.
25. If it only picks up at central locations.
26. If it delivers to every house.

1.	c	27.	b
2.	d	28.	a
3.	b	29.	a
4.	b	30.	c
5.	c	31.	a
6.	c	32.	b
7.	d	33.	b
8.	b	34.	c
9.	b	35.	a
10.	c	36.	a
11.	c	37.	d
12.	d	38.	b
13.	d	39.	a
14.	c	40.	b
15.	c	41.	c
16.	a	42.	c
17.	a	43.	a
18.	c	44.	a
19.	b	45.	c
20.	c	46.	b
21.	a	47.	b
22.	a	48.	b
23.	a	49.	b
24.	b	50.	b
25.	c	51.	b
26.	d		

1. NF. One doesn't have to go back.
2. FF. One can pack as tightly as needed.
3. WF. There can be equal room in each box.
4. WF. This allows for some "error" or sawdust scraps.
5. FF. This keeps scraps large if possible.
6. 1
   2
   1 1 5 6
   5 7 4 3 2
7.   1
     1 4 1 6
   5 7 2 5 3 2
8. 1
   2
   1 1 5 6
   5 7 4 3 2
9.   1
       1
   2 3 4 2
   7 6 5 5 1
10.   1
        1
        2
       4 2
    7 6 5 5 3 1
11. 1 1
    2 2 4 3
    7 6 5 5 1
12.

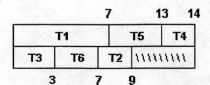

13.

14.

15.

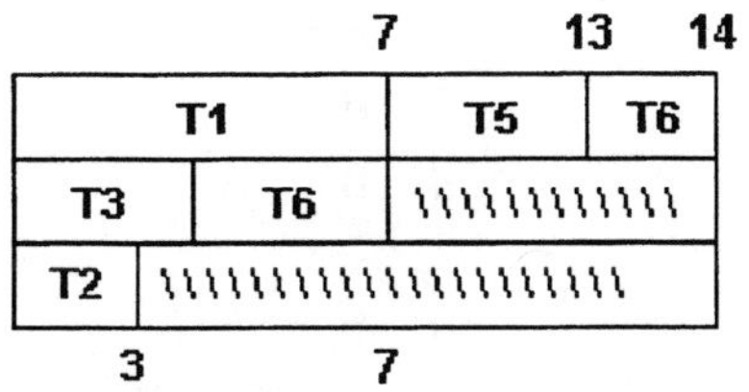

T1		T5	T6

T3	T6	\\\\\\\\\\\\\

T2	\\\\\\\\\\\\\\\\\\\\\\\

(markers above: 7, 13, 14; markers below: 3, 7)

16. 20 minutes
17. 32 minutes
18. For example,
    T1 (5) --> T3 (6) --> T4 (5)
                ^
                |
                |
    T2 (1) --> T5 (1) --> T6 (1)
19. For example,   T1 (3) --> T2 (3) --> T3 (4)
                   T4 (2) T5 (6) T2 (1)
20. For example, 6,6,6,6,6,6.
21. For example, when the capacity is 10 lbs. The weights are 7 lbs, 6 lbs, 5 lbs, and 5 lbs.
22. For example, when the capacity is 10 lbs. The weights are 7 lbs, 6 lbs, 5 lbs, and 5 lbs.
23. There are different situations and no best algorithm.
24. It produces good schedules because the bigger tasks are done early, allowing for smaller tasks to fill in the remaining time.
25. It completes "prerequisite" tasks early, but this is not always an optimal schedule.

1.	c	26.	b
2.	a	27.	d
3.	b	28.	b
4.	b	29.	c
5.	d	30.	b
6.	a	31.	d
7.	c	32.	a
8.	d	33.	c
9.	b	34.	d
10.	c	35.	a
11.	a	36.	c
12.	a	37.	c
13.	a	38.	a
14.	d	39.	c
15.	b	40.	b
16.	a	41.	b
17.	a	42.	d
18.	c	43.	a
19.	c	44.	a
20.	a	45.	b
21.	d	46.	a
22.	a	47.	b
23.	b	48.	b
24.	b	49.	b
25.	a	50.	a

1.

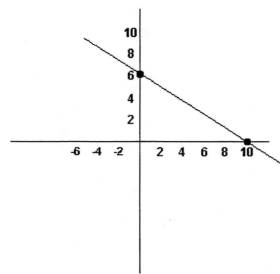

2.

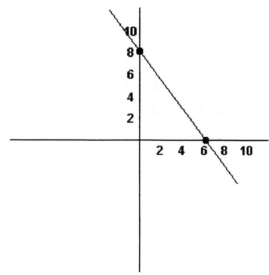

3.

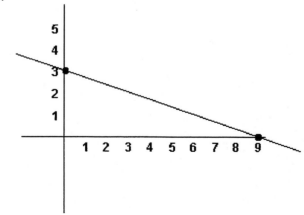

4.

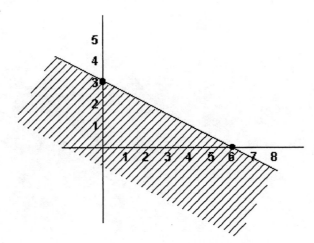

5.

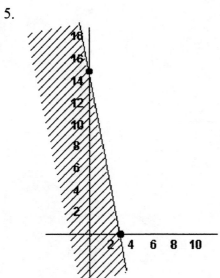

6.

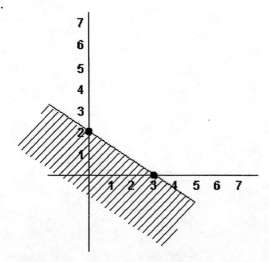

7. (4,1)
8. (3,5)

9. (2,4)
10. (6,7)
11.

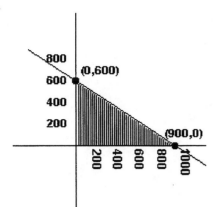

12.

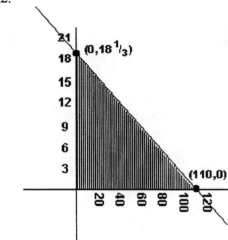

13.

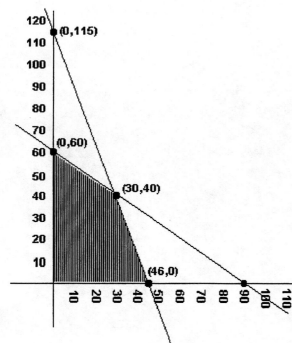

14.

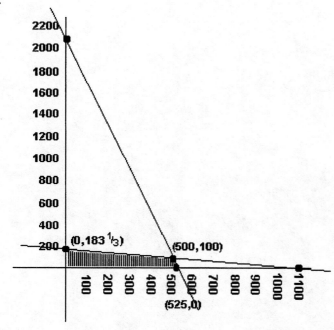

15.

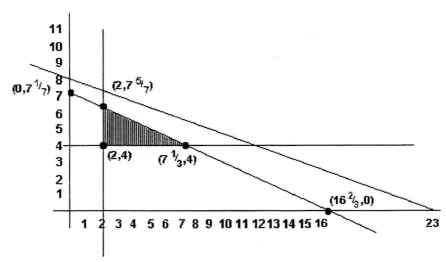

16. x is the number of wreaths produced and y is the number of table arrangements produced.

Constraint inequalities: $7x + 5y \le 30$
$$2x + 12y \le 100$$
$$x \ge 0$$
$$y \ge 0$$

Profit formula: $\qquad$ $23x + 26y = P$

17. x is the number of Plan A homes produced and y is the number of Plan B homes.

Constraint inequalities: $200x + 300y \le 900$
$$70x + 50y \le 260$$
$$x \ge 0$$
$$y \ge 0$$

Profit formula: $\qquad$ $P = 7000x + 8000y$

18. x is the number of regular sandwiches made and y is the number of special sandwiches made.

Constraint inequalities: $5x + 7y \le 350$
$$.7x + .6y \le 42$$
$$3x + 11y \le 330$$
$$x \ge 0$$
$$y \ge 0$$

Profit formula: $\qquad$ $P = 10x + 40y$

19. x is the number of cakes and y is the number of pies.

Constraint inequalities: $5x + 2y \le 165$
$$2x + 3y \le 110$$
$$1x + 4y \le 120$$

$$x \ge 5$$
$$y \ge 8$$

Profit formula: $P = 35x + 40y$

20. x is the number of vases and y is the number of bowls.

Constraint inequalities: $25x + 20y \leq 500$

$$5x + 10y \leq 160$$
$$x \geq 0$$
$$y \geq 0$$

Profit formula: $5x + 3y = P$

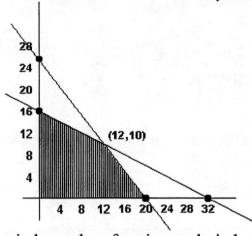

21. x is the number of receivers and y is the number of CD players.

Constraint inequalities: $8x + 15y \leq 160$

$$1x + 2y \leq 26$$
$$x \geq 0$$
$$y \geq 0$$

Profit formula: $P = 30x + 50y$

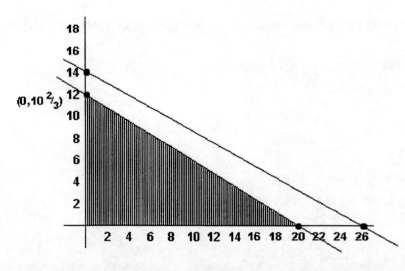

Maximum profit occurs at (20,0). Make 20 receivers and no CD players.

22.   If the optimal production policy for a linear programming problem is represented by a point on the x-axis, it means that profit is optimized by making only one type of product.

In order to maximize profit, the company needs to drop from its product line the item represented by the variable y.

23. A linear programming mixture problem with two products has a feasible region which is represented by a convex polygon in Quadrant I of the Cartesian plane.

24. Two alternatives to the graphical approach are the Simplex algorithm and Karmarkar's algorithm.

25. Answers may vary. A linear programming problem might have minimum constraints other than 0 if the company had standing orders for some number of its products which must be filled and cannot be canceled.

26. In a linear programming mixture problem, x and y represent the number of two different products to be made. Since it is impossible to produce negative numbers of products, the feasible region must be in Quadrant I.

1.	b	26.	a
2.	a	27.	d
3.	b	28.	a
4.	a	29.	c
5.	b	30.	b
6.	a	31.	a
7.	c	32.	b
8.	b	33.	d
9.	a	34.	c
10.	b	35.	c
11.	a	36.	a
12.	b	37.	b
13.	b	38.	a
14.	a	39.	b
15.	d	40.	b
16.	c	41.	b
17.	b	42.	a
18.	c	43.	d
19.	c	44.	a
20.	d	45.	a
21.	c	46.	b
22.	a	47.	b
23.	a	48.	d
24.	d	49.	a
25.	c	50.	c

1. The population is all registered voters in the state.
2. The population is all fish in the lake.
3. The students who are being surveyed are commuters who drive to campus and are likely to have different views on parking services than the general student body. This sampling technique would leave out the opinions of students living on campus or others without cars.
4. Convenience samples are drawn from individuals who are the most easily available and therefore they are unlikely to draw from all of the target population for a survey.
5. Variability refers to the natural differences in results that occur from one random sample of a population to the next. Variability in sampling results cannot be avoided, but the overall pattern of variability can be described. Bias in sampling results refers to a systematic error caused by poor sampling technique or a poorly worded survey.
6. Obtain a list of currently enrolled students from the university registrar. Number the list of students and then use a table of random digits to select 500 numbers corresponding to students on the enrollment list and contact these students.
7. The sampling technique described uses self-selection. Only those residents with extreme views on the new plan are likely to respond to the advertisement. A second problem with the poll technique described is that not all residents who will be affected by the new trash collection plan are likely to read the newspaper. The opinions of a large number of residents are therefore unlikely to be included in the results of the poll.
8. A simple random sample is one in which every group from the population has an equally likely chance of being chosen.
9. We can not eliminate variability in the results of sampling. Variability refers to the natural differences that occur from one sample to the next in a population.
10. Those chosen would be: 02 Brown, 10 Jones, 17 Quayle, and 19 Stevens.
11. We can number the names on the roster using the labels 00, 01, 02, 03, . . . 96, 97, 98, 99. This list includes 100 distinct labels. (Using this list instead of 001, 002, . . . 098, 099, 100 would result in a more efficient use of the random digits table. Every 2-digit portion read from the table would refer to a name on the roster where only 1/10 of the 3-digit portions would be useable)
12. Answers may vary. First, the Marketing Department would break the state up into many contiguous areas, possibly using county borders. They would randomly select several of these counties. Each county selected would be broken up into smaller regions, perhaps neighborhoods. Several neighborhoods in each selected county would be randomly chosen. Within each chosen neighborhood, several individual families would be randomly chosen to be surveyed.
13. Taking every 25th name from an alphabetical listing of students is not a valid simple random sampling technique since no two students who follow one another on the list could ever be part of the sample. This contradicts the idea that in a simple random sample, every collection of individuals has an equal chance of being chosen.
14. 480/2500 = 19.2%
    The sample proportion of residents in favor of naming the grasshopper State Insect is 19.2%.
15. 950/1500 = 63.3%
    The sample proportion of the survey of shoppers who would visit a store more frequently if it were open Sunday evenings is 63.3%.
16. The results of an opinion poll are unlikely to match exactly the views of the whole population. Instead, those reporting poll results can be confident that the actual population results fall in an interval around the poll results. The margin of error defines the size of this interval.

17. An observational study observes individuals and measures some variable of interest, but does not try to change the behavior or conditions of the subjects. In an experiment, the researcher imposes some treatment or condition on some of the individuals in the study and then observes their response.

18. Answers may vary. In the four months since the curfew began, school would also have started. It is possible that teens are now home doing homework after dark and would have been even without the curfew. It is also possible that the cooler temperatures associated with fall months led to a decline in teens in the square after dark.

19. Answers may vary. The farmer randomly divides his chickens into two groups. Keeping all other conditions (housing, food, etc.) the same, he plays classical music to one randomly-chosen group. The other group of chickens will be in a coop without music. After two months, the egg production of the two groups of chickens will be compared.

20. Answers may vary. Children in the district will be divided randomly into two groups. This random division will, hopefully, minimize differences between the groups on IQ, parental education level, or other factors the superintendent believes may have an impact on children's test scores. One group is chosen to receive the new approach to reading instruction. The other group is taught reading using traditional methods. (It would be best if the same teacher taught both groups, changing only the instruction method.) The standardized test scores of the two groups are compared at the end of the year.

21. The meeting of parents, teachers, and students may have brought to the attention of parents problems associated with absenteeism in the school. Parents may have reacted with measures to increase their children's attendance in ways unrelated to the experimental program.

22. In a double blind experiment, neither the participant nor the person collecting the data knows who is taking the experimental treatment and who is taking the placebo. This is done so that when participants report on their health they are not swayed in their own assessments by the thought of being on an experimental treatment. Also, recorders will not unconsciously exaggerate participants conditions since they do not know which treatment participants are receiving. Running a study as double blind helps to combat the placebo effect.

23. The placebo effect refers to the effects of a dummy treatment on the subjects of a study. People who believe they are receiving an experimental treatment designed to make them perform better, may actually have a better performance do to the power of suggestion, regardless of the actual effectiveness of the treatment.

24. In a randomized-comparative experiment, subjects are randomly divided into two groups, one of which receives the experimental treatment and the other the traditional treatment. Since the two groups are chosen at random, any possible confounding variables should act equally on both groups. This allows differences in outcomes to more confidently be attributed to the treatment.

25. The results of an experiment are called "statistically significant" if they are greater than one would expect to occur by chance from a group drawn at random from the population of the study.

1.	b	26.	c
2.	c	27.	b
3.	c	28.	a
4.	a	29.	b
5.	b	30.	a
6.	b	31.	b
7.	d	32.	b
8.	c	33.	c
9.	b	34.	d
10.	c	35.	b
11.	c	36.	b
12.	a	37.	c
13.	c	38.	b
14.	d	39.	a
15.	c	40.	b
16.	c	41.	c
17.	a	42.	a
18.	d	43.	c
19.	a	44.	b
20.	b	45.	c
21.	d	46.	a
22.	b	47.	b
23.	a	48.	b
24.	c	49.	b
25.	a	50.	b

1.

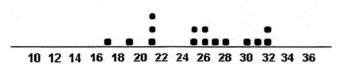

2.

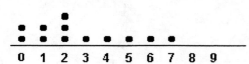

3.

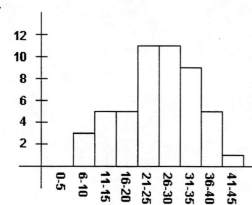

The distribution is not quite symmetric.

4.

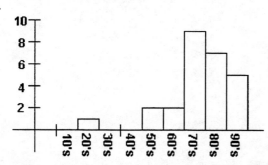

5. The median score is 73.
6. The median income is $25,000.
7. The mean is 27.56.
8. The mean age is 14.11 years.
9. The first quartile is 13 years. The third quartile is 16 years.
10. The five number summary is: 37, 58, 73, 81.5, 98.
11. The five number summary is: 1, 2, 9, 15, 18.
12.

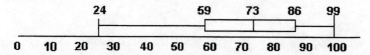

13.

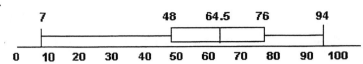

14. The variance is 1269.33.

15. The variance is 40.

16. In town A, the mean income is $30,000 and almost all residents earn between $20,000 and $40,000. The standard deviation of $2600 says incomes do not vary much among residents of the town. In town B, since the standard deviation is $25,000 we know that there are very poor residents and very rich residents even though the mean income is also $30,000.

17. The standard deviation is 6.32.

18. The standard deviation is 6.23.

19.

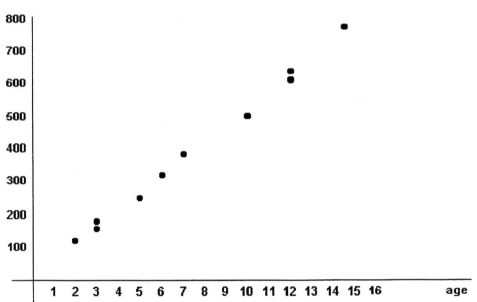

20.

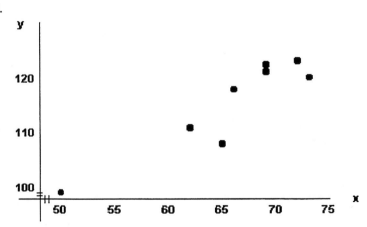

21. Yes, the advertisement could be true. The presence of a car or cars with a sale price of $200 (the outlier(s) on the histogram) could lower the mean sale price to $12,000.

22. Since the distribution is skewed, the five-number summary would be the better choice to describe the data shown in the histogram.

23. The least squares regression line would not be useful to describe the relationship between the variables. While there does appear to be a strong relationship between the variables, the relationship does not appear to be linear.
24. The missing number must be 4.
25. Answers may vary. Any value greater than 8 would be correct.

1.	d	26.	a
2.	c	27.	a
3.	a	28.	c
4.	c	29.	a
5.	c	30.	d
6.	c	31.	b
7.	a	32.	b
8.	b	33.	c
9.	b	34.	a
10.	a	35.	c
11.	a	36.	b
12.	b	37.	d
13.	d	38.	d
14.	c	39.	c
15.	a	40.	d
16.	c	41.	a
17.	d	42.	a
18.	a	43.	c
19.	b	44.	c
20.	d	45.	a
21.	d	46.	b
22.	c	47.	d
23.	a	48.	c
24.	b	49.	d
25.	b	50.	b

1. { (1,H), (2,H), (3,H), (4,H), (1,T), (2,T), (3,T), (4,T) }
2. { HHH, HHT, HTH, THH, HTT, THT, TTH, TTT }
3. Sam counts 36 outcomes in the sample space by observing the number rolled on each die. Sally counts 11 outcomes by observing the sum rolled on the die.
4. The probability Toni wins is 0.1.
5. The probability Kerry does not get an A is 0.18.
6. The probability of getting exactly 2 heads is 3/8 or 0.375.
7. The probability of rolling a sum greater than 9 is 6/36 or 0.167.
8. Answers may vary. Any spinner face which shows half the face labeled "1" is correct.
9. The probability of drawing a three or a heart is 16/52 or 0.308.
10. 650,000
11. 210
12. 6500/650,000 = 1/100 = 0.01
13. 30/210 = 1/7 = 0.143
14. 1/32 = 0.03125
15. The mean number of automobiles owned is 1.6.
16. The mean value of one trial is $0.60.
17. The mean value gives the win or loss after a very large number of trials. In this case, a player would lose an average of 5 cents for each trial.
18. The middle 50% of all scores lie between 433 and 567.
19. Jane must study more than 25.238 hours.
20. 50
21. 0.16
22. 99.7%
23. 95% of all diameters will be between 4.996 and 5.004 mm.
24. 0.000447
25. 225 pages

1.	c		26.	d
2.	a		27.	b
3.	d		28.	b
4.	d		29.	c
5.	c		30.	d
6.	b		31.	c
7.	b		32.	c
8.	a		33.	b
9.	b		34.	b
10.	b		35.	c
11.	b		36.	a
12.	d		37.	d
13.	d		38.	d
14.	d		39.	b
15.	c		40.	d
16.	c		41.	a
17.	c		42.	a
18.	a		43.	a
19.	d		44.	a
20.	a		45.	a
21.	c		46.	d
22.	c		47.	b
23.	d		48.	a
24.	c		49.	d
25.	b		50.	a

Chapter 8 Free-Response Answers

1. 55% is a statistic since it is a value found from a sample, not the entire population.
2. 49.8 g is the value from the sample so it is the statistic. 50g is the mean of the whole population so it is the parameter.
3. 13% is probably a statistic. It is unlikely that every voter in the nation was surveyed, so the value of 13% is likely based on a sample of voters.
4. 1980/2500 = .792 or 79.2%
5. 200 + 1300 = 1500 students surveyed.   200/1500 = .133 or 13.3%
6. proportion = 1100/1500 = .733

The standard deviation is $\sqrt{\dfrac{(73.3)(26.7)}{1500}} = 1.14$

7. The standard deviation is $\sqrt{\dfrac{(27)(73)}{500}} = 1.99$

8. $2.5 = \sqrt{\dfrac{(65)(35)}{n}}$

So, $n \cdot (2.5)^2 = 2275$ and n = 364

Three hundred and sixty four shoppers should be surveyed for the standard deviation of the sampling distribution to be about 2.5%.
9. No. If the staff surveys 2000 voters, and the level of support is 60%, the standard deviation of the sampling distribution would be only 1.1%. This means that a sample proportion of 40% is very unlikely.
10. The standard deviation of the sampling distribution for this mean is $.03/\sqrt{25} = .006$ inches.
11. The sample size, n, must satisfy $.0008 = .004/\sqrt{n}$, so n must be 25.
12. While it is true that the confidence level of the reported results of a survey can depend on the sample size, these values are not directly proportional to one another. Doubling the sample size for a poll has the effect of decreasing by a factor of $\sqrt{2}$, or about 1.414, the standard deviation of the sampling distribution. If results are to be reported with the same margin of error, this would allow for an increase in the level of confidence, but not close to a doubling of confidence.
13. A 96% confidence interval for the proportion who favor the candidate's stand on gun control is 78.5 ± 1.3%
14. Since $2\sigma = 2\%$, the standard deviation must be 1% so a 99.7% confidence interval would be 70 ± 3%.
15. A 95% confidence interval for the proportion of residents in favor of the budget cutting plan is 85 ± 1.6%.
16. .01 inches
17. Increasing the sample size from 25 to 100 would cut in half the standard deviation of the sampling distribution of the mean length of the wires.
18. 4.23 ± .02 inches
19. The store is asking the polling company to reduce the margin of error, and hence the standard deviation of the sampling distribution by a factor of 3. The polling company can do this by surveying 9 times as many shoppers.
20. 95% control limits would be 1.5 ± .0016 inches.
21. 95% control limits would be 1.5 ± .0016 inches or 1.4984 inches to 1.5016 inches. A sample mean of 1.4998 inches falls within these control limits.

22. By using a process control chart and sampling 25 parts each hour, the company can maintain a very high level of confidence about the mean diameter of parts produced without the time or expense necessary to evaluate every part produced.

23. 25/30 = 83.3% of 10-year-olds make first team for soccer.

24. 38/152 = 25% of all children enrolled for baseball make first team.

25.

	10-year-olds	11-year-olds
1st team	55	108
2nd team	125	52

When combined, it appears that 11-year-olds make first teams at a significantly higher rate than do 10-year-olds. For each individual sport, the same percentage of each age group will make first team, but larger numbers

1.	a	26.	b
2.	c	27.	b
3.	a	28.	a
4.	b	29.	b
5.	a	30.	a
6.	c	31.	d
7.	c	32.	d
8.	a	33.	a
9.	a	34.	b
10.	a	35.	b
11.	b	36.	c
12.	a	37.	b
13.	b	38.	a
14.	b	39.	a
15.	d	40.	b
16.	b	41.	a
17.	a	42.	b
18.	b	43.	c
19.	a	44.	b
20.	a	45.	b
21.	b	46.	c
22.	b	47.	a
23.	c	48.	a
24.	d	49.	b
25.	c	50.	a

1. Yes. All single errors except exchange of 0 and 9 are detected.
2. Not always. If it is replaced by 9, the error is undetected.
3. Yes. The check digit will detect the error.
4. Yes. It is the check digit and will be wrong.
5. Should be 8.
6. Yes. The sum will not be correct.
7. No. It is 5.
8. Yes. The sum will be incorrect.
9. Yes. The change affects the sum.
10. No. Final digit should be 6.
11. Yes.
12. Yes. The sum will no longer be a multiple of 11.
13. Yes. The sum will be incorrect.
14. No. Exchanges are not detected.
15. Yes. The sum will be incorrect.
16. It requires the use of "X".
17. There are different requirements and different costs for error in various codes.
18. Used on letters to automate address routing.
19. End marks to frame Postnet code.
20. For example, credit cards.
21. No. Theum will be unchanged.
22. Yes. Digits have different weights.
23. Yes. Digits have different weights.
24. Yes.
25. No. Change to 0.

1.	c	26.	a
2.	b	27.	b
3.	a	28.	b
4.	b	29.	b
5.	b	30.	b
6.	a	31.	b
7.	d	32.	b
8.	b	33.	b
9.	a	34.	b
10.	b	35.	c
11.	a	36.	d
12.	c	37.	b
13.	c	38.	d
14.	d	39.	d
15.	c	40.	c
16.	c	41.	b
17.	c	42.	a
18.	b	43.	d
19.	b	44.	d
20.	b	45.	d
21.	c	46.	d
22.	c	47.	b
23.	a	48.	b
24.	a	49.	c
25.	a	50.	c

Chapter 10 Free-Response Answers

1. Detects all singles, doesn't correct all.
2. Detects all singles, doesn't correct all.
3. Yes. Weight is 3.
4. Yes. Weight is 4.
5. Detects all single errors, doesn't correct all. Does not detect all double digit errors.
6. For example, $c_1 = a_1 + a_2$; $c_2 = a_2 + a_3$; $c_3 = a_3 + a_4$; $c_4 = a_4 + a_5$. Detects all singles, doesn't correct all.
7. For example, $c_1 = a_1 + a_2 + a_3$; $c_2 = a_2 + a_3 + a_4$; $c_3 = a_3 + a_4 + a_5$. Detects all singles, doesn't correct all.
8. For example, {111000000, 000111000, 000000111, 111000111, 111111000, 000111111, 111111111, 000000000}.
9. For example, {11111111, 11110000, 00001111, 00000000}.
10. It detects and corrects all single and double errors.
11. DEDQGRQ KRSH
12. ALL IS WELL
13. If a code has weight t, then t-1 errors can be detected.
14. If a code has weight t, then if t is even, (t-2)/2 errors can be corrected; if t is odd, (t-1)/2 errors can be corrected.
15. 1
16. 4
17. 45
18. 13
19. 2
20. 6
21. For example, choose r = 3. Then 23^3 mod 55 is 12.
22. As above, if r = 3 and m = 20, s = 7. So 7^7 mod 55 is 28.
23. For example, if r = 7, then 13^7 mod 391 is 55.
24. If r = 7 and m = 176, then s = 25. So 7^{25} mod 391 is 44.
25. It is a public key scheme that is effectively impossible to break.

1.	a	26.	b
2.	b	27.	d
3.	b	28.	d
4.	a	29.	d
5.	a	30.	a
6.	b	31.	b
7.	a	32.	b
8.	b	33.	c
9.	c	34.	c
10.	d	35.	b
11.	b	36.	a
12.	d	37.	b
13.	c	38.	a
14.	c	39.	b
15.	c	40.	a
16.	c	41.	a
17.	c	42.	a
18.	a	43.	d
19.	a	44.	d
20.	b	45.	c
21.	b	46.	a
22.	a	47.	b
23.	b	48.	b
24.	c	49.	b
25.	b	50.	c

Chapter 11 Free-Response Answers

1. Majority rule is not a good way to choose among four alternatives because it is possible that none of the four will get a majority of the vote.
2. For any voting system it is possible to find a set of voter's preferences that will cause the voting system to violate a condition deemed desirable for a fair voting system. These conditions may include the Condorcet Winner Criterion and the Independence of Irrelevant Alternatives condition.
3. A voting system satisfies the Condorcet Winner Criterion if the winner of an election is also the Condorcet winner, if a Condorcet winner exists.
4. Sincere voting means submitting a ballot that reflects the voter's true preferences. Strategic voting means submitting a ballot that does not reflect the voter's true preferences but will lead to an outcome the voter likes better than would occur if the voter voted sincerely.
5. Six candidates can be ranked in 720 ways if ties are not allowed.
6. Only Sequential Pairwise voting satisfies the Condorcet Winner Criterion.
7. Plurality, the Borda count, and the Hare system all satisfy the Pareto condition.
8. Plurality, the Borda count, and Sequential Pairwise voting all satisfy monotonicity.
9. Rock is the Condorcet winner.
10. There is no majority-rule winner.
11. B wins in a straight plurality vote.
12. A wins.
13. A wins.
14. No. They cannot make B win the election and if they switch any rankings to place C higher, then C would win and this is their least desirable outcome.
15. North Carolina wins with 51 points.
16. Yes. If these four voters ranked candidate T first, T would win with 7 votes. Since the voters prefer T to R, this outcome would be more desirable.
17. S wins.
18. D wins.
19. B wins.
20. B wins with 51 points.
21. With the given rank system, candidate B wins. Under a Borda Count, candidate B also wins.
22. No. They do not have enough votes to make C win under any possible ranking. Their second choice is B, who is the winner.
23. No. The six voters who most prefer applicant K represent a majority of the committee. No matter how the three voters rank the applicants, K will win.
24. Applicant K is chosen.
25. Three candidates can be ranked in 13 ways if ties are allowed.

1.	b	26.	b
2.	c	27.	b
3.	c	28.	c
4.	a	29.	b
5.	c	30.	c
6.	c	31.	b
7.	d	32.	c
8.	a	33.	d
9.	b	34.	a
10.	b	35.	b
11.	b	36.	c
12.	a	37.	b
13.	a	38.	a
14.	d	39.	d
15.	b	40.	b
16.	c	41.	d
17.	c	42.	a
18.	d	43.	b
19.	c	44.	b
20.	b	45.	a
21.	a	46.	d
22.	a	47.	a
23.	b	48.	b
24.	d	49.	d
25.	d	50.	a

Chapter 12 Free-Response Answers

1. Answers may vary. One solution is [q: w(A), w(B), w(C)] = [9: 6, 5, 2]
2. The system given is not a legitimate weighted voting system since the quota is exactly half of the total vote weight. Two different complementary coalitions exist with vote weight total of 13, (A, D), and (B, C, E).
3. Answers may vary. One solution is: In the system [q: w(A), w(B), w(C), w(D), w(E)] = [14: 10, 6, 5, 3, 2], the coalition (A, D) is a blocking coalition since (B, C, E) has only 13 votes. (A, D) would not be a winning coalition by voting "yes" since (A, D) has only 13 votes.
4. (A, D) (A, C) (B, C, D) (A, B, C) (A, B, D) (A, C, D) (A, B, C, D)
5. (A, B) (A, C) (A, B, C) (A, B, D) (A, C, D) (A, D) (B, C) (B, C, D) (A, B, C, D)
6. (A, B) (A, C) (B, C, D)
7. (A, B) (A, C) (B, C, D)
8. (A, B) (A, C) (A, B, C) (A, B, D) (A, C, D) (B, C, D) (A, B, C, D) (A, D) (B, C)
9. There are 16 coalitions of 4 voters:
   Ø, (A) (B) (C) (D) (A, B) (A, C) (A, D) (B, C) (B, D) (C, D) (A, B, C) (A, B, D) (A, C, D) (B, C, D) (A, B, C, D)
10. No. A voter with veto power has enough votes to block any measure, but not necessarily enough to pass any issue. A dictator has enough votes to pass any issue on his or her own.
11. 10
12. 792
13. (6, 2, 2)
14. (10, 6, 6, 2)
15. (32, 20, 20, 20, 20, 20)
16. The Banzhaf power index of any dummy voter is 0.
17. Answers may vary. One solution is: [q: w(A), w(B), w(C)] = [15: 10, 8, 6]
18. Answers may vary. One solution is: [q: w(A), w(B), w(C)] = [32: 20, 15, 10]
19. Yes, A is a critical voter. Without A, the coalition becomes (B, C) which has only 11 votes; no longer enough to win.
20. A critical voter in a winning or blocking coalition is any voter who has sufficient weight so that the coalition would no longer be winning or blocking the remaining vote. The order of voters in the coalition does not matter. There can be more than one critical voter in a coalition. A pivotal voter is the first voter who joins a coalition and gives that coalition enough votes to win. Each permutation has exactly one pivotal voter.
21. $C = \dfrac{8*7*6}{3*2*1} = 56$
22. (5/12, 1/4, 1/4, 1/12)
23. (2/3, 1/15, 1/15, 1/15, 1/15, 1/15)
24. Answers may vary. One example of each of the five distinct voting systems is:
    [3: 3, 1, 1]
    [4: 2, 2, 1]
    [2: 1, 1, 1]
    [3: 2, 1, 1]
    [3: 1, 1, 1]
25. Answers may vary. One solution is: [q: w(C), w(V), w(M_1), w(M_2), w(M_3)] = [7: 3, 3, 2, 2, 2]

1.	b	26.	a
2.	a	27.	c
3.	c	28.	d
4.	a	29.	d
5.	d	30.	a
6.	a	31.	d
7.	c	32.	c
8.	b	33.	b
9.	d	34.	a
10.	b	35.	a
11.	b	36.	c
12.	d	37.	b
13.	c	38.	c
14.	a	39.	a
15.	a	40.	b
16.	d	41.	c
17.	a	42.	d
18.	c	43.	c
19.	c	44.	b
20.	a	45.	a
21.	b	46.	c
22.	c	47.	a
23.	d	48.	a
24.	c	49.	c
25.	b	50.	b

1. Alex gets the textbooks, the barbells, the desk, and 16/21 of the novels. Bob gets the rest.
2. Management gets its way with regard to incentive pay, opportunity for promotion, and employee accountability, and 60% of its way on the issue of the retirement package. Labor gets its way on the rest of the issues.
3. The husband gets the house, the boat, the television, the stereo, and 20% use of the car. The wife gets the cabin and 80% use of the car.
4. The administration gets its way on the mandatory meal plan, and 11/12 of its way with regard to weekday fraternity parties. The student body gets its way on the rest of the issues.
5. Henry receives the house and gives Lisa $62,250.
6. The first person receives the painting and gives the second person $5,577.50.
7. John receives the painting and pays $15,600. Ken receives $8,400 and Linda receives $7,200.
8. Yes. Her bid should be just slightly lower than John's and higher than Ken's. Her new bid is $25,194.
9. The first child receives the farm and pays $11,250. The second child receives the house and pays $62,500. The third child receives $57,500 and the fourth child receives the piece of property and $16,250.
10. The first person receives objects A and B and pays $8,025. The second person receives object C and pays $250. The third person receives $4,175 and the fourth person receives $4,100.
11. Bob makes a vertical cut in the middle of the fourth column. Carol chooses the piece on the left. Bob thinks he gets 8 square units of value. Carol thinks she gets 8.5 square units of value.
12. Bob will like the results better if he is the chooser. If he is the divider, he will divide the cake into two pieces he thinks are both worth 8 units and so the piece he is left with is worth 8 units in his mind. If Carol divides, Bob can choose a piece Carol thinks is worth 8 units but Bob believes is worth 10 units.
13.   If Bob cuts, he makes a vertical cut between the fourth and fifth column. Carol chooses the piece on the right. Bob thinks he gets 8 square units of value. Carol thinks she gets 12 square units of value.
            If Carol cuts, she makes a vertical cut two-thirds of the way across the fifth column. Bob chooses the piece on the left. Carol thinks she gets 8 square units of value. Bob thinks he gets 10 square units of value.
14. Bob makes a vertical cut almost two-thirds of the way across the fifth column. Carol chooses the piece on the right. Bob thinks he gets almost 10 square units of value. Carol thinks she gets slightly more than 8 square units of value.
15.

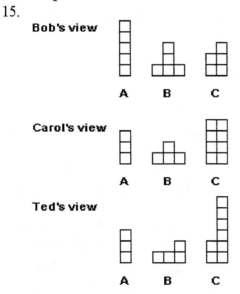

16.

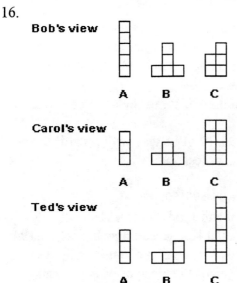

Carol approves of only piece C, and Ted approves of only piece C. Thus, Bob is the only one to approve of piece A. Bob is given piece A. Carol and Ted use divide-and-choose on pieces B and C recombined. If Carol is the divider, she makes a vertical cut in the middle of the fifth column. Ted chooses the piece on the right. Bob thinks he gets 5 square units of value. Carol thinks she gets 6 square units of value. Ted thinks he gets 7 square units of value.

17. Bob makes a vertical cut between the second and third column. The piece made up of the first and second columns is, in Bob's eyes, 4 out of the 16 units of value, and thus one-fourth of the cake.

  Carol sees this piece as 7 out of 16 square units of value, so she trims it by making a vertical cut between the first and second column. The piece made up of column one is, in Carol's eyes, one-fourth of the cake.

  Ted passes, as does Alice, because they both think column one represents no more than one-fourth of the cake.

  Carol takes this piece (column one) and exits the game.

  Bob now makes a vertical cut between column three and four. The piece made up of column two and three is, in Bob's eyes, 4 square units of value.

  Ted passes, as does Alice, because both think the piece represents no more than one-fourth of the cake.

  Bob takes this piece, column two and three, and exits the game.

  Ted and Alice now use divide-and-choose on the rest of the cake (the fourth, fifth, and sixth columns).

  Ted, as divider, makes a vertical cut between the fifth and sixth column.

  Alice chooses the piece made up of columns four and five (she thinks there are seven square units of value).

  Ted receives the piece made up of column six (he thinks there are 5 square units of value).

18. Alice makes a vertical cut between the fourth and fifth column. The piece made up of the first four columns is, in Alice's eyes, 4 out of 16 square units of value, and thus is one-fourth of the cake.

  Ted sees this piece as 8 out of 16 units of value, so he trims it by making a vertical cut between the first and second column. The piece made up of column one is, in Ted's eyes, one-fourth of the cake.

  Carol passes, as does Bob, because they both think column one represents no more than one-fourth of the cake.

  Ted takes this piece (column one) and exits the game.

Alice now makes a vertical cut one-sixth of the way across column five. The piece made up of columns two, three, four, and one-sixth of column five is, in Alice's eyes, 4 square units of value.

Carol sees this piece as 5.5 out of 16 square units of value, so she trims it by making a vertical cut between the third and fourth column. The piece made up of columns two and three is, in Carol's eyes, one-fourth of the cake.

Bob passes because he thinks this piece represents no more than one-fourth of the cake.

Carol takes this piece (columns two and three) and exits the game.

Alice and Bob now use divide-and-choose on the rest of the cake (the fourth, fifth, and sixth columns).

Alice, as divider, makes a vertical cut 11/12 of the way across the fifth column.

Bob chooses the piece on the right (1/12 of column five plus column six).

Alice receives the piece on the left (column four plus 11/12 of column five).

19.   Player 1 cuts between the third and fourth column, viewing the piece made of column one, two, and three as worth 5 square units of value and so one-third of the cake.

Player 2 views the piece made of the first three columns as worth 7 square units of value and so trims between the first and second column. The piece made up of the first column is, in Player 2's eyes, worth one-third of the cake.

Player 3 views this as worth no more than one-third of the cake and so passes.

Player 2 receives the piece made up of column one and exits the game.

Player 1 and Player 3 now use divide-and-choose on the remainder of the cake (columns two through six).

Player 1 cuts the cake half way through the fifth column. Player 3 chooses the part made of columns two, three, four, and half of five, for a total (in Player 3's eyes) of 8 square units of value. Player 1 is left with the portion made of half of column 5 and column six for a total, in Player 1's eyes, of 6 square units of value.

20. a)

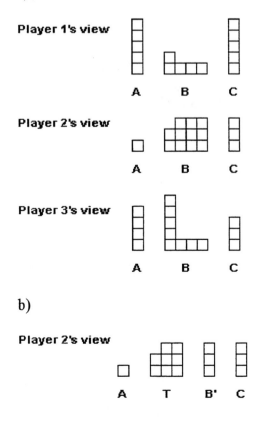

b)

Player 2's view

c) Player 3 will choose A (which he thinks is worth 4 square units).
Player 2 will choose B (which he thinks is worth 3 square units).
Player 1 will receive C (which he thinks is worth 5 square units).

21. a)

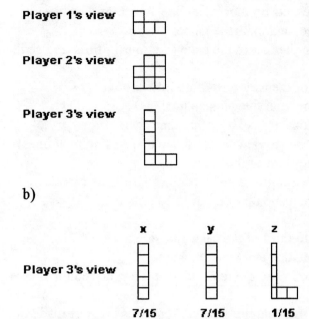

b)

c) Player 2 chooses first and will take Z. Player 1 chooses next and takes either X or Y (he considers them equal). Player 3 receives the remaining piece.

22. Chris gets the stereo and pays Terry $158.33.

23. Ariel gets $3862.50.
Binky gets the painting and pays $3918.75.
Chris gets the sculpture and $56.25.

24. Divide-and-choose is envy free because the divider believes both pieces are of equal worth and the chooser gets to pick a piece he believes is worth at least half.

25. Tom divides the yard in the middle of the third column. Jerry chooses the left side to rake.

1.	a	26.	c
2.	b	27.	a
3.	b	28.	a
4.	b	29.	d
5.	b	30.	d
6.	a	31.	b
7.	a	32.	d
8.	a	33.	c
9.	c	34.	a
10.	a	35.	c
11.	b	36.	a
12.	d	37.	d
13.	c	38.	b
14.	b	39.	b
15.	a	40.	a
16.	c	41.	b
17.	b	42.	d
18.	a	43.	c
19.	d	44.	b
20.	d	45.	a
21.	d	46.	a
22.	b	47.	c
23.	d	48.	d
24.	b	49.	a
25.	c	50.	a

1. The Alabama paradox occurs when a state loses a seat as a result of an increase in the house size. It can happen when an increase in house size causes the quota for some states to increase more than others and a state that originally assigned its upper quota then receives only its lower quota.

2. The population paradox occurs when one state's apportionment decreases and another state's apportionment increases even though the first state has gained population and the second state has lost population.

3. The quota in an apportionment problem is the exact share that would be allocated if a whole number were not required. A method is said to satisfy the quota condition if each state's apportionment is equal to its lower quota (the largest whole number no more than the quota) or its upper quota (the smallest whole number no less than the quota).

4. The geometric mean of 4 and 9 is $\sqrt{36} = 6$.

5. 3.67 rounds to 4
   9.42 rounds to 9
   2.46 rounds to 3
   6.49 rounds to 7

6. Greenville 9
   Riverdale 7
   Oceanside 5
   Parkview 4

7. A 7
   B 5
   C 3

8. North 5
   Central 2
   South 5

9. Greenville 9
   Riverdale 7
   Oceanside 5
   Parkview 4

10. A 8
    B 5
    C 2

11. North 5
    Central 1
    South 6

12. Greenville 9
    Riverdale 7
    Oceanside 5
    Parkview 4

13. A 7
    B 5
    C 3

14. North 5
    Central 2
    South 5

15. Greenville 9
    Riverdale 7
    Oceanside 5
    Parkview 4

16. A 7
    B 5
    C 3

17. North 5
    Central 2
    South 5

18. North 1242.86
    South 1400
    East 1200
    West 1166.67

19. A 49000
    B 45714.29
    C 51666.67

20. North .0008046
    South .0007143
    East .0008333
    West .0008571

21. A .0000204
    B .0000219
    C .0000194

22. 116.67

23. 5.77%

24. 6×10^{-6}

25. 5.79%

1.	a	26.	c
2.	a	27.	c
3.	a	28.	c
4.	a	29.	c
5.	a	30.	c
6.	a	31.	c
7.	c	32.	c
8.	d	33.	c or d
9.	a	34.	a
10.	c	35.	a
11.	c	36.	a
12.	c	37.	b
13.	c	38.	b
14.	c	39.	c
15.	b	40.	d
16.	d	41.	c
17.	b	42.	c
18.	d	43.	c
19.	a	44.	c
20.	a	45.	c
21.	a	46.	b
22.	a	47.	a
23.	b	48.	b
24.	b	49.	b
25.	b	50.	a

1. For example,

$$\begin{bmatrix} 0 & 1 \\ -1 & 0 \end{bmatrix}$$

2. For example,

$$\begin{bmatrix} 1 & -1 \\ -1 & 1 \end{bmatrix}$$

3. For example,

$$\begin{bmatrix} 0 & 1 \\ -1 & 0 \end{bmatrix}$$

4. For example,

$$\begin{bmatrix} 0 & 1 & 1 \\ -1 & 0 & -1 \\ -1 & -1 & 1 \end{bmatrix}$$

5. For example,

$$\begin{bmatrix} 1 & -1 & 0 \\ -1 & 0 & 1 \\ 0 & 1 & -1 \end{bmatrix}$$

6. For example,

$$\begin{bmatrix} 0 & 1 & 1 \\ -1 & 0 & -1 \\ -1 & -1 & 1 \end{bmatrix}$$

7. Has a saddle point at 4. Play 1st row and 1st column.
8. Has a saddle point at 5. Play 2nd row and 1st column.
9. No saddle point. Play 2nd row and 1st column.
10. Has a saddle point at 4. Play 1st row and 1st column.
11. Has a saddle point at 3. Play 3rd row and 1st column.
12. Has no saddle point. Play 1st row and 1st column.
13. Batter expects 1/2 Fastball and 1/2 Knuckleball. Pitcher plays 1/4 Fastball and 3/4 Knuckleball.
14. Batter always expects Fastball. Pitcher always plays Knuckleball.
15. Batter expects 3/4 Knuckleball and 1/4 Fastball. Pitcher plays 3/4 Knuckleball and 1/4 Fastball.

16.

$$\begin{bmatrix} 1 & -1 \\ -1 & 1 \end{bmatrix}$$

17. Yes. Yes.

18.

$$\begin{bmatrix} (-1,-1) & (1,-1) & (-1,1) \\ (1,-1) & (-5,-5) & (-5,5) \\ (1,-1) & (5,-5) & (-10,-10) \end{bmatrix}$$

19. Yes. No.

20.

	Insurance	No Insurance
Sue	$500	$5000
Don't Sue	$1000	$0

21. 1/4

22. 1/2

23. Dominating strategies: Player 1 chooses A, Player 2 chooses B.

24. For example, X (chair) has ordered preferences x, y, z. Y has ordered preferences y,z,x. Z has ordered preferences z, x, y.

25. A deceptive strategy can be used, where an announced preference differs from the actual choice.

1.	c	28.	b
2.	c	29.	b
3.	c	30.	b
4.	d	31.	c
5.	d	32.	b
6.	c	33.	b
7.	b	34.	d
8.	b	35.	a
9.	c	36.	a
10.	b	37.	a
11.	c	38.	b
12.	c	39.	a
13.	b	40.	b
14.	c	41.	b
15.	a	42.	d
16.	a	43.	c
17.	d	44.	b
18.	a	45.	d
19.	c	46.	b
20.	a	47.	b
21.	b	48.	a
22.	c	49.	a
23.	c	50.	b
24.	c	51.	c
25.	d	52.	a
26.	c	53.	b
27.	b		

1. The dominant strategies are column 1.
2. The Nash equilibria is (4, 3).
3. The NMEs are (4, 3) and (2, 4).
4. The dominant strategies are Row 2, Column 1.
5. The Nash equilibria is (3, 4).
6. The NMEs are (3, 4) and (4, 1).
7. The dominant strategies are Row 2.
8. The Nash equilibria is (3, 4).
9. The NMEs are (3, 4) and (4, 1).
10.

(4,3)	(4,3)
(2,4)	(4,3)

11.

(3,4)	(3,4)
(3,4)	(4,1)

12.

(3,4)	(3,4)
(3,4)	(4,1)

13.

(4,3)	(4,3)
(2,4)	(4,3)

14.

(3,4)	(3,4)
(3,4)	(3,4)

15.

(3,4)	(2,2)
(3,4)	(3,4)

16. It is cyclic in the clockwise direction only.
17. It is cyclic in the clockwise direction only.
18. It is cyclic in the clockwise direction only.
19. Moving power is effective for either player.
20. Moving power is effective for either player.
21. Moving power is effective for either player.
22. An example of a situation modeled by Success is Samson and Delilah.
23. An example of a situation modeled by Chicken is Dare.
24. An situation modeled by Prisoners' Dilemma is cheating students.
25. A situation modeled by Variation could be Samson and Delilah.
26. A situation modeled by Truel is selecting a chair for a group of 8 people.

Chapter 17 Multiple-Choice Answers

1.	b	26.	d
2.	b	27.	c
3.	b	28.	a
4.	a	29.	b
5.	b	30.	d
6.	a	31.	d
7.	a	32.	d
8.	c	33.	c
9.	d	34.	a
10.	d	35.	a
11.	b	36.	d
12.	b	37.	b
13.	d	38.	b
14.	c	39.	c
15.	c	40.	a
16.	b	41.	c
17.	b	42.	b
18.	d	43.	a
19.	d	44.	a
20.	c	45.	a
21.	a	46.	c
22.	c	47.	b
23.	a	48.	a
24.	a	49.	a
25.	d	50.	a

1. 8.5/24, approximately 0.3542
2. 8.5 inches × 10.625 inches
3. 11/24, approximately 0.4583
4. 11 inches × 13.75 inches
5. For example, amount of crust or toppings.
6. For example, ease in construction or operation.
7. For example, unusable scrap material.
8. For example, new hybrids are developed.
9. For example, root system.
10. For example, larger whales can hold more air.
11. No. For example, square and non-square rectangles are not similar.
12. Yes. All circles have the same shape.
13. No. For example, regular and non-regular pentagons are not similar.
14. $3\sqrt{(1/3)}$; $\sqrt{(1/3)}$ inch × $3\sqrt{(1/3)}$ inch × $3\sqrt{(1/3)}$ inch
15. For example, "Half-price rings now another 25% off" implies 75% discount.
16. For example, a bank building scaled by 3 representing triple assets is actually 27 times as large.
17. Approximately 1980.
18. Approximately 1916.
19. The Great Depression.
20. No. The actual material should be about 1/5 the weight of the model.
21. The weight is supported by a small surface area.
22. The weight is supported by a larger surface area.
23. Children's features grow by different proportions.
24. Approximately, a = 0.9526, b = 40.6429.
25. Approximately, a = 4.1405, b = 9.4350.

1.	a	26.	a
2.	c	27.	b
3.	b	28.	c
4.	d	29.	c
5.	c	30.	c
6.	b	31.	c
7.	c	32.	d
8.	b	33.	d
9.	a	34.	b
10.	b	35.	a
11.	b	36.	d
12.	c	37.	c
13.	d	38.	b
14.	c	39.	b
15.	c	40.	a
16.	a	41.	b
17.	c	42.	a
18.	d	43.	c
19.	b	44.	a
20.	a	45.	b
21.	b	46.	c
22.	d	47.	c
23.	c	48.	d
24.	c	49.	b
25.	d	50.	a

1. 6.25% compounded quarterly will pay more interest.
2. 6.5% compounded monthly will pay more interest.
3. 6.4% compounded daily will pay more interest.
4. 6.5% compounded quarterly will pay more interest.
5. $8186.27
6. $7360.09
7. Approximately 16.05%.
8. Approximately 9.68%.
9. APY are bounded by 1-e^.1, approximately 10.52%, APY for continuous compounding interest.
10. No. It is not effective for high interest rates.
11. Approximately 7.18%.
12. Bi-weekly payments would be less than half of a monthly payment.
13. Purchase price is $50424.89. Paying $400 per month, the mortgage is paid in approximately 23 years.
14. Purchase price is $64626.57. Paying $550 per month, the mortgage is paid in approximately 23.6 years.
15. Approximately 4.12%.
16. Approximately 77 months.
17. Yes. Theoretically, the payment could only pay the interest and never reduce the principal.
18. $1230.40
19. After approximately 28 years.
20. After approximately 18 years.
21. If a sample weighs P now and weighs A after t days, the half-life $T\_1/2 = t \ln (1/2)/ \ln (A/P)$.
22. For example, carrying capacity.
23. Exponential reserve assumes a percentage change in usage.
24. Future populations are reduced in size.
25. For Example, limited food supplies starve most of the large population.

1.	d	26.	d
2.	b	27.	c
3.	b	28.	c
4.	b	29.	c
5.	c	30.	b
6.	c	31.	c
7.	b	32.	c
8.	c	33.	d
9.	a	34.	c
10.	b	35.	a
11.	d	36.	a
12.	d	37.	b
13.	b	38.	d
14.	a	39.	d
15.	b	40.	b
16.	d	41.	c
17.	a	42.	b
18.	b	43.	b
19.	a	44.	b
20.	c	45.	d
21.	c	46.	b
22.	a	47.	c
23.	a	48.	c
24.	d	49.	c
25.	a	50.	a

1. Elliptic > Euclidean (180 degrees) > Hyperbolic
2. Elliptic > Euclidean (450 degrees) > Hyperbolic
3. The angle sum is less than 360 degrees, so there cannot be 4 right angles.
4. The angle sum is greater than 360 degrees, so there cannot be 4 right angles.
5. For a line and point not on the line, many parallels go through the point.
6. There are no parallel lines.
7. Yes. For example, form a triangle with two equal sides and reflect across the third side.
8. Yes. For example, form a triangle with two equal sides and reflect across the third side.
9. Yes.
10. Yes.
11. For example, four points, six lines, each line determined by every pair of points.
12. For example, three points, three lines, each line determined by a pair of points.
13. For example, four points, four lines, represented by a square.
14.

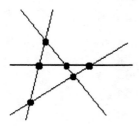

15.

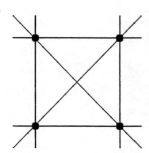

16. For example, a point on a line means a store stocks a product.
17. For example, a point on a line means a product is stocked by a store.
18. For example, three points, five lines, each line contains exactly two points, each point is on exactly two lines.
19. Shortest paths (geodesics) are great circles.
20. Latitudes are not geodesics, longitudes are geodesics.
21. They preserve angles, or length, but not both.
22. Hyperbolic
23. For example, it allows space to "curve".
24. Velocity exceeds ($\sqrt{.99}$)c.
25. Measure angles and sum. Angle sums can determine the geometry of space. Unfortunately, round off errors can affect such an experiment.

1.	c	26.	b
2.	c	27.	a
3.	a	28.	b
4.	a	29.	b
5.	c	30.	a
6.	b	31.	c
7.	a	32.	b
8.	a	33.	c
9.	b	34.	d
10.	c	35.	c
11.	d	36.	c
12.	a	37.	b
13.	c	38.	b
14.	b	39.	d
15.	a	40.	c
16.	b	41.	c
17.	c	42.	c
18.	b	43.	a
19.	a	44.	c
20.	d	45.	a
21.	b	46.	a
22.	c	47.	a
23.	b	48.	a
24.	c	49.	a
25.	a	50.	b

1. 1, 1, 2, 3, 5, 8, 13
2. 1, 4, 5, 9, 14, 23, 37
3. 2, 1, 3, 4, 7, 11, 18
4. The numbers drift toward the golden mean.
5. The numbers drift toward the golden mean.
6. Approximately 1.618 - (1/1.618) = 1.618 - 6.18 = 1
7. The geometric mean is less than or equal to arithmetic mean.
8. Length = 1/[√(golden mean)] Width = √(golden mean)
9. E.g.,

10. E.g.,

11. E.g.,

12. E.g.,

13. E.g.,

14. E.g.,

15. E.g.,
QQQ
QQQ
QQQ
16. E.g.,
SSS
SSS
SSS
17. E.g.,

18. E.g.,

⌐L⌐L⌐L
⌐L⌐L⌐L

19. E.g.,
    XXX
    XXX
    XXX

20. The identity, 1/4 turn, 1/2 turn, 3/4 turn, horizontal reflection, vertical reflection, left diagonal reflection, right diagonal reflection.

21. The identity, and vertical reflection.

22. It's hard to decide if the imperfections are intentional.

23. They describe patterns in a formal scheme.

24. There are rotations and reflections around lines through the center.

25. Rotation and reflection through plane through the center.

1.	b	26.	b
2.	b	27.	a
3.	c	28.	c
4.	c	29.	a
5.	d	30.	b
6.	d	31.	c
7.	c	32.	a
8.	b	33.	c
9.	b	34.	b
10.	b	35.	b
11.	a	36.	b
12.	a	37.	a
13.	a	38.	c
14.	b	39.	c
15.	b	40.	c
16.	b	41.	a
17.	b	42.	a
18.	d	43.	b
19.	d	44.	a
20.	b	45.	a
21.	d	46.	c
22.	c	47.	b
23.	a	48.	b
24.	a	49.	b
25.	b	50.	c

1.

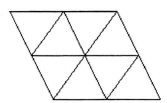

2.

3.

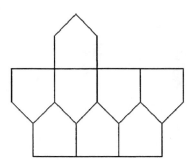

4.

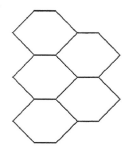

5.

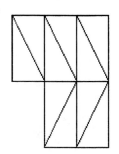

6.

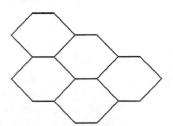

7.

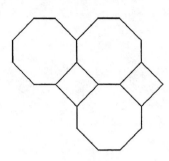

8.

Yes.

9.

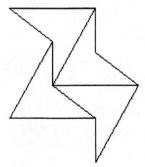

Yes.

10.

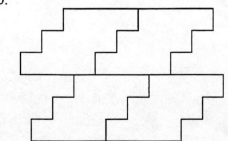

11.

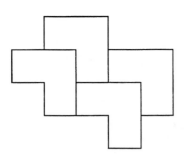

12.

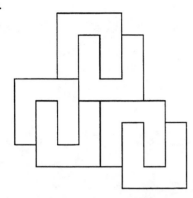

13. See illustration in Spotlight 21.2, for example.
14. Angles do not evenly divide 360 degrees.
15. Angles do not evenly divide 360 degrees.
16.

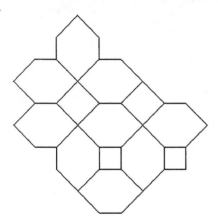

17.

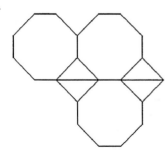

18. See Figure 21.10, for example.
19. See Figure 21.12, for example.
20. See Figure 21.11A, for example.

21. See Figure in Spotlight 19.4, for example.
22. For example, they describe the structure of quasicrystals.
23. p1
24. For example, stack them as alphabet building blocks.
25. For example, stack them as cinder blocks.